INTERCOUNTRY ADOPTEES TELL THEIR STORIES

INTERCOUNTRY ADOPTEES TELL THEIR STORIES

Heather Ahn-Redding and Rita J. Simon

LEXINGTON BOOKS

A Division of

ROWMAN & LITTLEFIELD PUBLISHERS, INC.

Lanham • Boulder • New York • Toronto • Plymouth, UK

LEXINGTON BOOKS

A division of Rowman & Littlefield Publishers, Inc.
A wholly owned subsidiary of The Rowman & Littlefield Publishing Group, Inc.
4501 Forbes Boulevard, Suite 200
Lanham, MD 20706

Estover Road
Plymouth PL6 7PY
United Kingdom

British Library Cataloguing in Publication Information Available

Library of Congress Cataloging-in-Publication Data

Intercountry adoptees tell their stories / edited by Heather Ahn-Redding and Rita
J. Simon.
    p. cm.
 Includes bibliographical references and index.
 ISBN-13: 978-0-7391-1855-9 (cloth : alk. paper)
 ISBN-10: 0-7391-1855-2 (cloth : alk. paper)
 ISBN-13: 978-0-7391-1856-6 (pbk. : alk. paper)
 ISBN-10: 0-7391-1856-0 (pbk. : alk. paper)
 1. Intercountry adoption. 2. Adoptees—Biography. I. Ahn-Redding, Heather.
II. Simon, Rita James
 HV875.5.I53 2007
 362.734092'2—dc22   2006035391

Printed in the United States of America

∞™ The paper used in this publication meets the minimum requirements of
American National Standard for Information Sciences—Permanence of Paper
for Printed Library Materials, ANSI/NISO Z39.48-1992.

CONTENTS

*Denotes a pseudonym.

INTRODUCTION

Over the past several decades, people have often posed the question, "Does transracial adoption work?" Critics and those skeptical of the transracial aspect of adoption maintain that children should be raised by parents of similar ethnicities. Others predict that identity formation will be an arduous, if not impossible, process for transracially adopted children. Sensationalized reports of abused adoptees often instigate waves of doubt regarding the merits of transracial adoption. But whether adoption "works" cannot be answered by a simple "yes" or "no," because just as there is no single adoption experience, there is no single correct response. Nor is this a question that we seek to answer. Rather we must begin to understand that the voices of today's adult transracial adoptees—many who represent the first and second generation of children adopted from overseas—have much to teach us about the multidimensional aspects of adoption and identity.

In 2000, Rita Simon and Rhonda Roorda set out to explore the experiences of black adults who were transracially adopted by white families as children. They sought out adult adoptees to hear, in their own words, about their experiences growing up black in white families and to understand their perceptions of transracial adoption. *In Their Own Voices* contains transcripts of in-depth interviews with the twenty-four adult adoptees from across the country who volunteered to share their adoption experiences.

This current study extends Simon and Roorda's research to include a wider range of transracial adoptees. Born overseas or within the United

States, all of the respondents in this study were transracially adopted. The Korean War initiated a wave of international adoptions that brought to the United States many Korean orphans who were adopted by white families. Similarly, the war in Vietnam increased the number of transracial adoptions. Today, many families are adopting African American children and opening their homes to children born in Asian, European, and Latin American countries. While adoption is typically depicted as white parents adopting a black or Asian child, the faces of adopted children—and adoptive parents—are changing.

This volume includes a more diverse transracial adoptee population than those interviewed in *In Their Own Voices*. We conducted in-depth interviews with adult transracial adoptees born in other countries in order to understand their experiences and to examine their attitudes towards identity, culture, race, and parenting within a multicultural household. We sought out individuals reared in "unconventional" transracial adoption combinations—such as white and Hispanic children adopted by black and Asian families. We asked questions similar to those in *In Their Own Voices* to determine whether the stories and emotions that emerged from the present study bear any semblance to those in Simon and Roorda's research. What issues are unique to Asian adoptees? To Latinos adopted by white families? By black families? To children reared by biracial couples? The perceptions and thoughts that were expressed in *In Their Own Voices* varied considerably regarding culture, parenting, racism, attitudes regarding adoption, and identity; thus, we wanted to explore the same issues as experienced by non-black transracial adoptees.

The men and women in this study offer us glimpses into their worlds, sharing with us many experiences that for some are private, uncomfortable, and difficult to discuss. They represent a range of positive and negative adoption stories. They describe the complexities of racial and ethnic identity formation that are recognized by almost all transracial adoptees. Each of the experiences related in this volume is unique not only in demographic characteristics, such as age of adoption or family composition, but in the journey each participant has undertaken in his or her transition to adulthood.

What emerges from our interviews is a broad collection of voices speaking out from all corners of the country about their adoption. For some of these voices, adoption encompasses their entire identities, defining not only their racial and cultural selves, but also intensely shaping their social, political, and psychological sense of being. For others, adoption has a more peripheral influence upon their everyday lives and has been incorporated into their identities with less intensity. For some voices, adoption is coupled with positive, warm, and loving memories. Other voices express grief from losses following their adoption, either through the deaths of loved ones, parental divorce, or familial estrangement. Still others describe childhoods that were filled with the sadness and horrors of abuse. We thus hear the diverse voices of adoptees that embody the entire spectrum of the adoption experience.

By paying attention to the voices of adoptees—both young and old—prospective adoptive parents can gain a trove of valuable information. The memories that are recalled by the participants in this book, along with their current thoughts on adoption, can educate parents on the issues and questions that are often raised by transracial adoptees of all ages. Young children often ask the following:

- Where do I come from?
- Why don't I look like you?
- Why was I adopted—didn't my birth parents love me?
- How am I supposed to feel a sense of belonging when I look nothing like my friends and family?
- Will you be mad if I search for my birth parents?

Many of these questions linger into adulthood but are often complicated and confusing with a more heightened, mature perspective on adoption.

- Do I want my own children to learn of my heritage?
- What information or questions do I seek in my birth parent search?
- Why do I sometimes feel "white" until I look in the mirror and am reminded of my different skin tone?
- How can I feel a sense of belonging without compromising my own identity?

None of these questions are easy to address, and there is certainly no set of correct responses. While many adoptees can and do discuss these questions with their families, there are many who remain silent but still yearn for answers. When the voices of adoptees are heard, we grow more aware of the process that many have undergone in their search for identity, belonging, and self. This book is a tribute to transracial adults in acknowledgment of their journeys from childhood to adulthood, of the questions they dared to ask, of the persons they have become, and of the inner strength found among them all.

I

INTERCOUNTRY ADOPTION

OVERVIEW

This overview covers the number of intercountry adoptions over the past fifty or so years, their country of origin, and a brief summary of empirical studies describing the social adjustments and racial identities of the children. Much of the material in this chapter is based on the work of Rita Simon and Howard Altstein that appeared in *Adoption Across Borders*.[1]

Between 1953 and 1962, approximately 15,000 foreign-born children were adopted by American families. The following eleven years, 1965–1976, saw an additional 37,469 foreign-born children adopted, of which about 65 percent came from Asia, mostly from the Republic of Korea (ROK). The years from 1977–1983 saw an additional 39,555 non-U.S.-born orphans adopted in the United States, 55 percent of whom were Korean-born.

Table 1.1 shows the overall number of intercountry adoptions from 1989 through 2002.

Table 1.2 reports the number of intercountry adoptions from 1989 through 1998 by the region of birth.

The variation in the number of intercountry adoptees during the fourteen-year interval described in table 1.1, from a low of 6,472 in 1992 to a high of 20,099 in 2002, can be explained almost completely by looking at the number of Asian children allowed to be adopted in the United States. In 1989 that figure was 5,112; by 1992 it dropped to 3,032.

Table 1.1.   All Intercountry Adoptions Per Year

2002	20,099
2001	19,237
2000	17,717
1999	16,363
1998	15,774
1997	12,743
1996	10,641
1995	8,987
1994	8,333
1993	7,377
1992	6,472
1991	8,481
1990	7,093
1989	8,102

Source: U.S. Department of State, The Bureau of Consular Affairs, Overseas Citizens Services, Office of Children Issues. "Numbers of Immigrant Visas Issued to Orphans Coming to the U.S." Retrieved January 20, 2004.

Until 1995, the Republic of Korea (ROK) has historically supplied the United States and the West with the majority of their intercountry adoptees. The origin for the large number of Korean adoptions is the Korean-American war that began in 1950 and lasted until 1953. Following the end of the Korean war there were (1) large population shifts from rural to urban areas; (2) a breakdown of the extended family; (3) large numbers of orphaned children, many of whom were "illegitimate"; and (4) an influx of Western ideas, values, and social institutions. To cope with the stagger-

Table 1.2.   Number of Intercountry Adoptions by Region, 1989–1998

Year	Europe	Asia	Africa	Oceania	North America	South America	Total All Regions
1989	120	5,112	36	13	910	1,757	7,948
1990	232	3,823	49	11	1,016	1,957	7,088
1991	2,761	3,194	41	16	1,047	1,949	9,008
1992	874	3,032	63	13	1,136	1,418	6,536
1993	1,521	3,163	59	1	1,133	1,471	7,348
1994	2,370	3,687	83	8	847	1,205	8,200
1995	2,660	4,843	104	9	764	1,004	9,384
1996	3,568	6,100	89	4	750	805	11,316
1997	5,176	6,483	182	4	1,228	548	13,621
1998	5,660	7,827	172	4	1,456	655	15,774

Source: U.S. Department of State and Immigration and Naturalization Service. Reported in "The Bulletin of the Joint Council on International Children's Services," (Spring 1999); and www.travel.state.gov/family/adoption/stats/stats_451.html "Immigration Visas Issued to Orphans Coming to U.S."

ing number of parentless children, the Republic of Korea, with the assistance and encouragement of American social welfare agencies, began to send its orphans to the West, especially to the United States.

From the 1950s until the early 1970s, Korea was the main provider of infants to the West. For some thirty years, Korea allowed thousands of its orphaned children to be adopted by foreigners. Although no exact figures exist, it is estimated that between the early 1950s and the mid-1980s, in excess of 100,000 Korean-born children were adopted by Western families.[2] But as shown in table 1.3, since 1995, China has taken over as the major source of intercountry adoptees. By 1995, only 1,666 ROK orphans were adopted by U.S. citizens, compared to 2,130 from mainland China.

The reasons for Korea's reduction have to do with national pride and the fact that Korea no longer is considered a developing country incapable of caring for its own. By the end of the twentieth century, Korea has become a major economic force in the world's markets, rich enough to provide for its own orphans. Nationalism and economics are twin factors in sharply reducing the number of Korean children sent abroad for adoption.[3]

Important, too, in reducing the number of Korean children adopted by Westerners was a 1980 statute liberalizing the availability of abortion services in the Republic of Korea. The legalization of abortion has had some impact, but other, more powerful factors also affect the reduction, not the

Table 1.3. Total Adoptions from Asia, 1989–2002

Year	Mainland China	ROK	Vietnam	Philippines	India
1989	201	3,544	*12	465	648
1990	**28	2,620	*53	421	348
1991	61	1,818	*17	393	445
1992	206	1,840	*23	357	352
1993	330	1,775	110	360	331
1994	787	1,795	220	314	412
1995	2,130	1,666	318	298	371
1996	3,333	1,516	354	229	380
1997	3,597	1,654	425	163	352
1998	4,206	1,829	603	200	478
1999	4,101	2,008	709	195	500
2000	5,053	1,794	724	173	503
2001	4,681	1,870	737	219	543
2002	5,053	1,779	766	221	466

*Source: Simon and Altstein 2000. Table 1.4, p. 13
**Source: Simon and Altstein 2000. Table 1.3, p. 8

least of which is North Korea's constant haranguing that by "selling" its children to the West, the Republic of Korea is engaging in capitalism at its worst.[4] In 1993, an official in the ROK's Health Ministry was quoted as saying,

> We are going to stop foreign adoption by 1996, although this will not include the handicapped. We believe we will by then be able to take care of our own children.[5]

Following the end of the conflict between the U.S. and Vietnam, the North Vietnamese government did not allow Vietnamese children to be adopted by foreigners, especially Americans. Prior to the conflict, in 1975, 655 Vietnamese children were adopted by Americans. The easing of tensions between the United States and the new government in Hanoi led to an increase in the number of children who were allowed to leave Vietnam for adoption by American families. Intercountry adoption from Vietnam jumped from twelve children in 1989 to 766 in 2002.

In 2002, 60 percent of all foreign-born adoptees came from three countries: Russia, China (only girls) and South Korea.

Federal statutes concerning intercountry adoption require that the state law where the adoptive parents reside must be satisfied, as must the law of the sending country of the child's origin. Second, the parents must be considered suitable to adopt, as shown by a home study conducted by an agency approved in the United States. And third, the child must satisfy the U.S. immigration law definition of "orphan."

Table 1.4.   Number of Intercountry Adoptions from the Three Major Countries

Year	Mainland China	Republic of Korea	Russian Federation
1992	206	1,840	324
1993	330	1,775	746
1994	787	1,795	1,530
1995	2,130	1,666	1,896
1996	3,333	1,516	2,454
1997	3,597	1,654	3,816
1998	4,206	1,829	4,491
1999	4,101	2,008	4,348
2000	5,053	1,794	4,269
2001	4,681	1,870	4,279
2002	5,053	1,779	4,939

Source: U.S. Department of State, the Bureau of Consular Affairs, Overseas Citizens Services, Office of Children Issues. "Numbers of Immigrant Visas Issued to Orphans Coming to the U.S." Retrieved January 20, 2004. www.travel.state.gov/family/adoption/stats/stats_451.html

In November 2003, the U.S. Citizenship and Immigration Services announced a Child Citizenship Act (CCA) Program to streamline the acquisition of Certificates of Citizenship for children adopted outside the United States. The CCA will automatically provide (without application or fee) these certificates to children whose adoptions were finalized overseas within forty-five days of entering the United States.

In January 2004, the United Nations Children's Fund (UNICEF) issued a position statement which recognized that intercountry adoption "may indeed be the best solution" when adoption within the country itself is not possible.

The following section reviews empirical studies conducted on intercountry adoptees (almost all Koreans) from the 1970s to the present time.

Empirical Studies of Intercountry Adoptions by D. S. Kim, in 1975 and 1976, examined 406 Korean children between twelve and seventeen years of age who were adopted by American families.[6] The research was conducted by the International Adoption Research Project at the University of Chicago and represented the first nationwide study of long-term adjustment by adopted Korean children. The major focus of the study was "to assess the identity and socialization patterns of teenage subjects." The study consisted of two groups: "Early group" children who were placed before they were one year of age and "later group" children who were placed at the age of six or older. The two groups were compared "in relation to the length of placement, transcultural factors, and family environment." Quoting D. S. Kim,

> The study shows that adopted Korean children tend to progress very well in all areas of their lives, indicating no special problems in their overall, long-term adjustment. Their self-concept was remarkably similar to that of other American teenagers (represented by a norm group in a standard scale with an impressively positive self-esteem). Also, their assessment of various socialization processes appeared to be very healthy. . . . It is significant here to note that a warm and supportive family environment was crucially important and responsible for positive outcomes.

But, Kim warned,

> With this positive evidence of progress and development, however, it should be recognized that these foreign children are still in the adolescent stage with an anticipatory socialization. It is questionable whether these positive indications will be maintained once they assume competitive adult roles in the larger society. There are some latent signs that seem to point to possible pathological symptomology among these children. For example, both sexes of adopted

Korean children appeared to be extremely concerned with their physical appearance, complaining of their small stature, dark skin, flat noses, short legs, and so on. With this kind of negative body image, they tend to reject their own racial background. More than 25 percent of all the subjects in the study believed that they belonged to the "American" group, only a little more than 8 percent identified with the "Korean" group, and the rest identified with the "Korean-American" group. Actually more than 60 percent of the subjects were, in fact, racially pure Korean.[7]

He went on to say,

In fact, it is necessary for the child to be aware of personal heritage to develop his full potential or to define his place in society. Therefore, while avoiding ethnocentricity or reverse racism, foreign children can and should be instilled with a positive ethnic identity. Such a positive identity formation can furnish children a useful inclination to self-assertion, advocacy, and determination for their full socialization.[8]

In October 1987, the *Open Door Society News* reported a study conducted by Edward Suh, in which he spoke with (an unmentioned number of) families in Iowa who adopted Korean-born children. Parents reported that their children's main areas of difficulty lay in their language development, physical ailments, and disciplinary problems.[9]

In 1993, three relevant pieces (of which two were dissertations) appeared on various aspects of intercountry adoption (ICA). The first dissertation assessed how a group of forty-eight five-, six-, and seven-year-old Korean adoptees ethnically identified themselves by examining factors such as (adoptive) parents' interest in Korea, community demographics, adoptive family support-group membership with other families adopting Korean-born children, and so on. What the author found was very little covariance. Additional measures derived from interviewing the children, along with interpreting their reactions to puzzles and dolls, contributed little to clarifying a child's perception of his or her ethnic identity.[10]

In late 1993, John Politte completed a dissertation entitled "Self-Esteem among Korean Adopted Pre-Adolescents."[11] His sample consisted of forty-one families with sixty-four children, fifty-one Korean adoptees and thirteen non-adopted siblings. The sample included forty-seven girls and seventeen boys. All (except four) were between the ages of eight and twelve. Politte measured variables traditionally used in this type of investigation; for example, self-esteem, school performance, conduct, and self-worth. He also spoke with parents and asked questions pertaining to their experiences as parents of racially different children, marital preferences for their children, and the extent to which they reinforced their child(ren)'s birth culture, racial perceptions, and so on.

Politte's results were consistent with previous findings in the literature. Intercountry adoptees did very well academically and scored especially high on measures of self-esteem and self-worth. Teasing a child about his or her Korean heritage did tend to minimally affect a child's self-concept and degree of social acceptance. Politte also found that the presence of another Korean adoptee in the family served to increase the scores of both on measures of social competence. Somewhat unclear was the effect on an adoptee's self-esteem of the parents' interest in having cultural artifacts in the home. No unusual results were found in the responses of the parents to Politte's questions regarding the previously described areas.

In April 1993, the General Accounting Office published a report entitled "Intercountry Adoption: Procedures Are Reasonable, but Sometimes Inefficiently Administered."[12] One of the appendices indicated the responses of 203 families to the question, "Why did you choose intercountry adoption rather than domestic adoption?"[13] Table 1.5 describes the families' responses.

The item receiving the highest score (51 percent of the families) was "Believed they were ineligible for domestic adoption." The lowest response (6 percent of the families) saw parents believing that "there were no children available to adopt domestically." Both categories of responses reflect the extent to which our country has failed to educate the public about adoption. Without having the demographic specifics, one could guess that many of those who thought they were ineligible to adopt an American-born child were indeed eligible. Second, it is surprising that much of the public was

Table 1.5. Parents' Reasons for Choosing Intercountry Adoption

Why did you choose intercountry adoption rather than domestic adoption?	Percent of Families*
Believed they were ineligible for domestic adoption	51
Believed intercountry adoption could be completed in less time than domestic adoption	38
Wanted to adopt a child with certain characteristics	27
Believed intercountry adoption would be easier than domestic adoption	20
Believed that intercountry adoption would cost less than domestic adoption	13
Were concerned about birth parent rights in domestic adoption	10
Wanted to help disadvantaged children	9
Were advised to pursue intercountry options	7
Had previous intercountry adoption experience	7
Believed there were no children available to adopt domestically	6

*N = 203 families. Families could indicate more than one reason.

and remains unaware that in excess of fifty thousand U.S.-born children were (and are) available for adoption.

In 1994, the Search Institute published *Growing Up Adopted*, a major report describing the results of interviews with 715 families who adopted infants between 1974 and 1980.[14] When the survey was conducted in 1992–1993, the adoptees' ages ranged from twelve to eighteen. A total of 881 adopted children, 1,262 parents, and 78 non-adopted siblings participated in the study. Among the 881 adoptees, 289 were intercountry and/or transracially adopted, of which the largest single group was 199 Koreans, making up 23 percent of the total sample. (In addition to the Koreans, there were 27 African Americans [3 percent of the sample], 39 Hispanics [4 percent], and 24 Native Americans [3 percent] included in the study.)

The Search study reported that 81 percent of the "same race" adoptees and 84 percent of the transracial adoptees (TRAs) (of whom 68 percent were Korean) said, "I'm glad my parents adopted me."

Various measures of mental health, self-esteem, and well-being were given to both inracial and transracial adoptees. The results are shown in tables 1.6, 1.7, and 1.8.

Table 1.9 reports the relative difficulties that transracial and intercountry adoptees had with their adoptions as compared against same-race adoptees. The large majority in all three categories report that adoption "has always been easy for me," and 5 percent and fewer report that it "has always been hard for me."

When asked, "Which has made growing up difficult for you: your race, being adopted, both, or neither?" we see in table 1.10 that although intercountry adoptees report the least amount of difficulty in being adopted (2 percent), they had more difficulty with racial differences between themselves and the rest of the world (35 percent as compared to 25 percent for all transracial adoptees).

Table 1.6.   Percent of Adolescents with High Self-Esteem

	Boys	Girls
National Sample*	51	39
All Transracial Adoptees	55	51
Asian TRAs**	53	53
Same-Race Adoptees	63	53

*National sample of public school adolescents; N = 46,799.
**In this study, transracial adoption is used in lieu of intercountry adoption.

Table 1.7. Four Measures of Psychological Health for Transracial
and Same-Race Adoptions

Measure of Psychological Health	Range	Scale	Average	Scale Average in Comparison to Same-Race Group
Index of Well-Being	0-16	All TRA	11.23	No difference
		Asian	11.40	No difference
		Same-race	11.08	No difference
At-Risk Behavior	0-20	All TRA	1.80	No difference
		Asian	1.55	No difference
		Same-race	1.78	
Self-Rated Mental Health	1-5	All TRA	4.10	No difference
		Asian	4.07	No difference
		Same-race	4.11	
Achenbach	1-120	All TRA	44.63	No difference
		Asian	43.94	No difference
		Same-race	42.29	

Table 1.8. Racial Identity Among Transracially Adopted Adolescents

Items	Asian	African American	Hispanic	Native American	All TRA
			Percent Agree		
My parents want me to be proud of my racial background	79	87	83	81	79
Other people of my racial background accept me as one of them	51	65	63	52	54
My parent(s) try hard to help me be proud of my racial background	66	74	60	71	66
I wish I was a different race than I am	22	13	23	14	20
I wish my parent(s) were a different race	4	9	3	14	5
I get along better with people of my racial background	34	35	17	33	30
I feel more comfortable with people of my racial background than I do with other people	9	9	3	19	9
I get along equally well with people of my own racial background and people of other backgrounds	80	73	63	86	78
N	173	23	30	21	247

Table 1.9.   Relative Difficulty with Adoption

	Percent All TRAs	Percent Asian ICAs	Percent Same Race
Being adopted has always been easy for me	70	70	68
Being adopted used to be hard for me, but now it's easier	17	20	14
Being adopted used to be easy for me, but now it's harder	10	8	13
Being adopted has always been hard for me	4	2	5

Regarding attachment to their families, the study found, as shown in table 1.11, that transracial and intercountry adoptees are more likely than same-race adoptees to be attached to both parents.

When the data on parental responses were examined, some interesting findings emerged. For example, parents' perception of how emotionally attached their children are to them reveals that they rated their intercountry adoptees as having stronger attachments to them (46 percent) than all other transracial adoptees (42 percent) or inracially adopted adolescents (40 percent). Their perception of "very strong" attachments showed similar scores between intercountry and transracial adoptees (33 percent) but lowest scores (28 percent) for inracial adoptees.[15] Thus, the parents' perceptions of how emotionally attached they think their children are to them are not inconsistent with how the parents are in fact perceived by their children.

Except for the study conducted by the Search Institute, empirical examinations of intercountry adoptees continued to rely upon comparatively small samples of less-than-adult-age adoptees.

In 1998, several interesting studies were reported that examined various aspects of ICA. In a study of 1,200 families who adopted children born in Eastern Europe, which appeared in the *Bulletin of the Joint Council on International Children's Services*, investigators found that the majority of the

Table 1.10.   Difficulty Growing Up: Race versus Adoption

	All TRAs (%)	Asian ICAs (%)	Same Race (%)
My race	25	35	1
Being adopted	3	2	13
Both my race and adoption	12	12	2
Neither	59	52	83

Table 1.11.   Attachment to Families in Percent

	All TRAs	ICAs	Inracial
I get along well with my parents	76	76	73
My mother accepts me as I am	85	87	81
My father accepts me as I am	85	87	78
There is a lot of love in my family	79	78	78
My parents often tell me they love me	83	86	82
I have lots of good conversations with my parents	61	65	67
My parents are easy to talk with	63	66	59

children were doing well in areas such as overall adjustment, attachment, emotional development, and health.[16]

The summer issue of the previously mentioned bulletin published another study of foreign-born children adopted by 206 families. Here, too, authors reported that almost all intercountry adoptees had positive adjustment patterns (bonding and attachment).[17]

Generally supporting these conclusions was an investigation from Canada of 155 intercountry adoptees who reported that although they experienced racism and discrimination, they also felt very attached to their adoptive families. As a group, these adoptees had higher levels of self-esteem than their peers in the general population.[18]

An article presenting a somewhat less optimistic picture than the three noted previously appeared in the *Journal of Family Issues* early in 1998. Here, investigators found an association between the lengths of time children stayed in Romanian orphanages and parental difficulty in behavior management.[19]

This last section reports a study conducted by Simon and Altstein that describes the experience of 124 white families all over the country who adopted 168 Korean children in the late 1960s and the 1970s. The major thrust of the report concerns the reactions that the currently adult Korean adoptees have to their Caucasian American parents and siblings and to growing up in the United States. We gained access to these families by contacting the Holt Adoption Agency and asking them to help us locate families who had adopted at least one Korean child sixteen or more years ago. Over 85 percent of the families the Holt Agency was able to locate agreed to participate in the study. We then wrote or phoned the parents to arrange to interview both the parents and their adopted adult Korean children. Most of the parents were surveyed by mail; the children's interviews were conducted by phone.

Making only minor changes, we used the same parent and children questionnaires that we had used in the 1991 phase of the twenty-year

Simon-Altstein study, except for substituting the appropriate racial background of the adoptees. The Korean "children's" questionnaire also included a few of the items asked of the TRAs in the 1983–1984 phase of the study.

The parents' questionnaire opened with this item:

> Think back, and with the knowledge of hindsight and the experiences you have accumulated, would you have done again what you did—adopt a child of a different race?

Ninety-five percent of the parents said "yes," they would have done what they did—adopt a child of a different race. Three percent were "not sure" and 2 percent said "no." When asked why, over 80 percent of the parents who said they would do it again answered, "It was a positive, enriching, rewarding experience," "Because he/she is our child and we love him/her," "He/she is like our birth child," and "Every child needs a home." Among the five families who said "no" or that they "weren't sure," two sets of parents said they had adopted their children when he and she were nine and seven years old, and that the children had had traumatic experiences prior to being placed with them; two others cited pre-existing physical and emotional problems; and one family said "because we think our child would have been better off with a family of his own ethnic background."

We then asked,

> With all the thought and preparation that had gone into your decision, what about the experience surprised you the most?

The most frequent responses offered by over half of the respondents were "There have been no major surprises," "How easily our family and friends accepted our Korean son/daughter," "How easy it was,"and "How quickly our child integrated/bonded with our family." Five percent of the families said the teen years were difficult, "particularly how much the child grappled with his/her identity."

Almost all of the parents said that the main impact that rearing a child of a different racial and cultural background had on their lives was that "it exposed us to a different culture," "to different groups of people that we either would not have known, or would not have known as well as we do," "it broadened and enriched our lives," "it made us more sensitive to racial issues, to what it means to be a minority," "it made us more tolerant of different kinds of people, from all walks of life," and "we saw that an adopted child is no different than a biological child."

Finally, we asked the parents this question:

Would you recommend that other families like your own adopt a child of a different race or culture?

Ninety percent answered "yes," they would recommend that other families like their own adopt a child of a different race. One percent said they would not, and 9 percent were not sure whether they would recommend transracial adoptions to other families similar to their own. Those who would recommend it said they would also tell the parents to love the child as if it had been born to them, to be aware that the child comes from a different culture and try to expose him or her to that culture, and to generally be aware of the responsibility they are taking on.

We turn now to the adoptees' responses.

Ninety-four percent of the 168 children were born in Korea, about half were born in Seoul, and the others came from Vietnam, India, Bangladesh, and Thailand. Thirty-eight percent were brought to the United States before they were one year old. Another 27 percent came before they were two years old, and 80 percent arrived before their fourth birthdays. At the time they were interviewed, 4 percent were still attending high school. The educational attainments of the others are described in table 1.12.

In two-thirds of the families, the parents have paid or are fully or partially paying their children's tuition, room and board, and other university expenses.

Almost all of the respondents reported living in their parents' home until they went off to school, married, or went to work full time. Two percent said they left because they were not getting along with their parents. Among those currently employed full time, the occupational distribution is described in table 1.13.

Table 1.12. Highest Degree Obtained Thus Far by Percent

High School Diploma	53
A.A. Degree	8
B.A./B.S.	24
M.A./M.S./M.B.A.	3
M.D.	1
Ph.D.	1
Other/N.A.	10*
N	168

*Only one respondent reported that he did not complete high school.

Table 1.13.   Occupational Categories by Percent

Professional	25
Administrative/Clerical	20
Service	20
Skilled/Laborer	7
Unemployed	12
Other	16

Thirty-six percent of the respondents were married at the time the interviews were conducted, none to a Korean. Seventy-seven percent are married to Caucasians, 8 percent to American blacks, and 15 percent to Hispanics and others. Twenty-four percent have children; four of the respondents adopted at least one child, and one of the adopted children is Korean.

The next section of the interview probed the ties the respondents have to the country in which they were born and from which most of them were adopted before they were two years old. Only one in five of the respondents reported having visited Korea. Among those who did, twelve went on a Holt Agency-sponsored "Motherland Tour," nine went with their parents or a sibling, five went alone, and the other eleven went with a spouse, a friend, or via the U.S. Navy. Although only 20 percent reported having visited Korea, two-thirds said they had artifacts, books, photos, and so forth, in their homes that describe some aspect of Korean society. But as the responses in table 1.14 indicate, the large majority can neither speak, read, nor write Korean.

When asked to describe the racial/ethnic characteristics of their three closest friends, when they were in high school and "now" (at the time of the interview), at least 80 percent of the respondents reported having white friends.

In response to questions about the types of people they dated when they were in high school, 72 percent answered "white American," 9 percent said "mainly whites, some blacks and other minorities," and 4 percent answered

Table 1.14.   Korean Language Facility

	Percent Speaking	Percent Reading	Percent Writing
Fluently	0.0	1.8	1.8
Fairly fluently	2.4	3.0	3.0
Hardly at all	13.7	5.4	5.9
Not at all	83.9	89.9	89.3

"Asians." Fifteen percent said they did not date in high school. In response to the follow-up question, which was "Why did you choose to date the people you did?" 52 percent said, "They were the people I was most attracted to on the basis of looks, common interests, and personality." Most of the others said their school was predominantly white, and there were "few other dating options."

Next we turned to a more detailed analysis of the respondents' memories and perceptions of their childhood. We started by asking, "In thinking back about your childhood, what were the most positive aspects about it?" followed by "What were the most negative aspects about it?" For the positive side, 68 percent said, "growing up in a warm, loving family," 30 percent said "having lots of friends," and 21 percent said "being afforded a wide variety of educational and other opportunities." Nine percent said "doing well in sports."

For the most negative aspects, 78 percent said they had none or so few that they could not describe them. No one said that in response to the question about the positive aspects of their childhood. The categories of negative experiences most frequently cited are listed in table 1.15.

Continuing to probe about their childhood, we then asked,

When you were a child, how did you feel about having a different racial and ethnic background than your parents?

Do you remember when you first realized that you "looked" different from your parents?

For those who had siblings born to their adoptive parents, we asked,

How do you think the fact that you had a different racial/ethnic background affected your relationships with your brother(s) and/or sister(s)?

Was being of a different race and ethnicity than your adoptive family easier or harder during various stages of your life (e.g., during childhood, adolescence, etc)?

Table 1.15. Negative Experiences Most Frequently Cited

	Percent
Difficulties getting along with my adoptive mother	19
Experiences I had related to racial prejudice	14
Difficulties getting along with my adoptive father	12
Difficulties getting along with my peers at school	11

How did people who were of the same ethnic background as you react to you when you were an adolescent?

Aside from the obvious racial/ethnic differences, did you ever feel that somehow you just did not fit in with your adoptive family, that your temperament and/or personality were different from other family members? If you did, please explain under what conditions, or in what situations they occurred.

Finally, we asked,

Did you ever attribute these differences between you and your adopted parents to the fact that in some way, from what you know, you were behaving like either of your birth parents?

Now for the responses! Sixty-four percent of the respondents said, "It simply did not matter that my parents were of a different racial background than I was." Fifteen percent thought of it as having "positive" aspects, and 12 percent saw some negative aspects to the differences. Only 39 percent remembered when they first realized that they looked different from their parents. Almost half of those who remembered said, "Immediately, as soon as I was adopted." They had all been adopted when they were at least four years old.

Like the responses to the item about being of a different race than their parents, most of the respondents said about being of a different race than their siblings(s), "it made little or no difference." Six percent viewed it as positive, and 9 percent viewed it negatively. As for which periods in their lives being of a different race was easier or harder, almost half (48 percent) of the respondents said they just didn't think about it and could not designate an easier or harder time at any stage of their lives. Ten percent said they had difficult periods throughout both childhood and adolescence, 24 percent said adolescence was the most difficult, and 13 percent said early childhood was the most difficult. Four percent said early childhood was the easiest, and 1 percent said adolescence was the easiest.

Only 38 percent could answer the question, "How did people who were of the same ethnic background as you react to you when you were an adolescent?" because the others said they encountered "very few or no" Koreans during their childhood and adolescence. Of those who answered, 17 percent said, "It didn't seem to matter to them." Eighteen percent said they responded positively, and 12 percent said the responses were usually negative.

Seventy percent said that they "never" felt that they did not fit into their adopted family (for whatever reasons, e.g., temperament, personality, etc.).

Among the 30 percent who did report such feelings, the most typical explanations were "I was much louder and more expressive than other people in my family," "I was quieter and more introspective," "I related to people differently," and "I had different interests." None of the explanations were shared by more than 5 percent of the respondents. But even among those who noticed differences between themselves and other family members, practically no adoptees attributed the difference to the possibility that their own behavior was similar to that of their birth parents, in part because hardly any of them had known or knew anything about their birth parents.

The next section examined the respondents' accounts of their current relationships with their parents and siblings. We first asked whether they lived in the same communities as their parents and found that 38 percent did. Of those who did not, 55 percent lived within two hundred miles of their parents. Among those who were not living at home, 25 percent said they see their parents at least once a week, 30 percent at least once a month, and the others said several times a year. Sixty-two percent reported talking with them on the phone at least once a week and 27 percent said at least once a month. None of the respondents reported no contact with their parents; two reported visits once every other year, and one every two to three years.

Table 1.16 describes the responses to these questions:

How would you describe your relationship at the present time with your adopted mother/father?

When you were an adolescent, how would you describe your relationship with your adopted mother/father?

The responses show that relationships had been close with both parents during adolescence and had gotten closer as the children became adults. Only 13 percent perceived their current relationship with either their

Table 1.16. Quality of Relationship with Parents in Percent

	Mother		Father	
Quality of Relationship	*Adolescent*	*Present*	*Adolescent*	*Present*
Very close	40.1	50.0	36.9	43.5
Fairly close	31.8	35.1	41.1	35.1
Quite distant	14.7	6.0	4.8	3.0
Distant	12.4	7.1	14.9	10.1
No Answer/Other*	1.2	1.8	2.4	8.3

*Three of the fathers had died when the respondents were adolescents and twelve of the fathers were deceased at the time the interviews were conducted.

mother or their father to be "quite distant" or "distant." When we asked those respondents who had answered "quite distant" or "distant" to explain why they were not close to their parent(s), most of the respondents said of their mother, "She doesn't accept the kind of person I am," "She doesn't approve of my lifestyle," and "She objects to my friends." About their fathers, more of them put the blame on the parent; for example, "He has a substance abuse problem," or "He is non-verbal," "unaffectionate," or "irresponsible." But those descriptions fit less than 15 percent of either the mothers or the fathers.

For those who told us that the relationship between them and their parents had changed from the time they were adolescents until now, we asked, "Why?" Most answered that there was a "natural break when I went off to college." Others cited different interests, and some cited changes in the family (e.g., deaths of fathers, divorces, illnesses) that brought parents and children closer.

Another way of assessing how close the respondents feel towards their adopted families is by examining their responses to the following question:

> If you had a serious personal problem involving, for example, your marriage, your children, your health, etc., who are the three people you would most likely turn to for help or advice?

We also asked the same questions: "If you had a serious money problem. . . ?" and "If you were in trouble with the law. . . ?" The results shown in table 1.17 clearly indicate that almost all the respondents—between 93 and 99 percent—would turn to their parents as one of the three sources. Friends are the next most frequently cited category, especially for a "personal problem," followed by a sibling.

It is worth noting that, within the "parents" category, mothers were consistently cited more often than fathers.

Table 1.17.   Type of Problem in Percent

Category of Person	Personal	Money	Law
Parent(s)	99.3	95.3	92.6
Friend(s)	73.0	41.9	52.7
Sibling(s)	48.0	34.0	40.0
Spouse/Boyfriend/Girlfriend	6.0	20.9	11.5
Other Relatives (Grandparents, Aunts, Uncles)	30.4	18.9	25.7
No One	2.0	0.7	—

The last part of the interview focused on policy issues concerning transracial adoption. We began by asking,

Would you urge social workers and adoption agencies to place Hispanic, Korean, Asian, black, or other nonwhite children in white homes?

Eighty-seven percent said "yes," 9 percent said "no," and 3 percent said they "weren't sure." We followed up with, "If 'no,' please explain why not," and "If 'yes,' would you make any stipulations in that policy?" Among the 10 percent who opposed the practice, almost all of them said, "Race and ethnicity are very important," and "Whites simply cannot understand what it means to be Asian." For the 87 percent who said "yes," they would urge adoption agencies to make transracial placements; about half made no stipulations. The others made comments such as "Yes, only if the adoptive parents are willing to make a commitment to expose the child to her native culture" and "Yes, such children should be placed in white homes only after an exhaustive search has been made to try to place the child in a home of her own racial/ethnic background." Others urged having the families live in multiracial neighborhoods. Most of the other stipulations focused on the importance of a "stable, loving family," "adopt when the children are very young," and "families may need counseling."

In response to the question, "How do you think being Korean by birth but reared by white parents has affected how you perceive yourself today?" one-third said, "It had no effect on my self-image one way or the other." Another third said, "It had a positive effect on my self-image" and "It broadened my view of different races." Thirteen percent stated that it had a negative effect on their self-image and an additional 5 percent said, "I feel like a banana."[20] The other 15 percent gave a range of "other" explanations.

For those respondents who were married at the time of the interview (one-third, and only one to a Korean), we asked, "How important was the racial or ethnic background of your spouse in your decision to marry?" Eighty percent said, "It did not matter." Most of the others said, in essence, "I cared more about personal characteristics than race." Although 22 percent have children, half of them were too young for the respondent to answer "How does your child identify his/her racial background?" Among the seventeen respondents who did answer, nine described some combination of "Korean," or "Asian/white," or "American."

When asked, "How would you describe yourself (focusing on racial/ethnic background)?" 30 percent answered "Korean," 32 percent said "Korean/Asian American," 5 percent said "Asian," 20 percent said "American,"

Table 1.18. Percent Preference for Adoption by Same Race Parent

No	80
Yes	7
Don't know	5
No answer	8

7 percent said "White," and the other 6 percent said Amerasian, Indian, Thai, and so forth. For some 73 percent of the respondents, their Korean-Asian heritage is very much part of their current identity.

An item near the end of the formal interview asked:

All things considered, would you have preferred to have been adopted by parents whose racial and ethnic background was the same as yours? If so, please explain why.

The responses are shown in table 1.18.

For those who answered "no," the explanations were mainly that "everything worked out well for me," "race should not be that important," and "my parents loved me."

And finally, we asked,

What advice would you give to white parents who have the opportunity to adopt a young child of your racial background about how he/she should be reared?

Responses fell into two major categories. One emphasized "Just do it" and "Be sure you love that child and treat him as yours." The other emphasized that parents "must be sensitive to racial issues," "show respect for his/her culture," "talk about her/his background," and "live in a mixed neighborhood." The overall impressions that emerge from these interviews are that Korean transracial adoptees are aware of their backgrounds but are not particularly interested in making them the center of their lives. They feel good about having grown up with the families they did. They are committed to maintaining close ties with their adopted families and are supportive of policies that promote transracial adoptions.

NOTES

1. Rita J. Simon and Howard Altstein, *Adoption Across Borders* (Lanham, Md.: Rowman & Littlefield, 2000).

2. Peter Maass, "Orphans: Korea's Disquieting Problem," *Washington Post*, December 12, 1988, p. 1.

3. National Broadcasting Corporation, 10:45 p.m., September 19, 1988; Maass, "Orphans," 1; Tamar Lewin, "South Korea Slows Export of Babies for Adoption," *New York Times*, February 12, 1990, p. 10B.

4. Bruce Porter, "I Met My Daughter at the Wuhan Foundling Hospital," *New York Times Magazine*, April 11, 1993, p. 24.

5. "South Korea to Restrict Adoptions by Foreigners," no author, *Baltimore Sun*, December 26, 1993, p. 16.

6. D. S. Kim, "Intercountry Adoptions: A Study of Self-Concept of Adolescent Korean Children Who Were Adopted by American Families," unpublished Ph.D. thesis, University of Chicago, 1976.

7. Kim, "Intercountry Adoptions," 56.

8. Kim, "Intercountry Adoptions," 84.

9. Edward Suh, "Life Adjustment Problems among Adopted Korean Children," *Open Door Society News* (October 1987): 3.

10. Jill C. Cole, "Perceptions of Ethnic Identity among Korean Born Adoptees and Their Caucasian American Parents," Dissertation Abstracts International-A, vol. 54, no. 1 (July 1993): 317. University Microfilms, #9504358, also cited in FACE FACTS, (July/August 1995): 24–26; Kevin Lee Wickes, "Transracial Adoption: Cultural Identity and Self-Concept of Korean Adoptees," Dissertation Abstracts International-B, vol. 54, no. 8 (February 1994): 4374. University Microfilms, #9504358, also cited in FACE FACTS (July/August 1995): 24–26.

11. John Politte, "Self Esteem Among Korean Adopted Pre-Adolescents," University Microfilms, #9504358, 1993.

12. "Intercountry Adoption: Procedures Are Reasonable, but Sometimes Inefficiently Administered," GAO/NSIAD-93-83.

13. "Intercountry Adoption," no. 17, p. 59.

14. Peter L. Benson, Anu R. Sharma, and Eugene C. Roehlkepartain, "Growing Up Adopted: A Portrait of Adolescents and Their Families," Search Institute, Minneapolis, Minn. (June 1994).

15. Benson et al., "Growing Up Adopted," 99; "Intercountry Adoption," no. 20, p. 109; "Intercountry Adoption," no. 20, p. 107; "Intercountry Adoption," no. 20, p. 103.

16. Mary Essley and Linda Perilstein, "Eastern European Adoptions," *Bulletin of the Joint Council on International Children's Services* (Spring 1998): 8; and www.cradlehope.org/survey.html.

17. D. Clauss and S. Baxter, "Rainbow House International Survey of Russian and Eastern European Children," *Bulletin of the Joint Council on International Children's Services* (Summer 1998): 6.

18. Anne Westhues and Joyce S. Cohen, "The Adjustment of Intercountry Adoptees in Canada," *Children and Youth Services Review* 20, nos. 1–2 (1998): 115–34.

19. Henry Mainemer, Lorraine C. Gilman, and Elinor W. Ames, "Parenting Stress in Families Adopting Children from Romanian Orphanages," *Journal of Family Issues* 19, no. 2 (March 1998): 64–80.

20. Spokespersons for the National Association of Black Social Workers have dubbed black children adopted by white families "oreos," that is, black on the outside with white psyches. The "banana" simile evokes the same image for Korean transracial adoptees.

II

INTRODUCTION TO INTERVIEWS

INTRODUCTION TO INTERVIEWS

Of the twenty-one respondents included in this study, seven are men and fourteen are women. Nine of the respondents were adopted from Korea, four from Vietnam, one from Haiti, one from the Philippines, and three from Colombia and Mexico. One is a black American adopted into a white family and two are white Americans who were adopted by black families. The female respondents range in age from eighteen to forty-three, the men from eighteen to thirty-five. Twelve of the respondents were adopted before they were six months old: one was four days old and another one day. Six were adopted between the ages of one and three years, and three were between five and nine years of age. Nine of the fourteen women are single, as are five of the seven men. Four women are married, one is divorced, and one man is married and the other is divorced. Five of the respondents, four women and one man, hold a postgraduate degree (a master's degree). Six, three men and three women, completed a bachelor's degree. Three women and two men are currently students working towards a bachelor's degree, three women have high school diplomas, and one woman dropped out of high school in the eleventh grade.

The respondents live in all parts of the United States except the deep South. One lives in Toronto.

Each of the interviews lasted between one and three hours, and all but three were conducted over the phone. The interviews were conducted by Heather Ahn-Redding and Rita J. Simon. One participant, Flutie, was interviewed by Elisha Marr, a doctoral student at Michigan State University. Most of the respondents were recruited through online postings on chat rooms and bulletin boards and a large majority contacted us directly. The names of the interviewees that appear in these transcripts were those they wished to be identified by. The names of relatives, places of birth, childhood homes, and names of schools attended are also those the interviewees agreed could be identified. In cases where interviewees preferred using a pseudonym, that is so indicated in the transcript. The interviewees were given an opportunity to review their transcripts before the materials were sent to the publisher. Any deletions or additions they made were noted and included. With the exception of one individual, none of the persons who initially agreed to participate in this study changed their minds and refused to have their interviews included. All of them believe, as we do, that their stories are important and worth telling. All of them hope that their experiences will help other transracial adoptees better understand themselves and their relationships to their families, have a clearer image of their racial and social identities, and live richer, happier lives.

III
INTERVIEWS

JODI

GENDER:	Female
AGE AT TIME OF INTERVIEW:	22
RACE:	Korean
MARITAL STATUS:	Single
OCCUPATION:	Student

Jodi was adopted from Seoul, Korea, by Caucasian parents when she was twelve months old. At the time of the interview, Jodi was twenty-two years old and attending Indiana University at South Bend.

Jodi's parents were both raised Amish, although they converted to the Mennonite faith prior to Jodi's birth. Jodi grew up in Nappanee, Indiana with two older sisters, ages fourteen and sixteen at the time of her adoption, both of whom are her parents' biological daughters.

During her childhood, Jodi was not exposed to other Asian children. She describes Nappanee as very rural, country-like, slow paced, and religious. She attended public schools where the students were predominately white and middle class and she "stuck out like a sore thumb." At times she was teased because of her physical appearance. In high school, she was very involved in golf, basketball, track, and cross-country and was on the English academic team.

Within her family, she was "spoiled growing up." She received a lot of attention from her parents and extended family at reunions. Her grandparents treated her "extra special." Due to the age gap between Jodi and her sisters, she felt as if she was raised as an only child. As a kid, she displayed little interest in Korean culture.

In 1998, Jodi traveled to Korea for the first time on a trip that was sponsored by the Korean Consulate. Her memories of Seoul are enjoyable, as she had fun traveling around the city and visiting the countryside. When asked if she has any interest in locating her birth parents, she expressed no desire.

Presently, Jodi lives in South Bend, one of Indiana's largest cities. Though the area is quite diverse, she has seen "a lot of stereotypes being fulfilled in this town." At times, she was complimented on her English skills.

Jodi has several Korean American friends, many of whom are adopted. She stresses the need for adoptive parents to educate themselves on their child's birth country through counselors, adoptive agencies, academia, and other adoptive families. Jodi describes herself as "career-oriented" and is currently studying criminal justice. She looks forward to attending law school or business school in the future and is interested in learning Korean.

TELL ME ABOUT YOUR PARENTS' UPBRINGING AND THEIR EXTENDED FAMILY.

Both my parents were raised Amish. My father actually grew up in a small town south of South Bend, Indiana. He decided to establish his family miles from where he grew up. I'm really happy for him. He's happy and that's the happiest thing that I can say that I feel towards my dad. He has a really open mind and a very humble heart and is very patient. And I feel like those are absolute necessities for somebody to live a non-stressed life in today's society. We are not Amish anymore. My parents switched over to Mennonite. I was raised Mennonite till age eighteen, and now they attend a non-denominational church, and I currently claim no affiliation with the church. My mother was raised Amish in Pennsylvania and then they moved to Indiana. She attended college at first, but then she got married. My parents are just fun loving, and they've had the perfect marriage. They're very open, and they've actually counseled others in marriages. They have done the best they can in raising me. I hold them in high regard, and I love them to death.

YOU WERE ADOPTED FROM KOREA WHEN YOU WERE A YEAR OLD?

Yes. I flew into Chicago.

ARE YOUR PARENTS CAUCASIAN?

Yes. They both are as white as a snowman.

WHEN YOU WERE GROWING UP, DID YOU KNOW ANY OTHER ASIAN CHILDREN?

No.

ARE THERE ANY ASIANS WITHIN THE MENNONITE DENOMINATION?

Not that I know of.

WAS THAT A PROBLEM FOR YOUR FAMILY?

No.

WAS IT A PROBLEM FOR YOU?

No. I stuck out like a sore thumb. I got all the candy; I got all the presents. I can't complain.

DID THE CHILDREN EVER TEASE YOU BECAUSE OF YOUR BACKGROUND?

Yes. As I look back, I feel like they were just being honest. They would never make any truly degrading remarks. They were just making a point.

THEY WERE JUST ACKNOWLEDGING THAT YOU ARE DIFFERENT?

Yeah. And actually they were kind of curious. I would always give them dirty looks, but then I would have to be the bigger kid in that sense and understand where they were coming from. So I was like, "Yeah, I know I'm different. I'm adopted, all right?" They were like "ok" and that was it.

DID YOUR PARENTS KNOW ANY OTHER ASIAN FAMILIES? OR ANY FAMILIES OF COLOR?

No, we were the first in our area, and actually several families have now adopted some kids because of my parents. They were like a walking advertisement.

DO YOU KNOW WHAT INFLUENCED THEIR DECISION TO ADOPT?

Yes. They had two children, and they couldn't have any more. They talked to a cousin on my mom's side who had just come back from China. They said, "Asian kids are cute," and they said, "Ok, we'll get one."

WHAT WAS YOUR CHILDHOOD LIKE, WHAT WAS YOUR RELATIONSHIP LIKE
WITH YOUR PARENTS?

I got a lot of attention. The town did an article on me. I represented the
minority in my school, so I always stuck out. At family reunions they would
always make a note to give me attention and things. Both of my sisters were
in high school and college before I started kindergarten, so I was basically
raised as an only child. She didn't work before I started kindergarten, so I
got a lot of attention. I don't think I was spoiled in other aspects, and I definitely learned the value of work and the value of money, so in that respect
I was saved. The amount of time I got was more than the average kid.

DID YOUR PARENTS DO ANYTHING DIFFERENT TO ACKNOWLEDGE KOREAN
CULTURE? OR ASIAN CULTURE?

They tried, but I was very unreceptive.

WHAT KIND OF THINGS DID THEY TRY?

Well, let's see. They got books; they tried to educate themselves. It wasn't
working. First of all, I felt like the extent of their education was so limited,
it was pathetic. Second of all, my interest in it did not encourage them at
all. I just wasn't interested.

AND THEY SENSED THAT?

I told them in every way possible I wasn't interested.

WHAT IS YOUR RELATIONSHIP LIKE WITH YOUR SISTERS TODAY?

They're good. My one sister travels all over the world, so I only see her
on various occasions.

ARE YOU ABLE TO TALK ABOUT ADOPTION ISSUES WITH THEM?

Yeah, but it's never been an issue. I mean it's never ever been, "Oh, God,
you're an alien."

YOU SAID YOU DON'T IDENTIFY WITH THE MENNONITE CHURCH ANYMORE?

No.

IS THERE SOMETHING THAT TRIGGERED THAT CHANGE, OR HAVE YOU
ADOPTED A NEW SORT OF SPIRITUALITY, OR HOW WOULD YOU CHARACTERIZE
THAT?

I was just sick of church in general. I was doing my own thing. It felt like
I got religion jammed down my throat and I was just sick of it. It's nice to
sleep in on Sunday. I have a Bible and I read and I do my own thing. And

I haven't strayed as far as my own beliefs on any sort of new "Jodi philosophy tangent," but you know, it seemed like I needed time away from the people in this area, from church, from everything, and I just want to enjoy life.

NOW GOING BACK TO YOUR PARENTS. HAVE THEY EVER TRAVELED TO KOREA?

No.

HAVE THEY HAD ANY INTEREST IN DOING SO?

Yes.

DO YOU THINK THEY WILL?

I don't know. My mom's never flown in an airplane and she doesn't plan to. They actually were very interested, and when I went to Korea in 1998, they really wanted to come along, but I was like, "I don't want to be seen with you guys."

TELL ME ABOUT YOUR TRIP.

It was really fun. It was sponsored by the Korean Consulate so everything was paid. We had excellent tours and excellent sessions with qualified individuals as far as heritage, culture, economics, the times, and where they are planning on going—just pretty much every aspect of the country that we could get.

DID YOU EXPERIENCE ANY DISCRIMINATION OR STEREOTYPES BECAUSE YOU ARE A KOREAN ADOPTEE?

No. They could definitely tell that we were American by the way we dressed and the way we walked and things like that. But for the most part, the cities and places we visited were very much like the western culture, so they were cool with us.

TELL ME MORE ABOUT THE AREA THAT YOU LIVE IN RIGHT NOW.

South Bend is the fourth or fifth largest city in Indiana. I live right in the middle of town, and so I'm really close to everything. It's definitely of the working class. There are not a whole lot of opportunities to employ people with higher education.

IS IT A DIVERSE AREA?

It's getting better. They have a very respectable percentage of Asians. I think a lot of them are actual immigrants because they're very groupy and they're very unique. That kind of clued me in on some cultural differences that seem weird. There are a high percentage of African Americans as well, but I wouldn't call the area very diverse because they're very segregated, and there's a lot of racism going on with the police. There are a lot of stereotypes being fulfilled in this town.

YOU MENTIONED IN YOUR EMAIL THAT YOU WOULD NOT WANT TO MARRY ANOTHER KOREAN MAN. CAN YOU TELL ME WHY?

I prefer Caucasian men to any other race.

WHAT HAVE YOUR EXPERIENCES BEEN IN INTERRACIAL DATING?

Good and bad. For a lot of gentlemen, it's the first time dating an Asian. I still get shown around a lot, like "Look who's by my side"—stuff like that. I just don't appreciate that.

WHEN YOU'RE DATING SOMEONE, DO YOU EVER TALK ABOUT ADOPTION ISSUES? IS IT A TOPIC THAT YOU BRING UP TODAY?

Recently I have with a gentleman, but for the most part it's not really an issue. I love to talk about it, so it's never been tense.

SO IT'S NOT SOMETHING YOU'RE REALLY UNCOMFORTABLE WITH?

Oh, no.

YOU ALSO MENTIONED THAT YOU DON'T THINK YOU WILL HAVE CHILDREN?

Yeah. I'm definitely sure I'm not going to have children.

WHAT IS YOUR REASON FOR BEING SO DECISIVE?

I'm very career-oriented, and I'm very selfish with my money. I feel like I live once, and I want my toys. It goes beyond just that. The more I'm learning about children and the effects of the juvenile delinquency, I know if I would be a mother, I wouldn't be there for that child.

TELL ME MORE ABOUT YOUR EXTENDED FAMILY.

Country white people. That's about the extent of it.

ANYTHING ELSE? ARE THEY ALL MENNONITE?

No.

ARE THEY AMISH?

Some are, yes. Most attend a non-denominational church. They go to the same church as my parents.

GROWING UP, DID YOU HAVE ANY ASIAN ROLE MODELS OR ANYONE WHO YOU ADMIRED WHO WAS ASIAN?

Nope.

NOW YOU MENTIONED THAT DURING YOUR ADOLESCENCE YOU HAD SOME ROCKY PERIODS, AND YOU EXPERIMENTED MORE WITH DRINKING. DID YOU EXPERIMENT WITH DRUGS OR ANYTHING?

No. And I have no idea why I decided not to go down that road. I think some of my friends were actually abusing illegal substances at the time, and I just saw their lives and how they were just out of control of themselves. I wasn't very attracted to that after seeing them strung out, and I've been turned off to it ever since.

WAS THERE A TIME IN YOUR LIFE WHEN YOU WERE GOING THROUGH MORE OF A DIFFICULT TIME?

Let's see. I would say a span of four years—my junior, senior, freshman, sophomore years—the end of my high school, beginning of my college.

DO YOU THINK IT WAS DIFFERENT THAN WHAT MOST TEENAGERS GO THROUGH?

Not at all. I think it was totally normal.

HOW DID YOU HANDLE THIS DIFFICULTY?

Not very effectively. If you're talking about how we discussed it as a family, there was a lot of yelling and things, but it was mostly my fault. I was very immature, and I didn't know how to handle things so I yelled when I didn't get my way. That's just selfishness. In my opinion, I think it was a result of all the attention I got when I was younger, and I just needed to grow up. I think I was very immature in high school. I just didn't realize it, and that was the worst thing.

HOW DID YOUR PARENTS DISCIPLINE YOU?

They were very strict. I got spankings all the time. I never received verbal or psychological or physical abuse.

HAVE YOU EVER ATTEMPTED TO LOCATE YOUR BIRTH PARENTS?

No.

DO YOU THINK YOU MIGHT DO THAT IN THE FUTURE?

No.

DID YOU EVER HAVE A DESIRE TO?

No.

WOULD YOU EVER HAVE A DESIRE TO LOCATE POTENTIAL BIRTH SIBLINGS?

No.

HAVE YOUR PARENTS EVER PRESSURED YOU TO? HAVE YOU EVER TALKED TO YOUR PARENTS ABOUT IT?

Yes. I think they mentioned something about some articles about some other adoptees and about feeling a void in their lives. I've never had that.

IS THERE ANYONE WHO YOU CAN TALK TO ABOUT PERSONAL ISSUES?

No, I usually just take care of it myself.

HAVE YOU EVER EXPERIENCED ANY SORT OF STEREOTYPES OR PREJUDICES BECAUSE YOU'RE ASIAN?

Oh, my word. Totally. Especially in this area. They're very naïve and highly uneducated, and they have no clue. I get complimented on my English, and I say, "Thank you." Hell, after twenty-one years, I sure as hell better know my language. I've learned not to take offense at that because I look at their face, and they're being honest with me. They're not putting me down. They don't know. I just chalk it up to them being naïve. They're just fucking stupid. I actually don't even say that though. To be honest, my response is just, "Thank you very much." What would I achieve if I were being sarcastic to them? They could take offense at me. I want to be the adult here. I always think about them first, and I respond accordingly.

HAVE YOU NOTICED ANY CLASHES BETWEEN KOREAN AMERICANS AND KO-REANS?

Actually, no, because I feel that the Koreans from Korea are very cliquish and very groupy. They go to their own groups and outside of that, nothing really matters. The friends that I have aren't part of that. They're like second and third generation, and we're all good. We don't talk bad about them.

DO YOU THINK GROWING UP IN A VERY HOMOGENOUS AREA AND IN A MUL-TICULTURAL FAMILY HELPED PREPARE YOU TO DEAL WITH RACISM AND DIVER-SITY ISSUES TODAY, OR DO YOU THINK THAT MADE A DIFFERENCE?

That's a good question. No, I feel like me learning on my own was essentially the key. I visit large cities, and I get as diverse as I want to get. I learn a lot naturally from inner city society—not the poor—but just being in a metropolitan area. That's where I want to live.

Do you consider yourself Korean American?

Yes, I do. I consider myself Korean American. I went a long time denying my identity. I think about my skin, and I might as well work with what I got.

What changed that?

The city. Not this city, but visiting cities. I go to Chicago and nobody's looking at you funny. I mean everybody is going about their business. Everybody's beautiful, and that's what I love about it.

You don't stick out there?

I feel very at home, and I like the way people are so different. I love that. It makes me feel more like a nobody, so to speak.

Have there been times in your life when your self-esteem has really suffered because of identity issues stemming from adoption issues?

Yes, I've had identity issues. I don't know how to explain it. I felt like I could never get the guys. And I never could get the guys because all my friends were blond-haired, blue-eyed chicks. That's what they wanted, and that's what they preferred. How can you make somebody like something else? It's not like I never got dates, but even then I had this in the back of my head, "They're settling on me because my friends are taken."

Do you feel accepted by the Asian community?

I don't know where the Asian community is here. No, I don't want to feel accepted by them. This isn't the area for me.

Do you have any adopted Asian friends?

Yeah, the people who I met in Korea. A lot of them were from California and D.C.

What are some similarities that you've noticed among your friends who were adopted?

All my friends enjoy life; they are very ambitious. They're happy with their lives; they're happy with the way things went.

Do you think it is possible for transracial adoptees to really formulate a sound identity and really understand who they are?

I think that is a relative concept. It's what you make of it yourself, it's how you feel, how you perceive yourself, and not what you want to accept from a previous heritage. So I feel like it's a very relative term.

BECAUSE YOU ARE A KOREAN ADOPTEE, DO YOU THINK YOU WERE PRESSURED AT AN EARLY AGE TO REALLY THINK ABOUT IDENTITY ISSUES?

No. I didn't feel any more pressure than any other kids growing up.

HOW MUCH OF AN ADOPTED CHILD'S HERITAGE DO YOU THINK PARENTS SHOULD BRING INTO THE HOUSEHOLD?

That's a very relative question because I feel like each child is going to go about that differently, especially growing up in the different locations. I think parents are going to react differently too. Essentially you have to go by the individual case.

NOW IF YOU HAD BEEN OLDER WHEN YOU WERE ADOPTED, DO YOU THINK IT WOULD HAVE BEEN BETTER FOR YOU TO HAVE BEEN ADOPTED INTO A KOREAN OR KOREAN AMERICAN FAMILY, ALL THINGS BEING EQUAL?

I don't think anything could be equal. I think my experience would be different even if you could call it equal. So I don't think I can really answer that.

DO YOU HAVE ANY SUGGESTIONS OR ADVICE THAT YOU WOULD GIVE TO PARENTS WHO ARE THINKING OF ADOPTING FROM OVERSEAS OR BIRACIALLY?

Yes. I think that they should read, read, read, and educate themselves tremendously, and talk to counselors and experts in the field and to adoption agencies. Talk to other families who have adopted. Interview children separate from the families. I feel like to get a really honest answer, they should talk to as many adoptees as possible. They're all going to be different answers. They're all going to give them another piece of the adoption schema.

DO YOU THINK THAT SHOULD BE A REQUIREMENT OF AGENCIES?

No, I don't think so, but it would definitely help them. I think adoption should be open the way it is. My parents didn't expose me to a lot of culture. They did the best they could, and they did it with love, and I could not ask for anything otherwise.

IT SOUNDS LIKE YOU GREW UP IN A WONDERFUL ENVIRONMENT WITH WONDERFUL AND LOVING PARENTS.

2

TERRY BOESCH

GENDER:	Female
AGE AT TIME OF INTERVIEW:	43
RACE:	Korean
MARITAL STATUS:	Married
OCCUPATION:	Real estate agent

Among the interviews we conducted, we have one that is filled with sadness and pain. Her story attests to the will to survive and the courage that accompanies the journey to recovery. The experiences we are about to report were described by a forty-three-year-old woman who was adopted by Caucasian parents when she was three years old. Terry has few memories of Korea but vividly recalls the day she arrived in the United States. Shuffled from "person to person," "foster home, and then orphanage, and then hospital, and then orphanage" prior to her adoption, Terry remembers thinking that she was going to be sold when she came to the United States.

Raised in Oregon, Terry was the first of nine children to be adopted by her parents. With a Chinese Irish brother, three Korean sisters, a Bolivian brother, a Japanese-Indian-Mexican sister, a biracial African American brother, a Caucasian sister, and being Amerasian herself, Terry and her siblings were "like a club." While she and her siblings enjoyed the common experience of being adopted, they were forced to endure severe verbal, physical, and sexual abuse by her mother and grandfather. Because her mother forbade her siblings to have accents, Terry had to teach her brothers and sisters English. An honor student in school, Terry "detached" herself from her home, where she was called "ugly, stupid, worthless."

When she was in her late teens, Terry's family moved from an all-white town in Oregon to Torrance, California, where for the first time she went to a racially diverse school. Graduating early from high school, Terry left home at the age of seventeen. Her parents divorced when she was eighteen, and although her father was "verbally abusive" during her teenage years, she remained close to him.

Despite her escape from a household of brutality and trauma, Terry found herself in abusive relationships with men. Further, she received unexpected news from Korea pertaining to her biological parents, which sent her spiraling into a depression. She later began therapy to treat her depression. Though she still faces issues regarding confidence, she has "recovered enormously" and would like to write about her adoption experience.

Terry is currently married and works as a real estate agent. She has several friends who are transracial adoptees, many of whom have had similar experiences of abuse. After connecting with other Korean adoptees, "reading about Korea and its history," and enjoying the "beauty of Asian culture," she has come to describe her identity as a "Korean adoptee." Not feeling completely accepted by the white or Asian communities, she still has a "sadness with Korea."

Today, Terry only speaks to two of her siblings. The rest "have very difficult lives" and have battled alcohol abuse and drug addictions. Despite the hardships she has endured, Terry stated, "I am glad that I am adopted, and I do believe in transracial adoption." By confronting her past and opening herself up to Korean adoption issues, she has found the strength to share her story with others: "I feel good that this will get out. I feel good."

WHAT IS YOUR NAME?

My name is Terry Boesch.

WHEN IS YOUR BIRTHDAY?

The given birth date for me is not my real birthday. It's May 13, 1958.

How old are you right now?

I am forty-three (about).

Where were you born?

I was born in Seoul, South Korea.

How old were you again when you were adopted?

About three.

Were you adopted through an agency?

No. My parents sent a relative over there to look for an Amerasian child. And so they found me through a little orphanage outside of Seoul. They were turned down by Holt because they were Catholic.

You are Amerasian?

Supposedly. I found out after my father died. I read the papers about me, and the lady that ran my orphanage came to see me a couple of times. She said that my father was an American serviceman, that he was Italian American.

Where did you grow up?

I grew up in Grants Pass, Oregon.

Do you have any memories about the orphanage?

Just a few. I knew I was going to be adopted, but I didn't know what "adopted" was. I thought I was going to be sold. I didn't like the Korean shoes that they put on my feet, and I kept kicking them off. They were taking my pictures. A lot of chaos. Dirt.

Do you remember any of your emotions when you arrived?

The day I arrived, I remember right after I got off the plane. From then on, I remember everything. My dad—my adoptive dad—tried to carry me from the airplane. I remember from that moment on that he had a really hard time carrying me, like I was really heavy. I kept staring at him. That night I knew I was going somewhere, but I didn't think their house was going to be the place. I kept repacking my suitcase, like, "Okay, I've had enough of this; I'm ready to move on." I thought I was going to go somewhere else. I didn't know I was staying. I remember everyone staring and smiling and taking pictures. I just tried to pretend I wasn't there.

DO YOU REMEMBER ANY OTHER CHILDREN FROM THE ORPHANAGE?

I don't remember anybody, but I had a picture of a girl who everyone told me was my girlfriend. When I was in my twenties, her husband came to visit me. She never got adopted, but I think she grew up fine, and she lives in Chicago. She's married and has two kids. But at that time, in my twenties, I wasn't interested in knowing anything about my past.

DID YOU MAINTAIN ANY KIND OF CONTACT WITH THE ORPHANAGE? YOU SAID THE WOMAN CAME TO VISIT YOU?

Yes. She came to visit me a couple of times. At that time, I didn't have any interest in knowing anything about my past. In fact, I was a little upset because my adoptive grandmother had gone to my orphanage twice trying to dig up my roots, and I wasn't ready to deal with it.

WAS SHE THE ONE WHO WENT OVER TO KOREA TO ADOPT YOU?

No, it was one of her relatives who found me. For me, my adoption was sad. For them it was the happiest moment of their lives.

WHAT WAS IT LIKE NOT KNOWING THE LANGUAGE?

I couldn't understand a word they said, and I kept asking, "Do you know my mother? Do you know my mother?"

DO YOU REMEMBER ANY KOREAN?

No, just "mother," "father," and "hello." That's it.

TELL ME ABOUT YOUR PARENTS.

My mother is French Canadian and Irish. My dad is Swiss.

DO YOU HAVE ANY BROTHERS OR SISTERS?

I have eight adopted brothers and sisters. I was the first one. And I have a Chinese Irish brother, three adopted Korean sisters, one Bolivian brother, one sister who is Japanese-Indian-Mexican, and then a brother and sister— one is half black and the other is white.

WHAT IS THE AGE SPAN BETWEEN ALL OF YOU?

The oldest is my Bolivian brother. He is three years older than me, so he is forty-six. The youngest must be about twenty-one.

WERE MOST OF THEM ADOPTED WHEN THEY WERE YOUNG?

My Bolivian brother was adopted when he was eight or nine and it was very difficult for him. He has a lot of memories of Bolivia and his twelve brothers and sisters, so his childhood was very hard on him, very hard. Three of my adopted Korean sisters were adopted into other families first, and then they were given up for adoption.

THEY WERE GIVEN UP FOR ADOPTION AGAIN?

Yes. They were all adopted as infants, and one was put up for adoption when she was three—the parents didn't want her anymore. And the other two were nine and ten, and the parents were getting a divorce. Their father was having an affair with their older sister, so the mother gave up the Korean girls for adoption again. So we got them together. Even though they are not blood sisters, they were raised together since they were infants.

WHAT WAS IT LIKE GROWING UP IN SUCH A LARGE HOUSEHOLD OF CHILDREN FROM SO MANY COUNTRIES?

That was fine. I think that in the beginning I was pampered, and we had money. The more children we got after three, became a real financial burden, and my parents became poorer and poorer. We all had to get jobs really early—like at fourteen years of age to support ourselves, so we could buy our own clothes. I think in the beginning having the three of us was really great, and then after that I felt like the second mother in charge.

WERE YOU FAIRLY CLOSE TO YOUR SIBLINGS GROWING UP?

Growing up, yeah, we were kind of like a club; it was us against my mom. My mom was very mean. Verbally, physically—she had no patience. She felt that we should be grateful to even have her, that anyone would want us. She pretty much traumatized all of us—her mood swings, very unloving, uncaring. My father was very passive.

WAS SHE ABUSIVE?

Yes.

BOTH VERBALLY AND PHYSICALLY.

Yes.

WHAT KIND OF RELATIONSHIP DO YOU HAVE WITH YOUR BROTHERS AND SISTERS AND YOUR PARENTS TODAY?

I speak to two of them, and then the other ones have very difficult lives. One is in prison right now for stealing, theft; and one has had a stroke and has mental problems. The oldest brother is a mess. And then the youngest sister is in an unwed mother's home with two kids.

IT SOUNDS LIKE EVERYONE HAS HAD AN EXTREMELY DIFFICULT TIME.

Yeah. It's rough when you don't have any parents. My father passed away thirteen years ago. I feel like I am still the parent.

ARE ANY OF YOUR SIBLINGS CLOSE TO YOUR MOTHER?

No.

WERE THEY EVER CLOSE TO YOUR FATHER?

I was close to my father.

DID THAT CHANGE AS THEY CONTINUED TO ADOPT CHILDREN?

Actually, I wasn't close to him as a child. My parents got a divorce when I was eighteen. A couple of years after that, my dad was my best friend. And I helped him out for twelve years.

HOW OLD WERE YOU WHEN YOUR YOUNGEST SIBLING WAS ADOPTED?

I was in my twenties.

DID ONE OF YOUR PARENTS ADOPT AFTER THE DIVORCE?

My mom adopted with her second husband. She wasn't any better to them than she was to us even though she had money, so it wasn't money.

WERE YOU CLOSE TO YOUR STEPFATHER—HER SECOND HUSBAND?

No. I was already grown up when they got married.

DID YOUR PARENTS TREAT ANY OF YOU DIFFERENTLY?

Yes.

HOW DID YOU PERCEIVE THE DIFFERENCES?

My mother loved my brother, my older brother.

AND HE WAS ADOPTED AFTER YOU?

Yes.

HOW DID SHE SHOW HER AFFECTION?

Sexually.

DID SHE SEXUALLY ABUSE ANY OF YOUR OTHER SIBLINGS?

Not that I know of.

WAS YOUR FATHER AWARE OF ANY OF THE ABUSE GOING ON?

Yes. We were all aware of it. I think it happens a lot. Half of the adoptees I meet, females, we've been molested or abused. I'm one of them.

I THINK THERE'S A MYTH THAT ADOPTIVE PARENTS DON'T ABUSE CHILDREN.

They do.

HAS YOUR MOTHER EVER ACKNOWLEDGED THAT SHE DID THIS?

Oh, yes, she has.

WAS YOUR FATHER EVER ABUSIVE?

He was verbally abusive to me when I was a teenager. He had a lot of problems.

WHEN DID YOU LEAVE HOME?

I left home at seventeen. I graduated early. Actually, I was supposed to graduate from high school early at sixteen. But she wouldn't let me go. She wouldn't let me go to college; she wanted me to work in her doughnut shop.

WHAT ABOUT YOUR FATHER? WHAT KIND OF WORK DID HE DO?

He was a physical laborer in Oregon, and we moved to California in my late teens, and we had a doughnut shop. So we all worked in that.

DID YOUR PARENTS GO TO COLLEGE?

No.

HOW WERE THEY RAISED?

My father came from an alcoholic, abusive father. His mother and my adopted mother were both teenaged wives—his mother was sixteen when she got married; my mother was seventeen when she got married, and I think that was part of the problem. They were immature and young.

DO YOU KNOW WHY YOUR PARENTS DECIDED TO ADOPT SO MANY CHILDREN?

I have my own feelings. Number one, my father couldn't have children; number two, my mother didn't want to work, so she'd rather boss a bunch of little kids around than have to work. I think the grandparents wanted kids, and I think my grandparents pressured them.

DID YOUR MOTHER ACT VERY DIFFERENTLY IN PUBLIC?

Yes. Totally different. And my cousins and everyone have seen that.

DID ANY OF YOUR TEACHERS KNOW THAT YOU WERE BEING ABUSED GROW-
ING UP?

Yes.

DID THEY DO ANYTHING?

No. They tried to be supportive of me in high school. I tried to tell them
what was going on at home, and all they could say was that my mother loved
my brother, but I never went into details. They knew something was going
on at home, and I told them that my mother hated me. I thought of all of
us being split up—that's what my dad said. Three of my adopted sisters and
brothers had already been adopted before. If this came out, we would all be
put up for adoption again. That eventually wore me down after two or three
years—when I became around twelve or thirteen. I didn't want to see my
younger brothers or sisters going to different homes.

BEING ONE OF THE OLDER CHILDREN, I'M SURE YOU FELT THAT YOU HAD
SOME SORT OF RESPONSIBILITY, THOUGH OBVIOUSLY IT WASN'T YOUR RESPON-
SIBILITY.

My phys. ed. teacher also was really caring for me. She knew when I
could barely keep from crying at school, and I was the most depressed child
in the class. They knew something was going on but I had to keep quiet.

HOW DID YOUR SIBLINGS REACT TO THE ABUSE? WHAT WERE THEY LIKE IN
SCHOOL?

Lousy. My older brother got into drugs. He was only a year ahead of me
in school even though he was three years older. When he was in tenth
grade, he didn't want to be with my mother anymore, so she kicked him out.
So he moved out on his own. He was eighteen anyway. He wanted to leave.
He wanted to date girls his age, and she wouldn't let him so he moved out.
And that's when my mom decided to move us all back down to California.

DID YOUR PARENTS HAVE ANY FRIENDS WHO WERE ASIAN OR ASIAN AMER-
ICAN?

There were no Asians in town. My sisters and I and my brother were the
only ones. There were no blacks, no other minorities except us. And then
we moved to California and the school had a lot of Japanese, Korean Clubs,
and stuff like that, but we just felt really separate from the Korean people.

They tried to have us join their club, but you know we were into being American.

WERE YOU ABLE TO TALK WITH YOUR BROTHERS AND SISTERS ABOUT ADOPTION ISSUES?

Not growing up.

HOW ABOUT NOW?

I'm trying to get them to talk about it now.

HAS IT BEEN DIFFICULT?

It is painful for them.

DID YOU PARENTS EVER TRAVEL TO ANY OF YOUR BIRTH COUNTRIES?

My parents couldn't afford to even take us on vacations. We had no money.

SO TRAVELING OUT OF THE COUNTRY WAS NOT AN OPTION?

Traveling out of the state was not an option.

DID THEY KNOW ANYTHING ABOUT KOREAN CULTURE?

Nothing.

HOW ABOUT ANY OF THE OTHER CULTURES?

Nothing.

WHEN DID YOU START LEARNING ENGLISH?

First grade. She never talked to me. My mother never talked to me. She would only scream at me.

WAS IT THE SAME WITH YOUR BROTHER AND SISTER?

Well, they were older. I was almost six when we started adopting other children. I was alone for a while. So they didn't talk until I taught them.

DID SOCIAL WORKERS COME TO DO HOME STUDIES?

Yes. They came and she'd threaten me before they'd come. If I didn't behave—this is just my interpretation because I didn't speak any English—she would take care of me later on. She always threatened me before we went out in public. So when the social worker came over, I was just all pretty in my little party dress and looking all beautiful. Then as soon as that door shut she was back to her mean self.

MANY ABUSIVE PARENTS HAVE MASTERED THE ABILITY TO CLOAK THE ABUSE AND THEY KNOW HOW TO MANIPULATE EVERYONE.

I have even seen her on TV say how much she loves children, throw arms around two of the youngest ones—it just made all of us sick.

DID EITHER OF YOUR PARENTS EVER SHOW ANY INTEREST IN ANY SORT OF CULTURE?

No. In fact my mom would scream at us, "There are no accents in this family. We will all speak perfect English." And she pounded on my brother constantly. He was nine years old. He spoke no English and had a real problem with a couple of words. She was just very mean about it.

DO YOU BELONG TO ANY RELIGIOUS ORGANIZATION TODAY?

No. But I do consider myself a spiritual person. I always had this faith inside that if I would make it through my childhood, it would be a great story, and there would be some good that would come out of it. And that's what kept me going. I'm still going through it. Self-esteem is a huge problem . . . having any kind of confidence. Every day is a growth process for me and my brothers and sisters because when you grow up with abuse and feel worthless, and then being an orphan on top of that, you end up having horrible abusive relationships. All my brothers and sisters have had that, including me. It is horrible that you just repeat what you have lived through.

ARE YOU CURRENTLY MARRIED?

Yes. And he is controlling and overbearing.

IS HE ABUSIVE?

Sometimes he is verbally abusive. I don't tell anybody, but it makes me sick. I do what I did in my childhood, "You're right, I'm stupid," or "I'm an idiot," or "You're right, I'm worthless; I'm nothing."

WHERE DID YOU MEET YOUR HUSBAND?

He is my (adopted) cousin. His dad and my dad were brothers.

HAVE YOU BEEN ABLE TO TALK ABOUT YOUR ADOPTION ISSUES? DOES HE KNOW ABOUT THE ABUSE THAT WENT ON IN YOUR HOUSE?

Yes, he's known for quite some time. When my parents got divorced, everyone knew why.

HOW WOULD YOU DESCRIBE YOUR HUSBAND?

He's controlling. He always has to be right. But he is interested in adoptees. I think he's interested in them for different reasons than I am. He's interested in them recreationally, and I'm more interested in that I have a lot in common and have stories to share. I want to help people who may have gone through what I have gone through. And I've met a lot. I'd say half the adoptees who I've met have gone through what I have. I don't know if it's my age group or because I wasn't willing to admit what I'd been through until I was in my thirties. So when the younger ones tell me their life was wonderful, I don't believe them because I used to do that rather than have to talk about it.

I hate to say this, and I don't know if it was because they were older parents or because they were so naïve about foreign children, but I often wonder if they thought we were subhuman. One time my dad told me that someone at work said that people with darker skin don't feel as much pain. What an ignorant, stupid thing to say. And why would my dad repeat these things to me unless he thought that that might be kind of true? They treated us like we would suffer no pain.

They came from abusive, alcoholic families. Both of them had alcoholic parents, and I started thinking that they don't check backgrounds. Maybe they do now, but back then, did they check and see if my parents had alcoholic parents? That is not a great environment to bring a child into, adult children of alcoholics. The chaos my dad went through was nothing compared to what I went through. My dad had to watch his mother being beaten by a drunk every night, so of course my dad hitting me would be nothing because at least my teeth are still in my mouth, and he's not drunk. I think social workers ought to find out what these parents' childhoods were like before they go and adopt, and make sure they deal with these issues before they adopt children.

If you look at my sisters and brothers, half of them are being supported by the government. My brother is an alcoholic. He's being taken care of by a Mormon Church, and his children are all in foster homes. My sister is in prison; her son is in prison—seventeen years old and he's going to be in prison until he's thirty. When I think about that, that really makes me angry. I think that they don't want to spend the money to do a psychological profile on these adoptive parents.

I also have had times when I couldn't function because of my depression. I've had to rely on the social services and almost free therapy where I only had to pay five dollars an hour to help me survive my life without being a suicide victim. So I think that, yes, that definitely they should spend the time, spend the money to do psychological profiles, get help for these people. When they interview the children after they've been adopted—my mother was still in the room, staring at me. What was I supposed to say? And I didn't speak English. All I knew how to do was nod my head yes. "She's staring at me. She's going to beat me up later on as soon as the doors shut." I feel to this day that my life is probably better, even with all the abuse, better than it would have been in Korea. Isn't that awful? And that even though I was treated horribly, I think I might have been treated even more horribly there.

IS YOUR YOUNGEST SIBLING OUT OF THE HOUSE?

The two youngest ran away.

HOW OLD WERE THEY?

About seventeen and sixteen. But I'm living a pretty good life. I still go to therapy. I've been in therapy for over thirteen years. I went today. That helps me because I had all those years when I didn't have a mother. My childhood is the story that I want out. I've recovered enormously, but I still every day have trouble with confidence and having a happy marriage. My marriage is ok, but it is not great.

IT SOUNDS LIKE YOU'VE COME A LONG WAY NOW THAT YOU ARE ABLE TO SPEAK OUT ABOUT IT, SHARE IT, AND TALK ABOUT IT.

It helps me.

SURVIVORS OF PHYSICAL AND SEXUAL ABUSE, ANY KIND OF ABUSE—IT SWALLOWS THEM WHOLE SOMETIMES.

I was a good child, a great child, a people-pleaser, a good student. If I had been in a good family, I feel that I would have graduated from college, but instead I spent many years just wandering and depressed.

TELL ME WHAT YOU DID AFTER YOU LEFT HOME.

I got a job as a file clerk, and then I got a job in a bank, and a job at USC. My self-esteem was starting to get a little bit better, and then the people from Korea came and brought my past back into my face. Then my self-esteem went downhill.

DID THEY TRACK YOU DOWN?

Yes. My grandmother has been keeping in contact with them.

WHAT WAS THEIR AGENDA?

She said that she contacted all of the girls who were adopted. There were five of us—two of us were half Korean and three of us were full Korean. There were only five who were adopted to the United States from her orphanage, so she wanted to see all of us. They told me that my mother was a prostitute, and my father was an American serviceman. I was just trying to build my self-esteem back, and I wasn't ready to deal with this.

HAVE YOU EVER BEEN TO KOREA?

No, I haven't.

IS THAT SOMETHING YOU THINK YOU'D LIKE TO DO?

Yeah. But there's something inside—part of it was I didn't like my adoptive mother, and it was so horrible just trying to get her out of my mind. It would be awful if I met my Korean mother and couldn't stand her either. I've never really wanted to go to Korea. I've had a lot of hatred for Korean people. I've been treated badly by some of them.

WOULD YOU EVER SEARCH FOR YOUR BIRTH FATHER?

My birth father is supposed to be American. It's really odd. I'd like to go to Korea as a tourist and maybe with other adoptees, but not necessarily to do birth searches. Like I've had too much family.

IT SOUNDS LIKE YOU NEED SPACE FOR YOURSELF.

I don't need another brother or sister. I don't need another mean mother. I don't need a poor Korean woman who doesn't have any money. I can barely function emotionally for myself. I like collecting adoptee friends who've had unhappy childhoods, and we're getting our lives together now.

I THINK IT'S ABOUT HAVING PEOPLE WHO CAN UNDERSTAND WHAT YOU'VE BEEN THROUGH. IT SOUNDS LIKE YOU'VE REALLY BEEN THERE FOR A LOT OF PEOPLE IN ADDITION TO YOUR BROTHERS AND SISTERS. YOU'VE BEEN THERE FOR OTHER ADOPTEES WHO HAVE BEEN THROUGH HELL AND BACK.
GROWING UP, HOW DID PEOPLE REACT TO YOUR FAMILY OR PERCEIVE YOUR FAMILY?

They saw my family adopting each child and coming in. When they got their citizenship it was like a big assembly at school, and all the girls were crying because they thought it was so wonderful that my brothers and sisters became American citizens. So actually it was more like a celebrity thing.

ARE YOU GLAD IT WAS LIKE THAT?

Kind of, but I had my depression. I was just cloaked in this sadness, but everyone was basically nice to me. I was very tall, very fair, no one ever bothered me or teased me. My sisters got teased a couple of times, but not me. I was being abused at home. My family, where I should be getting the love and support—they were treating me worse than anyone in the entire world to this day. I have no desire, no guilt, about ever contacting my adoptive mother again.

WHEN DID YOU FIRST START FEELING DEPRESSED?

I told my therapist I was four or five.

HAVE SOME OF YOUR BROTHERS AND SISTERS DEALT WITH DEPRESSION?

Yeah, a lot of them take care of it with alcohol and drugs. The major problem in my family is drugs and alcohol. That's why my sister is in the rehab. She's an alcoholic and has been one since she was sixteen. The one in prison is in therapy because she has a drug problem, and that's why she steals.

WHAT WAS YOUR EXTENDED FAMILY LIKE?

My grandparents—well actually I was sexually abused by my grandfather, my dad's mother's third husband. My mother made me take naps with him, so I was sexually molested by him. My mother MADE me take naps with him for two years, until I moved to Oregon. So that was part of my depression. I always felt ugly and stupid, and I hated men. All my life I hated men.

YOUR FATHER—WAS HE PHYSICALLY ABUSIVE?

Not really. You know, pulling your hair. I later told him that hurt, and he did apologize before he died about how he treated me. My father had a lot of growth problems. He had some kind of dwarfism, I think, and I was really tall. That was some kind of threat I can understand now, but I couldn't as I was growing up. He was treating me like crap for three years because I was growing as a normal person. And there was a lot of sickness, like telling me the reason why I'm an orphan is because I was a bad mother in one of my past lives. Things like that. A lot of crazy made-up stuff. And then saying if I ever used my looks for money, I would have epilepsy in one of my next lives, things like that. He made up a lot of crap.

DID YOU EVER FORGIVE HIM?

I forgave him, yeah. But when he died, it took me three years. I suffered another big depression then. So the two major depressions were in puberty and then when I hit thirty.

IN PUBERTY, HOW DID YOU COME TO GRIPS WITH THE DEPRESSION? HOW DID YOU DEAL WITH IT?

Well, the counselor and my phys. ed. teacher.

DID YOU EVER GO THROUGH A DRUG OR ALCOHOL PROBLEM?

No. In my twenties I went out drinking, and I'm not really a drinker. I think it was a way to avoid pain, but I don't have an addictive personality. I was drinking for a while.

NOT HAVING AN ADDICTIVE PERSONALITY PROBABLY KEPT YOU TOGETHER AND HELPED YOU GET THIS FAR.

I had to deal with my sadness. I couldn't bury it.

SO YOU COULDN'T SELF-MEDICATE LIKE YOUR BROTHERS AND SISTERS SEEM TO HAVE DONE?

I can't do it. My body just physically cannot handle alcohol or drugs. I'm not an addictive person. I've never even smoked a cigarette.

WAS THERE A POINT IN YOUR LIFE WHEN ADOPTION REALLY BECAME A CENTRAL PART OF YOUR IDENTITY?

It is now. It's who I am, and I think it's made me feel a lot better. I identify with Korean adoptees or anybody who has been adopted, internationally especially, because I remember not being able to speak English.

ARE MOST OF YOUR FRIENDS TODAY TRANSRACIAL ADOPTEES?

Yes, by now, the last two years.

HAVE YOU EVER DATED AN ASIAN OR ASIAN AMERICAN MAN?

I dated some Japanese guy when I was younger.

WHAT WAS THAT EXPERIENCE LIKE FOR YOU?

I tended to get along with Japanese Americans better than Koreans because they didn't expect me to be Japanese. Koreans expect me to be Korean. The Japanese Americans had been here longer, so even though I was first generation here, I felt like I was second generation because I had American parents. So I got along with Japanese Americans a lot better, especially if they were half Japanese and half American.

I DON'T KNOW IF YOU ARE FAMILIAR WITH A STATEMENT THAT CAME OUT IN 1971 WHEN THE PRESIDENT OF THE NATIONAL ASSOCIATION OF BLACK SOCIAL WORKERS SAID, "BLACK CHILDREN BELONG PHYSICALLY, PSYCHOLOGICALLY, AND CULTURALLY IN BLACK FAMILIES IN ORDER THAT THEY RECEIVE A TOTAL SENSE OF THEMSELVES AND DEVELOP A SOUND PROJECTION OF THEIR FUTURE." I WAS WONDERING IF YOU HAD ANY THOUGHTS ON THAT STATEMENT IN LIGHT OF YOUR OWN EXPERIENCE?

I don't agree with that. A sense of self is a sense of self as an individual and not just based on what you look like, where you were born.

DO YOU THINK GROWING UP IN A MULTICULTURAL FAMILY HELPED PREPARE YOU TO DEAL WITH RACISM AND STEREOTYPES?

I think it helped me with my own racism. Because I grew up with different nationalities, I've come to believe that people are just people. Mexican, Indian, Japanese—everyone is a human being and has feelings, and you can hurt them. Color didn't matter in my family. My mother treated all of us like crap.

WHAT KINDS OF IDENTITY PROBLEMS HAVE YOU GONE THROUGH?

I did the Farrah Fawcett thing. I wished I was blond my whole life. I thought I was ugly. I hated my little eyes and my straight hair, and so I suffered the perm thing.

SO YOU SAID TODAY YOU WOULD DEFINE YOUR IDENTITY AS KOREAN AMERICAN?

Korean adoptee. I don't even say Korean American. I think we're in our own little subculture.

WHAT ARE SOME OF THE THINGS THAT HAVE HELPED YOU BUILD THAT IDENTITY?

Reading about Korea and its history has helped me a lot to understand the hardship that they went through, the war, the poverty. It helped me understand that it wasn't just because my mother was a horrible person and a prostitute, it was because Korea went through the Korean War and my mother was probably an orphan. She didn't come from a good family, wasn't able to marry anybody, and had to make a living. Women have no place in Korean society and she had to find some way to make money. She sees these American men and they have money, so she had no choice. And I've only come to realize that in the last few years.

I collect Korean dolls now. I'm not afraid to have them in my house. It's not like I have a swastika up in my room. That's how I used to feel. I can enjoy the beauty of Asian culture as much as I want to and as little as I want to.

DO YOU FEEL ACCEPTED BY THE WHITE COMMUNITY?

Yes.

DO YOU FEEL ACCEPTED BY THE ASIAN COMMUNITY?

Not really.

DO YOU THINK THERE IS MORE PRESSURE PLACED UPON TRANSRACIAL ADOPTEES BY OUR SOCIETY TO REALLY COME TO A SOUND CONCLUSION AS TO WHO THEY ARE AND WHAT THEIR IDENTITIES ARE?

Not by society.

BY OURSELVES?

I think for ourselves that's a real, real big issue for us. Because what happens if you have to avoid being Asian or a Korean adoptee? My husband says, "You guys talk about the hole in your heart. That's part of your identity." So you live with this big hole. Well, that's our identity, being an adoptee; being a Korean adoptee is our identity. My sisters are trying to forget it and are still drinking and everything, and the most painful thing is admitting that yes, you are a Korean adoptee, and yes, you have suffered, and yes, you can like yourself for it. After you go through the pain, you can also see the good in it. And the good is that you can help younger people who are going through it.

I THINK WE'RE NOW SEEING GENERATIONAL DIFFERENCES IN KOREAN ADOPTEES. SINCE THE '50S, ATTITUDES HAVE CHANGED, PRACTICES HAVE CHANGED, AND HOME STUDIES HAVE CHANGED.

When I see Korean adoptees around my age, we don't look alike at all. When you look at the younger ones, they all look very Korean. But us older ones, none of us look alike. Some look black, some look Mexican, some look Hawaiian. But when you look at the younger ones, they can pass for full Korean.

DURING THE '50S KOREA WAS EXPERIENCING THE RAMIFICATIONS OF THE WAR, SO MORE BIRACIAL CHILDREN WERE BEING ADOPTED. I THINK MORE CHILDREN ARE BEING ADOPTED WHOSE BIRTH PARENTS ARE BOTH KOREAN.

I have a sadness with Korea. I have an urge to write to a Korean paper, to write, "Yes, I understand why I was adopted." So I feel totally fine with that. I know that there was a Korean War. I know that my mother was probably a starving war orphan; her parents probably died during the war. I know that, and that she had no choice, and I accept that. But with younger adoptees, now that Korea is doing better, I feel that the country should find some way to help. I think they are starting to help the orphans stay there and keep their culture. Like the Korean woman told me—Korea is very slow to change, to accept unwed mothers, and to help them.

WHAT DO YOU THINK IS THE BEST SITUATION FOR A CHILD WHO IS TRANSRACIAL OR BIRACIAL?

Being alone, I was shuffled around from person to person a lot—foster home, and then orphanage, and then hospital, and then orphanage, and then stuck with some total stranger on a plane for almost a day, and then put in the family. Subconsciously, I don't trust anybody. Exposure to as few people as possible would help. I think going over and picking up the child eliminates about three or four other people. I think I was fed by a different person every day—breakfast, lunch, and dinner. There was no stability in my life, and I think that was why I never had much stability in my life as an adult. I didn't know why I wanted to move every six months, why I had to end every relationship every few months, until I started looking at the pattern in my life before the age of three.

DO YOU FEEL LIKE YOU ARE ABLE TO LOVE THE SAME WAY AS OTHER PEOPLE?

No. I hate to tell you this. I went to a retreat with six other adoptees, and two of them said they loved their mother. I asked, "Do you feel bonded to your mother?" and all six of them said no, they didn't feel a bond.

HAVE YOU EVER BEEN ABLE TO LOVE ANYBODY ELSE?

I thought I loved my first boyfriend. I was eighteen. I think I was infatuated. He was abusive, and the more abusive he was, the more I thought I loved him. So, no. I shouldn't speak for everybody, but I'll just say it. I think it is very difficult for adoptees to love somebody. Because I think that adoption is abnormal. I think it is against nature. It's a human thing that humans do.

WOULD YOU HAVE PREFERRED TO BE ADOPTED BY A KOREAN FAMILY IF YOU KNEW THAT THEY WERE A LOVING AND STABLE FAMILY?

I hate to say it, but probably. At least I could come home and be with someone that looked like me. Instead, I came home to blond-haired, blue-eyed people.

WHAT WAS THE MOST DIFFICULT PART ABOUT GROWING UP IN A MULTICUL-
TURAL FAMILY? WHAT WAS THE MOST ENJOYABLE PART? WAS ANYTHING EN-
JOYABLE?

The most difficult part was my identity. I don't look like my sisters even
though they are Korean adopted. I was never cute and little like them. I was
always very tall, angular, very white. The most enjoyable part was being
around my adopted brothers and sisters. That was the most enjoyable part
of my childhood—being with my adopted brothers and sisters, because we
shared that.

ARE YOU GLAD THAT YOU WERE ADOPTED?

I am glad that I am adopted. That's not my number one choice, but I am
glad that I am adopted. And supposedly being biracial, I think for me it was
the best thing.

DID YOUR SPIRITUALITY HELP YOU IN ANY WAY?

It helped me survive. I think I would have been a suicide victim.

SO IT WAS KEY TO YOUR SURVIVAL?

Yes. There was a voice that always told me: "If you just make it until you
grow up, life will be a lot better."

DO YOU HAVE ANY SUGGESTIONS OR ADVICE THAT YOU WOULD GIVE TO PAR-
ENTS WHO ARE THINKING OF ADOPTING TRANSRACIALLY?

They need to take care of their own issues first. And I've written this—
you should adopt totally out of no selfish reason for yourself.

ARE YOU WRITING?

Yes. I've been writing on chat lines, and I am publishing a book. I think
the last glitch for me was saying that I was molested because that was a big
part of why I felt so horrible about myself. I couldn't defend myself when I
was three, and my family not believing me—not even my husband. Just
now, recently, he has started to admit that he believes me. You know why it
was hard for him? Because his sisters took naps with [my grandfather] too,
and he's never asked them what happened. I think he had to admit finally,
and he said it was very painful for him to admit because my grandfather was
nice to him and my brothers. A nap with my grandfather for him was just a
nap, but a nap for me was in a private room with just him and me and no
English. Not speaking English, how can they even tell anyone what happened? I also told somebody, when these people give their children up
they're hoping for the best, but you might as well just throw the child up in

the air and hope it lands on its feet because as soon as you relinquish that child, there is no guarantee that they are going to a good family.

THEY HAVE NO WAY OF KNOWING WHAT WILL BECOME OF THEIR CHILDREN. I THINK THAT'S A GOOD POINT. BECAUSE THERE IS THAT BELIEF THAT AMERICAN HOMES ARE ALWAYS BETTER, HAPPIER. ARE THERE OTHER ASPECTS OF YOUR EXPERIENCE THAT YOU WOULD LIKE TO SHARE OR ARE THERE THINGS I FORGOT TO ASK YOU?

I think that no matter how horrible your childhood was, you can overcome it. You can.

I THINK YOU HAVE A POWERFUL VOICE THAT CAN ATTEST TO THAT.

I'm glad I survived to tell my story. It makes me really happy to see that children are adopted now, and on the surface they look like they're loved. Their parents allow them to write and talk to me, and I feel like that is a good sign. Even then, you may still have some identity issues. I told one girl, we all do. Even if you weren't adopted, there's a period where you have identity problems.

ARE THERE ANY OTHER PARTS THAT YOU WOULD LIKE TO TALK ABOUT?

No. I feel good that this will get out. I feel good.

3

CARRIE*

GENDER:	Female
AGE AT TIME OF INTERVIEW:	18
RACE:	Korean
MARITAL STATUS:	Single
OCCUPATION:	Student

Carrie, a junior at a large public university at the time of the interview, was adopted from Korea when she was only a few months old. Her parents were living in a large New York suburb at the time of her adoption. Carrie's mother came from a wealthy family, while her father grew up in a poor and sometimes abusive environment away from his own biological mother. With a biological son and no desire to have any more birth children, Carrie's parents decided to adopt. Interestingly, it was Carrie's brother who initially introduced the idea of adopting a child from Korea. With many multicultural marriages in her extended family, Carrie's family received support when they decided to adopt.

At the age of seventeen, Carrie's brother left home to join the military. Although he currently lives many states away, she still maintains a close

_____

*Identifying information about this participant has been omitted or changed.

connection to him. She has always felt comfortable talking to her brother about adoption issues, and has described him as her "sounding board."

As a child, Carrie recalls that her parents always told her that they loved her more than her brother, although she has no memory of being "treated more specially" than him. As a child who had seen very few other Asians, she never knew that Asians could have brown hair. Then, as an older child, she realized that her hair was actually brown. Her awareness of the lack of Asian visibility in magazines or movies was discomforting to her, and she would question her own looks. With pale skin and brown hair, she was often told that she looked "mixed." In addition, people would describe her as "exotic," which she interpreted as a sexual connotation rather than a reference to beauty.

Carrie recalled her middle school as being "absolutely awful." For the first time, she became aware of her physical differences. With the belief that she was the "biggest freak," she often came home from school crying. In her all-white school, kids would tell her, "You look like you ran into a brick wall," or they would make comments about her slanted eyes. With few friends, Carrie spent her time with her mother. With a love for sports, she would watch hockey and football games with her father. To this day, she remains very close to her parents.

Attending high school at an all-girls Catholic school was a better experience, although she was asked questions such as, "Who are your real parents" and "Do you eat dog meat?" To cope with such invasive and ignorant questions, Carrie sometimes lied about her family, or wouldn't deny certain assumptions about her family. Her parents taught her that "American didn't mean white" and she always felt comfortable being an American.

In college, Carrie is among a very diverse student population, where she has made many Asian friends. She described the transition from a homogenous high school to a diverse college as "liberating." Today, she identifies herself as Korean, whereas several years ago, she "would have no clue and it would scare [her] to death." While she has spent time reflecting upon cultural and identity issues related to her experience, she stresses the importance of focusing on school, family, and friends, and not just on adoption issues. With regards to conducting a birth parent search, she has no interest in doing so and states, "I am really happy here, and I know I am so totally blessed by God and everyone else around me. I'm lucky to be where I am and who I am." Carrie is currently pursuing a degree in biology and would like to become a doctor.

How old are you Carrie?

Eighteen.

Where were you born.

Korea, but two official documents have different cities on them, so we're not sure.

How old were you when you were adopted?

I was a couple of days over three months.

Where were you living before you were adopted?

With a foster mother.

What are your adoptive parents' backgrounds?

They are typical Anglos. My mother's German and Irish/Swedish. It depends what school of thought you come from, but her mother in the family was Jewish. Some people think that is an ethnicity, some think it just a religion or a culture somewhere between, so she has some Jewish roots in her family.

Do you have any brothers or sisters?

A brother, and he is twenty-nine.

Was he adopted?

No.

Growing up what kind of relationship did you have with your brother?

There was such a big age difference. He left the house when he was seventeen to join the military.

Have you ever been able to talk openly with him about your adoption?

Oh, yes. He is always my sounding board. Actually, when my parents didn't want to have any more birth kids, my brother was the one who found out about it and researched it. So he's always been there, a sounding board for me. Even if we're thousands of miles away, I can always call him.

Did you ever perceive any differences in the way you were treated by your parents?

Yes, my parents always told me they loved me more. It sounds horrible, but that's why my brother left when he was so young to join the Marine

Corps. He gave my parents a lot of grief, and I remember when I was a little kid, they were always screaming.

DO YOU THINK HE WAS EVER JEALOUS OF YOU OR YOUR SPECIAL TREATMENT BY YOUR PARENTS?

I don't think I was treated more specially than him. I just think, like they said, if you say you don't have a favorite among your children you're lying. When they say they love me more, I don't think they mean it literally. I think they maybe feel I've been a better kid than he was because of his behavior. My brother was in alcohol rehab when he was nineteen, and it put the family under a lot of stress.

CAN YOU TELL ME MORE ABOUT YOUR PARENTS, THEIR SCHOOLING, WHAT THEIR BACKGROUNDS ARE, WHAT THEY DO FOR A LIVING?

My mom came from a very wealthy family. Her father dropped out of high school a couple of months before he was about to graduate. He was the vice president of an HMO, and they always had a lot of money. For my mom's birthday, she got a new sports car. She always went to a private school and always had everything perfect and new. My father was the exact opposite. His father left him, and his mother couldn't afford to care for both him and his older sister. Since he was the youngest, he was sent to another house, and he was abused there. It was like a foster home.

HOW OLD WAS HE WHEN HE WAS SENT TO THIS HOME?

His father left at three or three and a half. His mother could only hold on for a few more months.

DID HE MAINTAIN CONTACT WITH HIS BIRTH MOTHER?

Yes. He was never adopted. She remarried later on, and as soon as she got money, she brought him right back. She said there was no money, and the electricity would be turned off. She sent him to where she knew there would be a warm roof over his head—to a distant relative to keep it in the family.

WHAT ABOUT YOUR PARENTS' EDUCATION?

My mother never went to college. My father started and then dropped out.

WHAT KIND OF WORK DO THEY DO?

My mother was a nurse, but then she started her own home care business, and that's what she is doing now. And my father works in an automotive factory. He was in the military full-time for a little while, and then he went into the Reserves.

DO YOUR PARENTS HAVE ANY FRIENDS WHO ARE ASIAN AMERICAN OR KO-REAN?

Well, only through me.

DO THEY KNOW A LOT ABOUT KOREAN CULTURE?

They know a few general assumptions. They would correct someone if someone said something like, "Does everyone eat dog there? Does everyone have an arranged marriage?" They would know that this is stereotyping.

WHAT WERE YOUR PARENTS' FRIENDS LIKE?

Just your typical middle-class Caucasian American. White Americans.

DO YOU HAVE ANY EXPERIENCES WITH OR THOUGHTS ON INTERRACIAL DATING?

Well, my parents wouldn't even let me talk to a guy now. They are very strict. My parents have told me when the age comes—I think it's about forty or fifty now—they are open to anyone as long as he treats me well.

WHAT ABOUT YOU?

Oh, I don't care. Give me purple with pink stripes.

WHAT IS IMPORTANT TO YOU IN A PARTNER?

He treats me well, respects me. Education level—maybe if they dropped out of first grade, I would be a little concerned. But if they're not college educated, it wouldn't bother me.

DO YOU THINK YOU'LL HAVE CHILDREN?

Hell, no. If the time comes, I would really like to adopt children instead, because I read that there are forty thousand kids abandoned throughout the world each day. It just gave me shivers up my spine.

WOULD YOU ADOPT FROM KOREA?

Well, they don't take singles do they? I'm not planning on getting married either.

My parents want me to adopt. They'd prefer me to adopt. They say, "Just go to any country that will take you."

IF YOU ADOPTED CHILDREN WHO WEREN'T FROM KOREA, DO YOU THINK YOU WOULD CELEBRATE KOREAN CULTURE WITH THEM? TEACH THEM ABOUT KOREA?

Well, I assume like all kids they would be curious, and I'd teach them what I know and can do. I don't think Korean culture is so important in my house—my parents just didn't get around to it.

WHERE ARE YOU GOING TO GO TO SCHOOL AND WHAT ARE YOU MAJORING IN?

University of Buffalo. I finished high school a year ago. I'm majoring in biology. Isn't it so quintessential Asian?

DO YOU KNOW WHAT YOU WANT TO DO WITH THAT?

I used to want to be a doctor.

WHAT WERE YOUR SCHOOLS LIKE BEFORE YOU STARTED COLLEGE?

Elementary school was really cool because no one really knew what was going on, no one really cared. They just want somebody to share their lunch with, you know? Middle school was absolutely awful. I came home crying every day. I thought I was the biggest freak. And then I just realized, "You know, I'm pretty normal. Some kids are really just mean."

WHAT WOULD THEY DO TO YOU? WOULD THEY TAUNT YOU?

They'd always say stuff like, "You look like you ran into a brick wall" or "slanted eyes."

WAS YOUR SCHOOL DIVERSE AT ALL?

Oh, God, no. In every single school I went to, I was the one and only. The only time that was not the case was when I was in elementary school. There was one girl of Asian descent.

WHAT KINDS OF THINGS DID YOU DO IN HIGH SCHOOL?

High school was a lot better because people kind of mature and calm down. It was an all-girls Catholic School. But instead of taunts, I was always getting questions like, "Who are your real parents?" and "Do you eat dog meat?"

HOW DID YOU USUALLY REACT?

It's really hard. It got to the point, and I hate to admit this, but actually sometimes I'd lie.

WHAT WOULD YOU SAY?

A lot of people knew my father was in the military, so they thought my mom was Asian. So I wouldn't say, "Yeah, my mom's Asian." I wouldn't say she wasn't either. I wouldn't deny anything, but I wouldn't make up stories.

WHAT WAS IT LIKE MAKING THE TRANSITION FROM A VERY HOMOGENEOUS HIGH SCHOOL TO A VERY DIVERSE COLLEGE?

It was the most liberating feeling. I mean, not the most liberating that I ever felt, but it ranks pretty high up there. It was pretty nice to be able to walk through the halls and not get stares or asked stupid questions.

DID YOU MEET OTHER ASIAN STUDENTS THAT YOU ARE FRIENDS WITH?

Oh, yeah. I have tons of them now. I was with my friends yesterday, and I don't think I have any white friends. I'm so happy to be in college. After middle school I thought, "Maybe I'm a social freak, maybe there's something wrong with me," but in college I'm so happy.

DO YOU FEEL GENERALLY PRETTY ACCEPTED BY THE ASIAN AMERICAN COMMUNITY AT YOUR SCHOOL?

There are a lot of Asian Americans there. But the Asians—you can tell when you see them—they're pretty exclusive, so not by them, no. Like I said, I just walk away. I don't dwell over it.

WHAT KINDS OF THINGS DO THEY DO THAT MAKE YOU FEEL UNCOMFORTABLE?

I am totally open to dating any race, I don't know any Asian guys; dating them is kind of difficult. If they see me walking with a white guy or something, they give me dirty looks.

GOING BACK TO YOUR CHILDHOOD. DID YOUR PARENTS DO ANYTHING SPECIAL TO CELEBRATE KOREAN CULTURE OR CELEBRATE KOREAN HOLIDAYS?

They weren't aware of any of the holidays. They did take me to Korean school, but I lost interest. They were really good. They would never force anything on me. "If you don't like it, then leave." I really had no interest in Korean culture growing up, so they did what they could.

DID YOU HAVE ANY ROLE MODELS OR PEOPLE YOU ADMIRE WHO ARE KOREAN OR ASIAN?

No. Do you read *Cosmo* or *Glamour*? When I was growing up, you'd never see anyone who was not white. Now you see a lot of blacks and Latinos, and like I said, in my neighborhood I am the only Asian here. Go up and down the streets—I am the one and only. I wouldn't know where to find these people.

WHAT WAS IT LIKE GROWING UP NOT DEFINITIVELY KNOWING YOUR RACIAL BACKGROUND?

I didn't even know until I was older that I actually had brown hair because it was so ingrained in me that Asians could only have black hair. My parents clued me in one day.

WHAT WAS YOUR RELATIONSHIP WITH YOUR PARENTS DURING YOUR ADO-LESCENT YEARS? DID YOU GO THROUGH ANY DIFFICULT PERIODS?

My mom was my best friend because I had no friends in middle school. My mom and I always went out. We always went to the mall; she took me out to eat. I was a typical teenage girl, but I also loved sports, so my father and I would watch the hockey and football games together, and he wanted me to go fishing together. So I am extremely close to both my parents, then and now.

WAS THERE A POINT IN YOUR LIFE WHEN ADOPTION ISSUES BECAME MORE OF A CENTRAL PART OF YOUR EVERYDAY LIFE, WHEN YOU BEGAN TO THINK MORE ABOUT HOW IT REALLY AFFECTED YOUR IDENTITY?

In middle school it was brought to my attention that I was different. But I have never intentionally sought it out.

DO YOU HAVE ANY INTENTIONS OF EVER GOING TO KOREA?

Oh, yeah, sure, I mean, why not? I've got a really close group of friends there, so I'd like to see them.

HAVE YOU EVER TRIED TO LOCATE YOUR BIRTH PARENTS?

No.

DO YOU HAVE ANY INTENTION OF EVER DOING THAT?

If I get some money, sure. I am really happy here and I know I am so totally blessed by God and everyone else around me. I'm lucky to be where I am and who I am.

SOME PEOPLE DON'T WANT TO MAKE CONTACT, BUT THEY JUST WANT TO SEE PICTURES.

Right. Just touch it on the surface. You know the questions. And I think none of those questions really jump out at me and grab me, so I don't think so.

IF YOU DID START A SEARCH, WOULD YOUR ADOPTIVE PARENTS BE SUPPORTIVE?

You know, my mom always said, "I'd be one hundred percent behind you," but I know my mother. I think there would be a little part of her that would say, "What did I do wrong that wants to make her go look?"

I THINK THAT'S A NATURAL FEELING. SHE'S YOUR MOTHER!

And I don't fault her for that. Maybe that's one of the reasons, because I don't want to hurt her. And the health reason thing is what people always bring up, a totally unemotional attachment. They just want the facts. With my mom being a nurse and everyone else in the family being a doctor, they say the best thing you can do is to take care of yourself—whether you're adopted or not—is to eat well, exercise. So even the health thing doesn't get me going.

IN 1971, THE PRESIDENT OF THE NATIONAL ASSOCIATION OF BLACK SOCIAL WORKERS SAID, "BLACK CHILDREN BELONG PHYSICALLY, PSYCHOLOGICALLY, AND CULTURALLY IN BLACK FAMILIES IN ORDER THAT THEY RECEIVE THE TOTAL SENSE OF THEMSELVES AND DEVELOP A SOUND PROJECTION OF THEIR FUTURE." DO YOU HAVE ANY THOUGHTS ON THIS?

I've heard that same expression. You know, I'm one of those from the school of thought that every child deserves a loving home regardless of race. We're all created in God's image, and race is so superficial. From the marriages in my family, we will have so many multiracial children.

HAVE YOU EXPERIENCED ANY IDENTITY CRISES OR PROBLEMS?

I've always been comfortable being American. I've never associated America with "white" because my parents always told me that American means you're a citizen of this country. But then I used to work in customer service, and of course when you're in customer service you get every question under the sun. People would always ask, "What are you?" I'd say "American," and they'd be like, "You can't be American." So every time someone would bring it up I'd think, "What do I do that people are convinced that only white people can be American?"

SO IS THAT HOW YOU WOULD DEFINE YOUR RACIAL IDENTITY, AS AMERICAN?

Nowadays, if they ask about ethnicity, I would definitely say Korean. A long time ago I would have had no clue, and it would have scared me to death.

WHAT ARE SOME OF THE THINGS THAT HAVE CONTRIBUTED TOWARDS SHAP-
ING WHO YOU ARE IN TERMS OF YOUR IDENTITY?

Well, I guess since my father was in the military for thirty years, I think
the whole concept of us being American was really emphasized. Like I said,
my parents always made sure that I knew American didn't mean white. So
I really think that shaped me. My parents were really good to me. "It's your
country too," my parents would always tell me.

HAVE THERE BEEN TIMES WHEN YOUR SELF-ESTEEM HAS REALLY SUFFERED
BECAUSE OF ADOPTION ISSUES, OR WHEN ADOPTION ISSUES HAVE BEEN ESPE-
CIALLY DIFFICULT TO DEAL WITH?

Growing up, I wasn't big on clothing and beauty and stuff, and I'd look at
magazines, and all I see are pages and pages of white people. Then I'd look
at the mirror, and then I'd think, "What is so ugly about people who look
like me that you can't put them in a magazine, or you can't put them in the
movies?" I don't think my self-esteem suffered so much because that has to
do with your self-confidence yourself, but I would just think, "What's wrong
with other people out there?"

TODAY I'VE NOTICED MORE ASIAN FACES IN MAGAZINES AND IN THE MEDIA,
BUT OF COURSE THERE'S ALSO THE STEREOTYPE THAT ASIAN WOMEN ARE EX-
OTIC.

People would always say I looked sexy, and I said, "Why?" They said, "Because you look exotic." I noticed they never described me as being beautiful or pretty; it's always "exotic." I did see some Asians in the magazine, but
I think they were half-Asian, like the one girl had an Asian face but blue
eyes.

YES, AND EVERYONE HAS VERY LIGHT SKIN.

Exactly. God forbid you put a one hundred percent Asian in a magazine.
They'd have a heart attack!

I REMEMBER READING THOSE MAGAZINES GROWING UP WHEN I WAS A
TEENAGER. I WOULD LOOK AT THOSE CHARTS THAT SHOWED YOU HOW TO PUT
MAKEUP ON AND WHAT COLORS LOOK GOOD, BUT I COULD NEVER FIND SOME-
ONE WITH MY SKIN TONE IN THE MAGAZINES. I'D READ THEM WITH MY
FRIENDS, AND OF COURSE IT MADE SENSE FOR THEM BECAUSE THEY WERE
BLOND-HAIRED AND BLUE-EYED, BUT I DIDN'T KNOW HOW TO DO ANYTHING.
AND I STILL DON'T!

And the whole thing about eye shadow—oh, that just threw me.

DO YOU THINK THERE IS MORE PRESSURE PLACED UPON TRANSRACIAL ADOPTEES TO REALLY COME TO A CONCRETE IDEA OF WHO THEY ARE, OF WHAT THEIR IDENTITY IS?

Oh, yeah. It seems to me that the only correct school of thinking is, "I'm Korean with Caucasian parents." It seems there's so much pressure to think that way. And you know what? I'm a big girl now, and I'm not going to deny that I'm of Korean heritage. It's like there's only one way to think right. The best thing I've found on all the Korean sites was people saying, "We don't have to justify ourselves to other people." I feel that culturally, I don't have to tell them what I am. "Why do I have to justify myself to you?" What I hate is that for some of these questions, I don't know the answer.

I THINK THAT ADOPTEES CHANGE THEIR IDENTITIES STARTING FROM WHEN THEY ARE CHILDREN THROUGH COLLEGE AND THEN BEYOND. OUR IDENTITIES ARE ALMOST ALWAYS SHIFTING BASED ON HOW WE'RE DEALING WITH ADOPTION ISSUES, OR IF WE'RE DEALING WITH THEM.

I say call me in five years and I'll tell you how I see myself. I can't even give you a time frame because who knows how I'll think tomorrow.

SOME DAYS I JUST FEEL COMPLETELY "AMERICAN." I ALMOST FORGET I'M A KOREAN. IT'S FUNNY, BUT I DON'T THINK ABOUT IT. AND THEN OTHER DAYS, IT'S VERY NOTICEABLE THAT I AM KOREAN. AND THEN OTHER DAYS I'M MORE KOREAN AMERICAN-*ISH*. I THINK A LOT OF US ARE IN PERPETUAL CULTURAL LIMBO. WE TOUCHED ON THIS BEFORE, BUT IN SELECTING A FOSTER OR ADOPTIVE HOME FOR A CHILD OF COLOR, WHAT DO YOU THINK IS THE BEST SITUATION FOR THEM?

The world is far, far from perfect, and we have to deal with it as best we can. Just look at the number of kids the world over who need homes. Adoptees are just as happy, or not as happy, as people in any other type of family. They produce just as many screwed up kids as all the rest of the families.

IN HOMES WITH ADOPTED CHILDREN, HOW MUCH CULTURE SHOULD THE PARENTS INTRODUCE TO THEIR CHILDREN?

I feel that the parents are shoving the culture down their throat. As far as I'm concerned, read all you can, get all the books you can, make yourself available. Some kids won't gravitate. I liked sports, and I liked shopping. Where would I have time for Korean culture? As far as I'm concerned, it's like another hobby. I think there was a backlash. There wasn't enough cultural information back when we were younger, so now these parents are trying to get everything down them as much as they can. I think if the kid wants it fine; but if the kid doesn't, it's not a sin.

I THINK A LOT OF PARENTS FEEL THAT THEY NEED TO LEARN EVERYTHING ABOUT THEIR CHILD'S CULTURE SO THEY ARE PREPARED WHEN THE CHILD ASKS QUESTIONS. ACTUALLY, I THINK MOST OF THE PARENTS ARE MORE ENTHUSIASTIC ABOUT LEARNING THE CULTURE THAN THE KIDS ARE. I'M SURE IT'S FRUSTRATING FOR SOME PARENTS WHO ARE SO ENTHUSIASTIC AND WHO TRY SO HARD BECAUSE NOT ALL KIDS ARE INTERESTED.

WHAT WAS THE MOST DIFFICULT AND ENJOYABLE PART ABOUT GROWING UP IN A MULTICULTURAL FAMILY?

The most difficult part? Definitely it would be what people would say. There are so many jerks out there. I'm an adult, and I'm better able to handle it, but when you're ten, or six, or seven, or eight or twelve, it's the last thing you want to hear. Someone smacking you in the face—you're different. Just like any other person, whether they're adopted or not, no one wants to stick out like a sore thumb.

CHILDREN ARE SO SUSCEPTIBLE TO EMOTIONAL TAUNTING OR TO ANYTHING THAT INDICATES THAT THEY'RE DIFFERENT.

Definitely the most enjoyable part was that my parents loved me enough, and they've never felt any differently. They've always been so good to me.

WHAT KINDS OF THINGS ARE ESSENTIAL IN RAISING CHILDREN OF A DIFFERENT CULTURE?

The openness and hearing them. Someone said the other day that it's so different parenting adoptive children, and it's so much harder. I think that's too glib of a statement.

DO YOU HAVE ANY SUGGESTIONS OR ADVICE FOR PARENTS WHO ARE CONSIDERING ADOPTING TRANSRACIALLY?

I wonder if my parents had gotten another child, if it would have been a little easier on me.

YOU HAVE A SISTER, RIGHT?

I have a younger sister who's adopted and a young brother who's adopted and an older brother who is not adopted.

WAS IT EASIER WITH YOUR SIBLINGS WHO WERE ADOPTED? LIKE A SOUNDING BOARD?

My sister and I never really talked about adoption issues. It's not like we felt we couldn't—it just wasn't really an issue. As we're getting older, we're starting to talk about it a bit more.

ARE THERE ANY OTHER ASPECTS OF YOUR STORY OR EXPERIENCE THAT YOU WANT TO SHARE OR THINGS THAT I'VE FORGOTTEN TO ASK?

About the culture stuff my parents do. Every October 14—the day my parents picked me up at the airport—we have a big celebration.

WHAT SORTS OF THINGS DO YOU DO?

It's like a second birthday. They bring me tons of gifts; they buy me a cake. And they make sure to make the day special. And I think my parents got the referral, whatever you call it, April 1, and it was the day my father returned from the war alive. So my father and I get to share that bond, and we celebrate that date together because it is like a new beginning for both of us. You know how Vietnam was, he was lucky to come back alive and in one piece and healthy.

Before, you asked, "Are you happy with yourself?" I'm happier than I've ever been. I have a great group of friends who like me for who I am. You know in high school, I wondered when they were going to stop asking me those stupid questions. In college, I brought it up, and we worked it into the conversation, and they don't even care. I am as happy as I can see myself, and I know I have been.

4

CHRISTINE SIMPSON

GENDER:	Female
AGE AT TIME OF INTERVIEW:	27
RACE:	Korean
MARITAL STATUS:	Single
OCCUPATION:	Fundraiser and event planner

Born in Korea and adopted at the age of eighteen months, Christine was raised by Caucasian parents who were living in Queens. Six months after she was adopted, her mother gave birth to her brother. Because they were so close in age, Christine and her brother had an almost twin-like relationship. Growing up on Long Island and in Queens, she lived in mostly white neighborhoods and went to schools with little diversity. From first to eighth grade, she attended Catholic school where there was only one other Asian student. Even though her friend was Filipino, other students would comment on their physical similarities. When she transferred to a school in a wealthy area of Long Island, she was the only Asian student in her class. Yet, she never noticed overt racism in the school, partially because she "didn't know what it was."

As a child, Christine expressed little interest in talking about her adoption issues, mostly because she was "never really comfortable with it." Fearful that she would not fit in with nor be accepted by her extended family, Christine's parents attempted to prevent "overt favoritism." During Christmas, if her brother received twelve presents, she would also receive the same number of presents. Christine also attended Korean immersion camp where she was exposed to Korean language and art. However, she described the experience as boring. Mostly, she just wanted to be "like everybody else," just "normal."

While attending Washington University in St. Louis, she participated in theatre for the first time and performed in an Asian American play. Playing the role of a first generation Asian American woman trying to identify a sense of belonging opened many doors to Asian American culture. Meeting other Asian Americans for the first time in her life has helped her to understand "why [she is] like this, why [she's] like that, why [does she] I do this. . . ."

As an "aspiring actress," Christine describes her participation in Asian American theatre as "incredibly freeing." Talking about adoption issues has not only strengthened her abilities as an actress—it has been beneficial in other areas of her personal life. As a child, she was wary of experiencing anger or sadness in fear of betraying her adoptive parents. Acting has helped her to recognize the similarities she has with her adoptive parents while also appreciating her differences. Participating in theatre has helped her to recognize and experience different emotions related to her adoption.

Although she has never dated an Asian man, she found that dating Caucasian men has become more difficult because she's often perceived as "basically white." Torn between the Asian American community and her Caucasian upbringing, Christine described her Korean heritage as an integral part of her identity.

At the time of the interview, Christine was twenty-seven years old. She has a bachelor's degree in English and a master's degree in English from Geneseo College. Today, she works as a fundraiser and event planner for a university in New York.

PLEASE START WITH YOUR NAME AND BIRTH DATE.

Christine Simpson. I was born on December 22, 1973. But like most adoptees, that's not my real birthday.

WHERE WERE YOU BORN?

Seoul, Korea. That's where I was adopted from.

HOW OLD WERE YOU WHEN YOU WERE ADOPTED?

I came to the states at a year and a half. I apparently had been abandoned at about six weeks.

ARE YOUR PARENTS CAUCASIAN?

Yes.

DO YOU HAVE ANY BROTHERS OR SISTERS?

I have a brother who is a natural child of my parents, seventeen months younger than me.

GROWING UP WHAT KIND OF RELATIONSHIP DID YOU HAVE WITH YOUR BROTHER?

It was pretty close. We got along really well. We were so close in age, it really was a little bit like we were twins. At that point, I was the dominant one. We lived in a neighborhood that didn't have a lot of little kids so we would play with each other. We had a surprisingly functional relationship. I know that most siblings don't. It's easy not to.

SO HE WAS BORN RIGHT AFTER YOU WERE ADOPTED?

Right. My parents always say that it really was like having twins. He was born in May, so it was about six months. I came in January. My parents had been trying for a very long time and my mother had been on fertility drugs. Once they knew that they were going to be able to adopt, something just clicked and my mom got pregnant. They had to fight really hard to make sure that they could still continue to adopt because at that time, a lot of agencies wouldn't give adoptees to parents who were going to have their own children for fear that they wouldn't love the adopted child as much.

DID SHE TALK TO YOU AT ALL ABOUT ADOPTION ISSUES GROWING UP?

It was never anything that was really discussed. Mostly because I didn't want to; I was never really comfortable with it. My brother is the one who comes up with some really interesting comments. He said something once that was really fascinating, that we had never talked about. For a thin person, I have a rather large appetite, and my whole family laughs at me. "You're going to be so fat when you get older! Why do you eat so much?" My brother one night at dinner goes, "You know what? If I had been starving as a baby, I would probably be eating like a pig now too." It was just really interesting.

DID YOU EVER PERCEIVE ANY DIFFERENCES IN THE WAY YOU WERE TREATED BY YOUR PARENTS GROWING UP?

No. That was a big issue for my mom. Every Christmas James got twelve presents and Chrissie got twelve presents. Mostly I think because my relatives were saying, "They're not going to get along; she's not going to fit in, people aren't going to accept her." So my mom and my dad really tried hard to be good parents. And it worked. There was no overt favoritism.

WHERE WERE YOUR PARENTS LIVING WHEN THEY ADOPTED YOU?

Queens. I grew up half of my childhood in Queens and half on Long Island.

WHAT WAS IT LIKE GROWING UP IN A MULTICULTURAL HOUSEHOLD?

Well, I wouldn't exactly call us multicultural. Basically it was just a white household with me in it. The neighborhoods we lived in were all white. My parents' friends are primarily white. Most of the kids I went to school with were white. I wouldn't say it was a multicultural background. I would say it was basically more Midwestern than anything else.

WHERE ARE YOUR PARENTS FROM?

They're from New York. They're both from Queens, actually.

CAN YOU TELL ME ABOUT THEIR SCHOOLING, THEIR WORK, ABOUT THEIR FAMILIES?

My mom is a nurse. She worked at Bellevue. My dad is an engineer, and he got his degree at West Virginia University. He has always worked for New York State. In fact, he just retired and went to work as a consultant for a contractor.

DO YOU KNOW WHY THEY CHOSE TO ADOPT FROM KOREA?

Initially when they were discussing about having children, the wait list for a white child was really long and they didn't see the need necessarily to adopt a white child. They had seen on TV all this stuff about the Vietnamese children who were needing adoption, but that wait list was incredibly long as well. And then someone had suggested looking at Korea because there were a ton of children available. They knew they wanted a girl. So they adopted from Korea.

DO YOU KNOW IF YOUR PARENTS RECEIVED POSITIVE SUPPORT FROM THEIR FRIENDS AND THEIR FAMILY?

I think it varied. I think some people thought it was great, and some people thought it was not such a good idea. From what I know, the people who

supported it were generally nice people, and the non-supporters were awful, generally.

WERE THEY UNSUPPORTIVE OF THE ADOPTION DECISION PER SE, OR OF
ADOPTING FROM OVERSEAS?

I think it was the overseas. It's like what you hear with biracial parents.
"What are the children going to be like? How are they going to fit in?" So
that's primarily what it was.

DID YOUR PARENTS EVER HAVE ANY FRIENDS WHO WERE KOREAN OR KO-
REAN AMERICAN OR ASIAN?

In terms of close friends, no.

DID THEY KNOW ANYTHING ABOUT THE CULTURE BEFORE THEY DECIDED
TO ADOPT?

No.

WERE THEY EVER INTERESTED IN JOINING A GROUP FOR ADOPTIVE PAR-
ENTS?

As far as I know Korean adoptees don't really have that much. We did the
immersion summer camp where I'd go and learn the language a little bit. I
would learn the arts, you know, meet other adoptees. I always thought it was
so boring.

WERE THEY ALL KOREAN ADOPTEES?

All Korean, yes. I thought it was really stupid. I was young. At that age all
you wanted to be was just like everybody else . . . to be normal

ARE YOU CURRENTLY MARRIED?

Single.

IN TERMS OF DATING, IS IT IMPORTANT THAT YOU BE WITH SOMEONE OF A
SIMILAR RACIAL BACKGROUND?

These are all things that I am still sort of sorting out in my head. I have
never dated an Asian person, and I have never really wanted to for basically
racist reasons. But I think a lot of it is just fear. It's sort of stupid that the
mommy bond is so strong, but it's like "if my mother didn't love me enough
to want to keep me, then why am I going to risk something with a partner-
ship?" Of course I'm over-intellectualizing this, but there definitely has
been a block in there for a long time, and I'm just slowly getting over that
now. Right now, this moment in my life is the moment I've had the most

Asian friends that I've ever had. It's kind of freeing. It's like I don't have to be paranoid when I walk into a Chinese restaurant. Even my incredibly Americanized friends still have this tinge of Asianness to them that connects them to something other than being an American in an Americanized culture. So I don't know. I guess as I get older, I just slowly came to accept that this is who I am and that it's ok.

WHAT HAVE YOUR EXPERIENCES BEEN WITH INTERRACIAL DATING?

I've actually only dated white guys.

DOES IT FEEL LIKE INTERRACIAL DATING?

No, it doesn't at all. Actually, I have to say that it is starting to more now, but I think that is because I'm not so much in denial about who I am and what I like. I'm an aspiring actress, and part of what's made me have to face certain truths about my identity and the way the world sees me is in the entertainment industry, where your appearance is everything. You can be a leading lady in your heart, but if you don't look like one, you ain't going to be cast as one. And being a minority, it even makes things harder. Having certain avenues obviously be open to me, like Asian American theatre, has introduced me to the whole Asian American culture. Being surrounded by more Asian Americans than white people for the first time in my life—it has answered a few questions as to why I am like this, why I'm like that, why do I do this. In some ways I'm very much like my adoptive parents, and in some ways I am so different from them. So being in this situation, I see it; and now that I can see it, I understand it, and I'm beginning to accept it. Dating white boys is getting a little bit tougher. I don't mean tougher. But I mean, it is different. They don't understand sometimes. And then they say, "Well, you're basically white. What's the matter?" and I say, "You don't understand. I am, but I'm not." That's what makes it hard. I've always likened it to being somewhat biracial because you feel torn between two cultures, because you don't know quite where to identify.

AND IT'S SO DIFFICULT TO DESCRIBE IN WORDS. IT REALLY CAN'T BE DE-SCRIBED.

WOULD YOU LIKE TO HAVE CHILDREN?

Oh boy. There's the million dollar question. I don't know yet.

AND TO ADD ON TO THAT, WOULD YOU EVER CONSIDER ADOPTING? OR WOULD IT BE IMPORTANT TO YOU TO HAVE BIOLOGICAL CHILDREN?

I don't know. I think I would consider adopting. But I think that I need to get over some issues first before I can start having kids. I would probably adopt before I'd have my own kids.

WOULD YOU ADOPT FROM KOREA OR ANY OTHER ASIAN COUNTRY?

I would probably adopt from an Asian country. Part of it is because people tell me that I don't look Korean, so that is always an issue with me. Part of my issue about having kids, and this is probably something that you hear all the time, is that there's a strange continuity when you have children. Like I can look at my brother and my parents and my grandmother, and I can see the familial relations. When I look at myself, it's just me that makes me special. And it's horrible being like, "What's going to happen if I have kids, and I suddenly don't like what they look like or what they do?" I don't want to be taking out my own neuroses on them. I guess that's not a healthy thing to do. I think kids pick up a lot of things you don't expect them to pick up, especially something as sensitive as neediness issues, abandonment issues, self-esteem issues. Those are all things I need to have straight in my head before I can even consider having kids, which of course doesn't stop millions of morons from having kids out in the world. But I would like to be somewhat responsible. I know people who have been adopted, and all they want to do is have kids because that's the one person who's going to love them. I actually cannot believe that at all. I think kids are very likely going to be the ones who reject you just by growing up. I think if you have abandonment issues already, that's going to be bad.

HAVE YOU BEEN INVOLVED IN THEATER FOR A LONG TIME?

No. It's really kind of funny. My first theater piece was in college. I was an English major and a friend of mine said, "Hey, somebody is doing an Asian American play. You should audition." "Me? What?"

I DIDN'T KNOW THERE WERE ASIAN AMERICAN PLAYS!

It was called *FOB* by David Henry Wong. It was basically about being Asian in America. So I auditioned, and for some reason I got cast, and man, did my issues just spill out on to the stage.

WHICH CHARACTER WERE YOU?

I was first generation. The person who is trying to figure out where she belongs.

This person just fully accepted the fact that she was confused, and I had not. This really opened the door for me to realize how much shit I needed to go through. But, of course, she scared the hell out of me, so I retreated back into my lovely intellectual English degree and then went to graduate school, hated graduate school, quit graduate school, had a bunch of really stupid jobs, and then got a job here at Columbia University doing fundraising and special events planning—mostly because I could take classes while I worked. Being the artsy person that I always wanted to be, I took a class and I love it, and now I've been doing different types of projects ever since.

It is incredibly freeing and theater is really—I hate to say it like this, but it really is therapy. You see, to fully embrace taking on another character is to be naked on stage and really just let yourself come into the character. So by having to do that, it really shows everything, who I am, and has enabled me to admit that, yeah, I have mom issues. I feel not good about myself a lot of the time, and I have big neediness issues because of the fact that I was abandoned when I was young.

IT SEEMS LIKE NOT ONLY DOES IT BRING UP EMOTIONAL ISSUES, BUT YOU REALLY HAVE TO KNOW YOURSELF.

And not be afraid to say, "You know, it's ok to be angry. It's ok to be sad; it's ok to be really, really, hurt." A lot times, especially when I was younger and a teenager, I wouldn't let myself feel those for a lot of reasons—that it wasn't right because I was guilty, that I was somehow betraying my adopted parents who were always good to me.

HAVE YOUR PARENTS ENCOURAGED YOU TO DO A SEARCH?

Oh, yes. They totally would be like, "You should do it."

HAVE YOU EVER INSTIGATED A SEARCH?

No, I'm not ready for that.

DID YOU EVER WANT TO AS A CHILD?

No. Like I said, I never thought about it as a child. All I wanted to be was just like everybody else.

CAN YOU TELL ME ABOUT THE SCHOOLS YOU WENT TO, YOUR FRIENDS, AND YOUR CHILDHOOD?

I lived in Queens, and I went to Catholic School from first to eighth grade, which may explain why I am so anti-religion. There was one other Asian woman there, Filipino, and we were friends. What was irritating was when people would say we looked like sisters. That was such a blatantly racist remark.

PEOPLE SEE WHAT THEY WANT TO SEE.

Then I transferred schools, and I was again the only Asian in my class. But see, that didn't strike me as weird.

DID PEOPLE EVER PICK ON YOU FOR BEING DIFFERENT?

Oh, no. They may have tried, but I think I was just too dense. Seriously, because I had never experienced it, I didn't know what it was.

DID YOU AND YOUR BROTHER GO TO THE SAME SCHOOL?

Yeah.

DID OTHER PEOPLE ASK YOU ABOUT YOUR FAMILY AND WHY DIDN'T YOU LOOK LIKE YOUR BROTHER?

They pretty much understood. People pretty much knew about adoption, and I don't think it was anything weird like that. It was more, I think, because it is Long Island and its proximity to New York City. I don't think things like that were as much of a problem as if I were living in the Midwest.

In terms of how I related to other people, it was pretty much normal. It was just that any problems that I had in high school were usually self-inflicted. I have to say one of the big things I am not real good at is long-term commitments. I don't have any real long-term close friends. Long-term relationships I can have, but after a while I stop participating. I don't know quite where that comes from.

DO YOU ATTRIBUTE THAT TO ABANDONMENT ISSUES? AFTER ALL, YOU WERE ON YOUR OWN FOR THE FIRST YEAR AND A HALF OF YOUR LIFE.

Yeah. That might be it. It's not that I don't want friends or to be around people. I make friends very easily, but maintaining a relationship is not always so easy for me.

DO YOU THINK THAT'S A FORM OF SELF-PROTECTION?

I think so, probably.

GROWING UP, WERE THERE ANY PERIODS DURING YOUR ADOLESCENCE THAT WERE PARTICULARLY ROUGH?

I think it would have been rougher had I been conscious of some of the things going on inside me. I think that I made decisions because I so desperately wanted to be loved.

WAS THERE A POINT WHEN ADOPTION DID BECOME MORE OF A FOCAL PART OF YOUR LIFE?

No, I don't think I ever realized that there was some intrinsic need for me to be loved. I'm still kind of doing it, looking for unconditional affection and nothing else. If it's not unconditional, it's not good enough. But if someone actually shows unconditional affection for me, I can't deal with it because then I'm like, "Why are you doing this? I am not worthy of this." It's really a double-edged sword. I'm interested in why I block myself so much from being happy.

WHAT IS IT LIKE WORKING WITH OTHER ASIAN AMERICAN ACTORS OR AC-TRESSES? YOU SAID THAT'S CHANGED SOME THINGS.

It's fine. That's been the strange thing because from high school and other experiences in college, most of the Asians were in a special club. And here it's given me an opportunity to see that I am pretty much like them, and they're like me, and we have the same facial features. It's sort of nice to be one of the group as opposed to someone who stands out. And here at least physically, visually, I am a part of the group. Though I have to say, the first time I went to an all-Asian American party I kind of felt sick to my stomach because I had never been in this situation before and I didn't know quite how to handle it.

DO YOU TALK AT ALL ABOUT ADOPTION ISSUES WITH OTHER PEOPLE?

I do occasionally, because I have to, because I think it is the key to unlock-ing who I am and will help me be a better actor. Also because it makes me a better person, let alone the acting part. I also don't want sensory overload, so I do it mostly when I have to. But I think about it. I do think about it.

I WANT TO READ YOU A STATEMENT THAT CAME OUT FROM THE PRESIDENT OF THE NATIONAL ASSOCIATION OF BLACK SOCIAL WORKERS IN 1971: "BLACK CHILDREN BELONG PHYSICALLY, PSYCHOLOGICALLY, AND CULTURALLY IN BLACK FAMILIES IN ORDER THAT THEY RECEIVE A TOTAL SENSE OF THEM-SELVES AND DEVELOP A SOUND PROJECTION OF THEIR FUTURE." WHAT IS YOUR IMPRESSION OF THE STATEMENT?

I think first and foremost having a loving family is more important than cultural identity. If you have a black child or Asian child in a loving interra-cial family, that's obviously going to be better than being in a same-cultural family that beat the shit out of them. I don't know. I really don't know. I've heard it before, that idea, but it's hard for me to answer. I joke that my par-ents are the most Asian white people I've ever met. When I talk to my Asian friends who are first generation with very Asian parents, my parents say and pull the same shit as their parents do, so I think a lot of things are univer-sal and transcend culture. I also think there is something to seeing yourself and having that lineage. My brother is the carbon copy—physically and ges-turally—he is the carbon copy of my dad. It's kind of nice to know that when my dad passes away that my brother will be there because I can see my dad. In some ways people need that.

HOW WOULD YOU DEFINE YOUR RACIAL IDENTITY TODAY?

Asian American.

HOW DID YOU COME TO THAT IDENTITY?

I've always identified as that. I just have never been quite comfortable with it. I'm not sure that I'm comfortable with it, but I am willing at this moment in my life to say, "This is the way the world sees me. And this is the way I see myself."

DO YOU THINK THERE IS MORE PRESSURE PLACED ON TRANSRACIAL ADOPTEES BY SOCIETY TO REALLY FORM AND SOLIDIFY THEIR IDENTITY?

I don't think any more than they put on anybody else. I think transracial adoptees feel it more because of themselves.

DO YOU THINK IT IS IMPORTANT FOR ADOPTIVE PARENTS TO INCORPORATE THEIR CHILDREN'S HERITAGE INTO THEIR UPBRINGING?

I think it depends on the child. My mom tried to force me to do that when I was a kid, and it made me go the opposite direction

ARE YOU GLAD THAT YOU WERE ADOPTED?

Yes. That's kind of like asking "Are you glad you're blond?" I don't really know any different. I am glad that I was adopted by a very loving, nurturing family who are not without their quirks, but I don't know any other way to be. Trying to imagine what my life would be in Korea is pointless. It could be anything because I don't know where I came from. I have all the horrible fantasies of drug addicts, prostitutes, being really poor. Or all the other fantasies—an illegitimate child of a politician or a movie star.

DO YOU HAVE ANY ADVICE THAT YOU WOULD GIVE PARENTS WHO ARE THINKING OF ADOPTING TRANSRACIALLY?

Just listen to your kid. If they want to talk about it, that's fine. If they don't want to talk about it, don't force it because it is not going to help the issue. And just love them for who they are, even if it is totally different than you want them to be. But that's like the parents for anybody, not just for transracially adopted. Be good parents and love your kid.

ARE THERE ANY OTHER ASPECTS OF YOUR ADOPTION OR YOUR EXPERIENCES THAT I FORGOT TO ASK OR THAT YOU WOULD LIKE TO SHARE?

I don't think so at the moment. I guess I just wish it wasn't so much of an issue.

5

CASEY STELL

GENDER:	Female
AGE AT TIME OF INTERVIEW:	18
RACE:	Korean
MARITAL STATUS:	Single
OCCUPATION:	Student

Casey, eighteen years old at the time of the interview, was adopted from Seoul when she was four months old and raised by Caucasian parents. Growing up in upstate New York, she described her childhood environment as "completely homogenous." At age four, she started to attend a Korean heritage camp for adopted children. Like many Korean adoptees, Casey portrayed her family as warm, loving, and welcoming. Yet, unlike many adoptees, she was adopted along with her twin sister. Though the two sisters did not talk about adoption issues much as children, their parents encouraged them to search for their biological parents during their teenage years.

At age sixteen, Casey's family traveled to Korea for the first time, and the agency through which Casey was adopted helped her conduct a search for her biological parents. Though initially hesitant to pursue the search, she described the "amazing experience" of meeting her biological mother and

father, as well as two older sisters and one younger brother. When her biological family and adoptive family met, Casey learned why her biological
mother had placed her and her sister for adoption. Through a translator, she
was told that the recession in Korea during the 1980s left her biological
family struggling financially. Her biological mother had given birth to the
twin girls in a clinic but later told her family they had died during childbirth. Even to this day, many of Casey's Korean relatives still believe that
the girls died at birth.

As a college student, Casey classifies herself as Korean American, although she expresses uncertainty as to where she fits in. Enjoying the diverse student population in her college, yet not quite feeling completely
part of one community, she continues to explore her self-identity. She maintains a strong interest in becoming involved in the Asian community and
would eventually like to study in Korea.

Today, Casey keeps in touch with her biological family, although the language barrier makes it difficult to communicate regularly. Both her biological and adoptive parents "try to keep [them] in contact." She has expressed
interest in returning to Korea to work in an orphanage. Presently, she is
studying international business and international economics in Washington,
D.C.

CASEY, HOW OLD ARE YOU?

Eighteen.

WHERE WERE YOU BORN?

South Korea.

HOW OLD WERE YOU WHEN YOU WERE ADOPTED?

Four months old.

WHERE WERE YOU LIVING IN KOREA WHEN YOU WERE ADOPTED? WERE
YOU IN A FOSTER HOME?

In a foster home in Seoul.

THROUGH WHAT AGENCY WERE YOU ADOPTED?

It was through Dillon International.

HAVE YOU MAINTAINED ANY KIND OF CONTACT WITH YOUR FOSTER PARENTS?

Actually, we didn't. We went back over there, and they asked us if we wanted to meet them, and I didn't want to. Some of my friends who we went back with did. I want to when I go back.

CAN YOU TELL ME ABOUT YOUR ADOPTIVE PARENTS?

My mom is Italian and my dad is Dutch and French.

YOU HAVE A SISTER WHO YOU WERE ADOPTED WITH?

Yes.

DO YOU HAVE ANY OTHER ADOPTED SIBLINGS?

No.

DO YOU AND YOUR SISTER TALK A LOT ABOUT ADOPTION ISSUES?

We knew we were adopted, but we didn't really talk about it too much when we were younger.

WHEN YOU WERE ADOPTED, YOU WERE LIVING IN NEW YORK. IS THAT WHERE YOU GREW UP?

Yes. We lived in upstate New York.

CAN YOU TELL ME MORE ABOUT WHERE YOUR PARENTS GREW UP AND THEIR PROFESSIONS?

My dad owns a landscaping business, and mom is a manager in the accounting section of an engineering firm. They grew up where I am living today.

HAVE YOU DECIDED WHAT YOU ARE GOING TO MAJOR IN?

International business and international economics.

DO YOU KNOW WHAT INFLUENCED YOUR PARENTS' DECISION TO ADOPT?

We talked about it a couple of times. They can't have children. At first they talked about adopting children from America but found out there was a very long waiting time. This was the early eighties. So they decided to adopt from Korea. I think Asia during the early eighties was one of the most popular places to adopt. They were asked if they wanted triplet boys but didn't end up adopting them. Then were offered two twin girls, but they died in a carbon monoxide fire. Then they got us.

DO YOU KNOW IF YOU HAVE ANY BIOLOGICAL SIBLINGS OTHER THAN YOUR SISTER?

Yes, we have. We went back to Korea when we were sixteen years old. Dillon was great. They searched for our parents. We didn't really want to, but our parents went ahead and did it anyway. We met our birth mom who hadn't told anyone that we were alive. So she went back and told our biological family. My birth father was so great. They came up to Seoul where we were and visited with us, and we found out we had two older sisters and a younger brother.

ARE YOUR BIRTH PARENTS MARRIED?

Yes, they were married when they had us.

HAVE YOU KEPT IN TOUCH WITH THEM?

We do randomly. It's hard in school. I'm not in my room much, and it's different time zones, but when I was home, we probably talked once a month.

WHAT WAS THAT LIKE WHEN YOU FOUND OUT ABOUT YOUR SIBLINGS?

It was weird. We thought that when we met our birth mom, it was going to be like picking a random person off the street.

DID YOU MAKE A CONNECTION?

Yeah. It was really amazing. We were only sixteen at the time, so I don't think we had thought too much about it. But when we actually did meet them, it was the most amazing thing to be sitting next to them and having the whole entire family look the same. That had never happened before in my life, and it was weird. But it was an amazing experience. Now that I look back, it is even more amazing. In our group there were mostly twenty-or thirty-year-olds trying to go back and look for their parents. It seemed like they were in that age where it was becoming more of an issue for them. I was only sixteen, so I was kind of like, "whatever." It wasn't really a big deal. But definitely I can see how it becomes more of an issue as people get older.

DID YOUR WHOLE FAMILY MEET YOUR ADOPTED PARENTS?

Yes. Carly and I didn't want to upset our parents, and it wasn't a big deal. We didn't really care if we met them or not. Our parents said they should look anyway, and when they came back, they told us we had two older sisters. So we said, "Ok, we'll meet them." I am really glad that they ended up doing that.

DID CARLY REACT THE SAME WAY? DID YOU BOTH HAVE THE SAME EXPERI-
ENCE MEETING YOUR BIRTH FAMILY?

I think so. We didn't really talk about it too much when we were in Korea. It was really emotional meeting them, but I think we were so very
young at that point. I think Carly wants to be involved with her background
less than I am. We're both definitely glad that we met them. I don't know if
it changed her—we didn't really talk a lot about it.

DID YOU LEARN WHY YOUR BIRTH PARENTS DECIDED TO PLACE YOU FOR
ADOPTION?

Yes. In the early eighties there was a big recession around the world. My
dad was laid off as a factory worker, and my mom couldn't work because I
was eight-and-a-half and Carly was seven-and-a-half pounds. We were
huge, and she didn't know she was having twins until three days before she
had us. So she decided at that point that she was going to give us up for
adoption. She didn't consult anyone else—she just went to the clinic where
she gave birth to us. She had a really tough labor, so she told everyone that
we had died at birth. And we were put up for adoption right then.

WHO ARRANGED THE REUNION?

I think it was mostly Dillon working with Eastern Social Welfare Society.

WAS THERE A TRANSLATOR?

Yes. My Korean sister is an English literature major so she has a very basic background. My other sister can speak English, but is nervous about it,
so she never speaks on the phone at all. And then my parents don't speak
English at all.

Of course, you don't talk *to* them. You talk through the translator, and
you're looking at them.

DO THEY SEEM LIKE FAMILY TO YOU? DO THEY FEEL LIKE EXTENDED FAM-
ILY, OR HAVE THEY BEEN INCORPORATED INTO YOUR FAMILY? HOW HAVE YOUR
ADOPTIVE PARENTS CHANGED?

My mom was always saying, "You have to call your birth family." I think
both sides try to keep us in contact, but it's hard because there's only one
sister as a go-between. It's hard having a family who just suddenly appeared
in your life for two days. It's been really weird knowing that I have family
over there who I can't speak to. We're half a world away in totally different
time zones, and it's hard to talk to each other. You know they are really important in your life, but you also wonder "How many times I will get over

there in my life and I see them?" and "How close a connection will there be?" I am going to be thirty one day and will I still be talking to them. It'll be weird.

DO YOU THINK THEY WILL EVER COME OVER TO THE STATES?

We tried to get my sister to come over here when I was a senior. We went to our representative in Congress, but they wouldn't give her a visa. I don't think my birth parents have the money to come over here. I think we'll be going back over there a lot sooner than they would come here.

GROWING UP WITH A TWIN SISTER IS VERY UNUSUAL, MOSTLY BECAUSE MOST ADOPTEES HAVE NEVER MET ANYONE WHO LOOKS LIKE THEM AND ARE ALWAYS WONDERING.

That is a big issue, but Carly and I would say it's not that big a deal. I've always had Carly, and I've always had that connection. I never felt like I didn't have an identity or that I'm missing part of me. She was that part of me that made me complete.

WHAT WAS IT LIKE GROWING UP IN A MULTICULTURAL HOUSEHOLD?

Carly and I were always the tomboys, and we played all sports. I never really had any issue being Asian growing up in a white area. Where I live is completely homogenous. There was one other Asian kid in my whole class, so I think that also affected it. If you grow up in a white area when you're younger, you want to be white; you want to be part of the white group. When I was younger I used to realize that if I never looked in the mirror or at Carly, I wouldn't think I was Korean at all. But then I got older, and we always went to Korean camp, and we'd learn our background and learn some language and culture. Whenever I was there I always wanted to be all Korean.

DO YOU STILL GO THERE IN THE SUMMER?

Yes. It's for adopted children. Korean families and their children would come and teach us heritage, culture, language, and cooking. It was so great when I was younger, and I made some very close friends. I want to marry a Korean boy now.

WHEN DID YOU START GOING TO THESE CAMPS?

When I was four, so I always had that Korean background.

ARE YOUR PARENTS OPEN ABOUT ADOPTION ISSUES? IT SOUNDS AS IF THEY ARE SINCE THEY ENCOURAGED YOUR BIRTH FAMILY SEARCH AND SENT YOU TO THE CAMP.

Yes. They definitely wanted us to have a sense of our culture. My parents have been very supportive of my taking language classes and wanting to go back.

BESIDES THE HERITAGE CAMP, DID YOUR PARENTS DO OTHER THINGS WITHIN THE FAMILY TO FOSTER CULTURAL AWARENESS OR BRING KOREAN CULTURE INTO THE HOUSE?

They bought us Korean Barbie dolls and books.

DID YOUR PARENTS RECEIVE A LOT OF SUPPORT FROM THEIR FRIENDS AND FAMILY WHEN THEY DECIDED TO ADOPT—ESPECIALLY WHEN THEY DECIDED TO ADOPT FROM OVERSEAS?

Yes, I really think that they did. They said that they cannot ever remember having negative things said to them and that the family was really supportive.

ARE YOUR PARENTS RELIGIOUS?

We go to church, but they didn't adopt for religious reasons. It was not to "save the children."

WERE YOU RAISED WITH A RELIGIOUS BACKGROUND?

Yes, Methodist.

DO YOU CONSIDER YOURSELF METHODIST TODAY?

Yes. My sister isn't quite into it.

DO YOU THINK YOUR PARENTS WILL GO BACK TO KOREA AGAIN?

Yes. I want to go back and study over there, and my dad wants to go back over when I'm there and work in the orphanages again. We all worked in an orphanage when we were there. When a child is given up for adoption and can't be adopted, they can stay in Eastern up to when they're eighteen years old. We went to one of the orphanages, and it is just so sad. You'd have two or three rooms with one person in it caring for five or six babies. It was just really sad. But Eastern is doing such a great job with them.

DID YOUR PARENTS KNOW ANYTHING ABOUT KOREAN CULTURE BEFORE THEY DECIDED TO ADOPT?

I don't think so.

ARE YOU CLOSE TO YOUR PARENTS' RELATIVES? TO YOUR EXTENDED FAMILY?

Yes. We are very close. I would say closer now that I've left because we try to stay in contact. But we are definitely close.

HAVE YOU HAD ANY EXPERIENCES OR THOUGHTS REGARDING INTERRACIAL OR TRANSRACIAL DATING, MARRIAGE, ETC?

When I was younger, I always saw myself marrying someone outside of the Korean race, but always having Korean babies. I don't know why. I don't think there's anything wrong with that, especially because I grew up in an all-white area. I think that tends to make you more attracted to white people or to whoever it was you grew up around, and I wasn't really growing up around Asian people. So I didn't really find Asian men that attractive. I don't think that there are problems with having interracial relationships.

DO YOU HAVE PERSONAL EXPERIENCES WITH THAT?

Yes, with white. But I don't see that as interracial.

HOW ABOUT TODAY?

It doesn't really matter. I kind of see myself with an Asian man, but I don't know if it will happen. It really doesn't make a difference what race they are, but it would be kind of cool having a Korean.

WHAT ABOUT YOUR SISTER?

She's with a white man right now. She's always dated white men.

WHEN YOU THINK ABOUT HAVING KIDS, DO YOU WANT TO INCORPORATE YOUR KOREAN HERITAGE INTO THEIR CHILDHOOD? WOULD YOU TAKE THEM OVER TO KOREA TO MEET YOUR FAMILY?

Definitely. I think that would be really cool. I really would love to be fluent in Korean someday and have it be spoken at home.

WOULD YOU WANT THEM TO BE CONNECTED TO YOUR BIOLOGICAL PARENTS?

Yes. Definitely. I think that would be so great. They're a part of me in a weird way. I don't know how much more of a connection we'll get because it's so far away, but I'd love to have a really close relationship with them. It's so hard to evolve a relationship because it is so far away.

WOULD YOU EVER CONSIDER ADOPTING?

Yes. I actually want to.

FROM KOREA? OR DOES IT MATTER?

No, it doesn't really matter. It would be cool to adopt from Korea. I definitely want to adopt children; I don't know from where though.

COULD YOU SEE YOURSELF ADOPTING WHITE AMERICAN CHILDREN OR EVEN EUROPEAN CHILDREN?

Oh, yes.

SO THE COUNTRY OF ORIGIN ISN'T A BIG FACTOR.

No.

WERE YOU EVER SUBJECTED TO RACIAL SLURS OR COMMENTS OR THINGS LIKE THAT GROWING UP?

My parents brought me up to believe that if someone said something to you, it was because of ignorance and not necessarily because of prejudice. So when I was young, I never would pick out people being prejudiced towards me. I would just realize they don't really understand. People ask really personal things when you are with your parents and you are Asian and you are a twin. But I don't really mind, and I don't think I ever thought of that being intrusive. I had one person once that called me "chink." She was joking, but I was really upset by that. My parents were always saying, "It's because of their ignorance, not because they are trying to be mean." People have generally been really accepting of my parents and Carly and me.

WHO WERE SOME OF YOUR CLOSE FRIENDS GROWING UP? WERE THEY KIDS FROM YOUR NEIGHBORHOOD OR KIDS FROM CAMP?

We have two very good friends from camp, but we didn't really talk too much except when we got together at camp. It's like you have some kind of adoption bonding, and you totally understand where they're coming from. You can't really explain it to your other friends because they don't really get it. It's something you understand. So that's really made us close even though we don't see each other very often. But my best friends at home were white.

DID YOU HAVE ANY ASIAN OR ASIAN AMERICAN ROLE MODELS GROWING UP? DID YOU KNOW ANY OTHER ASIANS OR ASIAN AMERICANS OUTSIDE OF YOUR CAMP?

Yes. Kristi Yamaguchi. I wanted to be her when I was younger! I can't think of anyone else. I don't think when I was younger I had that strong of a tie to being Korean.

WAS THERE A TIME YOU CAN REMEMBER WHEN YOU STARTED ASKING MORE QUESTIONS ABOUT YOUR ADOPTION?

I think our parents beat us to that. We definitely hadn't started asking a ton of questions or having identity problems or feelings that we weren't quite fitting in anywhere. When we went to camp, I definitely didn't fit in with the kids who were brought up in the Asian families, and sometimes I had the feeling that I didn't fit in with the white kids. But I didn't really get into it too much.

WHEN YOU WERE YOUNGER, DID YOUR PARENTS SIT DOWN AND EXPLAIN TO YOU WHAT ADOPTION MEANT, OR IS IT SOMETHING THAT YOU GREW UP UNDERSTANDING INNATELY.

I think because they always sent us to camp, that we always understood. We were so young when we started going.

CAN YOU TELL ME A LITTLE BIT ABOUT WHAT YOUR ADOLESCENCE WAS LIKE, ESPECIALLY AFTER MEETING YOUR BIOLOGICAL FAMILY? DID IT CHANGE YOUR TEENAGE YEARS?

I think it definitely changed them. It gave me a broader appreciation of living here—what they gave up for me. It's made me more grateful for what I have over here. When I was a freshman or sophomore, I was in a stage where I wasn't feeling—I didn't really want to be around my parents. Things weren't going right. And when I came back from Korea during my junior summer, I felt like I had so much to be thankful for, that I really shouldn't waste a day and waste my life being upset about things that really didn't have much importance. I think a lot of that came about from just meeting my birth parents and understanding more about my past. When I went over there, I didn't feel like I wasn't whole, but when I came back I realized that more of me was whole. It was a weird thing, because I never realized it at all. It still affects how I make decisions and how I think about what I'm doing.

HOW DID YOUR BIOLOGICAL SISTERS REACT TO MEETING YOU? DO YOU THINK IT WAS DIFFERENT OR DIFFICULT FOR THEM?

I don't know. I remember asking them if they remember when my mom was pregnant with us. My oldest sister was only four, but she said she kind of remembered it. I don't really know if my birth family ever told the rest of the family that we are alive. It would be such a big thing for her to tell them. For her to tell her husband in the first place, and then the family, was such a big deal. He was so amazing. He told her that he couldn't do anything about the past and that they would go to Seoul to meet us. My dad was so great, holding our hands and being really sweet.

DO YOU THINK YOUR ADOPTIVE PARENTS FELT A SENSE OF LOSS BECAUSE YOU ARE NOW CONNECTED TO YOUR OTHER FAMILY?

My mom and dad were so great. When we first met them, everyone was crying. My sister and I were the only ones not crying. And then my mom was a little tentative. She asked, "You don't want to stay over here, do you?" I told her that I wanted to go back home but that I wanted to come back.

HOW DO YOU CLASSIFY YOUR IDENTITY? DO YOU THINK OF YOURSELF AS AMERICAN OR KOREAN AMERICAN?

I classify myself as Korean American, but I really don't know where I fit. I know I don't feel Korean because I was brought up so white. It's a misnomer. I don't consider myself white either. No one at home asks me because they know I'm adopted, but when I came here to American University, I was asked, "Are you an international student?" And I said "no."

WHAT HAS IT BEEN LIKE BEING EXPOSED TO SO MANY OTHER ASIANS AND ASIAN AMERICANS IN COLLEGE?

It is really cool. I don't even think it is weird anymore to see a ton of Asian people walking around. It would have been odd six months ago. At home you wouldn't see it. You'd think there was a tour coming.

WHAT KINDS OF THINGS HAVE YOU DONE TO TRY AND GET MORE INVOLVED IN THE ASIAN COMMUNITY?

I want to go to the cultural center on Dupont Circle and take classes, and I'd really like to be part of the AFA [Asian Foreign Adoptees] group, but I haven't been. I'm kind of nervous about going to it because I don't know what to expect. I have a couple of Asian friends, so maybe we'll try it.

HAVE OTHER PEOPLE HERE ASKED YOU ABOUT YOUR ADOPTION? HAS THAT ARISEN WHILE TALKING TO OTHER ASIANS?

Not too much. I haven't met that many Asians—I have mostly white friends again. I didn't think that would happen at all, but my friends have asked me about adoption stuff.

ARE THERE OTHER THINGS THAT YOU'D LIKE TO LEARN ABOUT YOUR BIRTH PARENTS OR ABOUT YOUR BIRTH FAMILY THAT YOU HAVEN'T BEEN ABLE TO?

I would really like to be able to talk to them more and in Korean. I didn't learn as much as I want to about them. I want to understand more of their life over there.

IN 1971, THE PRESIDENT OF THE NATIONAL ASSOCIATION OF BLACK SO-
CIAL WORKERS CAME OUT WITH A STATEMENT THAT SAID, "BLACK CHILDREN
BELONG PHYSICALLY, PSYCHOLOGICALLY, AND CULTURALLY IN BLACK FAMILIES
IN ORDER THAT THEY RECEIVE THE TOTAL SENSE OF THEMSELVES AND DE-
VELOP A SOUND PROJECTION OF THEIR FUTURE." DO YOU HAVE ANY THOUGHTS
OR REFLECTIONS ON THAT STATEMENT?

The best interests of the children should be taken into consideration and
not policies. Parents obviously need to take this into consideration because
they're making a commitment. But if the children feel that they are well adjusted, and if they feel that despite growing up in a white family they can
deal with social issues, I don't feel there is a problem with transracial adoption. Especially when everyone is trying to say that prejudice shouldn't be a
big issue anymore. If we start with the children and teach them that white
children and black children can mix together and African children and
Asian children can be all in the same family, I think you are going to get a
better result.

WHAT FACTORS DO YOU THINK ARE THE MOST IMPORTANT IN CONSIDERING
THE PLACEMENT OF CHILDREN?

The best situation is that they are able to grow up in an environment that
teaches them that they are wanted and that they are loved and that they can
deal with the social issues. I don't feel that I'm unable to deal with social issues because I was brought up in a white family.

DO YOU THINK THAT HELPED PREPARE YOU BETTER?

Definitely for social and racial issues. So I feel like I can relate to Asian
Americans because I am Asian, but I also feel like I can relate to white people because of how I was brought up. I was really brought up with a sense
of knowing that I was loved and cared about, and I think that is the most
important thing, regardless of what race your parents are. It doesn't matter
what race they are or if its two men or two women who care for you—it's
that they love you and show you that.

DO YOU THINK THERE IS MORE PRESSURE PLACED UPON TRANSRACIAL
ADOPTEES TO DEVELOP THEIR IDENTITIES AND SAY "THIS IS WHO I AM"? ARE
TRANSRACIAL ADOPTEES PUT IN THE SPOTLIGHT?

I think you have identity issues because you don't know where you belong—in the Asian community? the white community? I think that it really
starts to wear on children who don't understand why their birth mother has
given them up. I think that is a lot of pressure for, especially, young children
to understand.

It's hard when you are that young. You should be out playing and being a child instead of having to focus so intently on identity.

For a lot of Asians, especially for myself, it would become an issue when I started thinking about it, but generally day-to-day I was well adjusted to what I was doing. I didn't really have problems with my identity and every-day issues. But deeper down there are.

Do you think it is important for adoptive parents to introduce their children to their biological culture and heritage?

In some instances, you get more culture being transracially adopted. If you're born into a family that has its own traditions, you have to make more of an effort to understand your background and your heritage, and I don't really know if I would have gotten more of it if I had lived with my biological family.

If you had been older when you were adopted, do you think it would have been better or easier if you had been adopted into an Asian or Korean family in the states?

I think when I was younger, I always wanted to have been older when I was adopted because I wanted to speak Korean. But I also think I wouldn't have understood a lot of American culture if I had been adopted when I was older. But definitely when you are older and you are adopted, it is harder. You have a lot of baggage that you bring with you.

What do you think was the most difficult part of growing up in a multicultural family? And what was the most enjoyable part?

I am kind of naïve because my parents brought us up in such a welcoming environment. On the surface I had a perfect childhood. We were a perfect example of children who grew up in a white family who had a cultural identity and felt that we belonged. But I would definitely say that as an adolescent, there was a feeling that I might not quite fit in with the white people, like white boys didn't like me. And the white girls—I was not quite white enough for them, but not Korean enough for Koreans. That's the hardest thing still—you're not white enough for the white community, but you're not Korean enough for the Korean community. The best part is the family I grew up in. They're so great. I had the best extended family that you could ask for. They always welcomed me, and I am so close to all of them. My parents worked so hard to have a really close family so we would be open to talking about anything and feel comfortable to be our selves. I think that was the best part because I don't know if I would have gotten the opportunities that I have if I was in Korea. I think there is definitely a tradeoff. My parents have given me everything that I could ask for, and I think that my birth parents gave us everything we could ask for by giving us up for adoption.

DO YOU HAVE ANY SUGGESTIONS OR ADVICE THAT YOU WOULD GIVE TO PARENTS WHO ARE CONSIDERING ADOPTING TRANSRACIAL CHILDREN?

My big advice would be to do it for the right reasons. If you have love to give to a child who needs to be adopted, I think it's great. I don't think it matters what race they are if they can give them that. If these parents want to give their love to you, you can have an environment where they can try to help you through these issues rather than being all by yourself in the world.

DO YOU THINK IT IS POSSIBLE FOR TRANSRACIAL ADOPTEES TO COME TO A SOUND CONCLUSION AS TO WHO THEY REALLY ARE?

I think so. I think it gets easier in time. The more you think about it the less it is "I'm this or this." It's just who you are. You take what you have from the Korean part of you and what you have from the white part of you. I think that's what's neat about transracial adoption. You're unique from everyone else, and you have a unique history to you.

4

KATE*

GENDER:	Female
AGE AT TIME OF INTERVIEW:	23
RACE:	Korean
MARITAL STATUS:	Single
OCCUPATION:	Student

Kate was twenty-three years old when she was interviewed. She was adopted from Seoul, Korea, when she was five months old. Raised by Caucasian parents, Kate has a younger brother and sister who are both Korean adoptees and an older brother who is Caucasian. Kate's parents had many friends with adopted children from Korea and felt very supported in their decision to adopt by friends and family.

As a child, Kate's family talked openly about adoption issues. Her parents encouraged Kate and her siblings to learn Korean, to meet other adoptees, and to integrate their heritage into their everyday lives. However, Kate resisted most of these efforts and was always conscious of how different she felt. The neighborhoods in which she was raised were somewhat racially diverse, although she was never connected with other Asian Americans.

---

*Identifying information about this participant has been omitted or changed.

When she was twelve years old, Kate and her family went to Korea for the first time through a Motherland Trip organized by Holt. She was able to visit her orphanage and gather some information about her biological parents. It was when she turned sixteen that Kate started to actively search for her biological parents. Though her search led to many dead ends, she still hopes to meet her biological family.

Kate's family adopted again from Korea when she was a teenager and she warmly welcomed her new brother into the family. Shortly after, she went to college and received her bachelor's degree in psychology. After her freshman year, she returned to Korea to continue her search. While she wasn't able to learn more about her past, she enjoyed the opportunity to stay with a local family in Seoul and learn more about Korea. During college, Kate had several Korean and Asian friends, although she never felt as if she belonged to that group. Though she was "dragged" to Asian American events or parties with some of her friends, she was more comfortable with the Caucasian culture in which she was raised.

Since the interview, Kate has married and started a career as an assistant professor.

FIRST WE NEED TO GET SOME DEMOGRAPHIC INFORMATION. HOW OLD ARE YOU?

Twenty-three.

AND HOW OLD WERE YOU WHEN YOU WERE ADOPTED?

I was five months old.

WHERE WERE YOU LIVING WHEN YOU WERE ADOPTED?

I was living in an orphanage in the northern region of Seoul.

AND SO FAR AS YOU KNOW, YOU WERE PLACED AT THAT ORPHANAGE AT BIRTH? DO YOU KNOW ANYTHING ABOUT THAT?

I was told that I was a couple of weeks old when I was dropped off, but I don't know how true that is.

AND DO YOU KNOW ANYTHING ABOUT YOUR BIRTH MOTHER OR FATHER?

When I went to Korea with my family, I was able to look in my file at KSS [Korean Social Services]. I was told that my birth parents were not married but living together. My birth mother disappeared, so my birth father took me to the orphanage. Again, I don't know how accurate this information is.

To the best of your knowledge, were your birth mother and father both Korean?

As far as I know they were. They have Korean names so I would assume so.

Now, in your adopted family, do you have siblings?

I have one adopted sister who is twenty years old from Korea, and a nine-year-old adopted brother from Korea as well, and a brother who is thirty-two.

And did your adoptive parents have any birth children?

Yes. My older brother is my father's biological son from a previous marriage.

Now, you were adopted by your family when you were five months old. They came to Korea?

No. I flew over.

Do you know the name of the adoption agency?

Welcome House.

Tell me something about the background of your parents. Where do they come from?

My parents are both Caucasian. My mother has some Russian and German on her side, and my dad has some German as well, maybe some Scottish. He was adopted within his own family by his biological aunt at birth. His biological mother, Naomi, later had a daughter, so he has a younger half-sister. However, Naomi died when my dad was still fairly young.

What is the religious background of your parents?

My mother was raised Jewish. My father grew up in the Church of Nazarene.

How were you raised in that family?

I was actually raised as a Quaker. My mother converted from the Jewish faith, and I don't think my father ever felt really connected with the Church of Nazarene. My family sometimes participated in Jewish holidays to be with the family.

And you are not married?

No.

HOW MANY YEARS OF SCHOOLING HAVE YOU HAD?

I have a master's degree, and I'm starting a doctoral program in a few months.

WHERE DID YOU GROW UP?

In the suburbs of Washington, D.C.

AND HOW WOULD YOU CHARACTERIZE THE MAKEUP OF YOUR NEIGHBOR-HOOD? AN INTEGRATED NEIGHBORHOOD WITH DIFFERENT RACIAL/ETHNIC GROUPS OR MOSTLY WHITE? DESCRIBE IT.

Over the years it became more diverse. When I was younger, it was mostly white. My best friend in elementary school was African American, but for the most part it was a very homogenous neighborhood. My school was somewhat diverse, although the students I was associated with were mostly white. I guess the minorities in our school were a little bit alienated from the rest of the population. I was in honors and advanced placement classes, and there were very few Asians, Latinos, or African Americans in my classes. There were a lot of immigrants, or so it seemed.

FROM WHERE?

From Vietnam, Southeast Asia, Latin America.

WHO WERE YOUR CLOSEST FRIENDS IN YOUR ELEMENTARY SCHOOL OR HIGH SCHOOL?

My closest friends were, I guess in terms of their cultural backgrounds, just normal white American kids. We were all the band geeks. My best friend since elementary school is Finnish. She was born in the United States but her family went back to Finland every year, so she was very integrated into Finnish culture.

DID YOU HAVE ANY PROBLEMS IN SCHOOL, EITHER ELEMENTARY OR HIGH SCHOOL, WITH ANYONE CALLING YOU DISPARAGING NAMES? DID YOU RUN INTO ANY DIFFICULTIES?

I remember a few times when people would make fun of my eyes, "Chinese eyes." Someone asked me when I was real young, "What's wrong with your eyes?" That stunned me because it was the first time I felt self-conscious about my appearance. This was really early on in elementary school, so I think it was more out of curiosity on their part, but of course it was very disturbing to me to have them come up to me and ask me these questions. In middle school and high school it wasn't really acknowledged.

Most of my friends were white, and we never talked about racial issues. It was almost ignored that I was from a different culture because I was so integrated into the "white" community, so to speak. They pretty much saw me as white, and so did I.

WHAT ABOUT IN YOUR HOME? DID YOUR PARENTS TALK ABOUT THE FACT THAT YOU AND YOUR SISTER AND BROTHER WERE FROM KOREA? WAS THAT A TOPIC OF DISCUSSION?

My parents tried to integrate Korean culture into our lives. We would celebrate the day that we arrived in the United States. They called them our *anniversaries* and we would go out and eat Korean food, and they would give us gifts. My parents would always try to buy us Korean dolls or Korean clothes for our dolls or Korean books. I was just about as interested in those things as I was in anything else. So I didn't treat these cultural things like they were special. Today, there are so many cultural resources for adoptive families. My younger brother has tons of books about Korea and about being adopted, and he seems more accepting of his Korean heritage than I was.

DID YOUR PARENTS HAVE ADULT FRIENDS WHO ARE KOREAN?

No.

WHO WERE YOUR PARENTS' FRIENDS?

Actually, they had some friends who adopted, but their families aren't transracial. They know a lot of adoptive families today. For a while, they kept in touch with a family whose adopted Korean daughter was somehow mixed up with my sister when they were adopted. When my sister arrived, we were expecting an eight-month-old baby. So when she arrived, my parents were expecting her to sit up. I'm sure they were confused when she couldn't. It turned out that she was actually five months old. She and another Korean baby somehow had their ID bracelets switched in Korea or on the plane. My parents were actually supposed to adopt another child. They realized this a few days later. They were so upset and so worried because they were already attached to my sister and didn't want to lose her. The other family in the situation felt the same way, so they left things as they were. Our parents stayed in contact for a long time.

DID YOUR PARENTS TALK TO YOU ABOUT WHY THEY ADOPTED CHILDREN— YOU AND YOUR BROTHER AND SISTER?

Mostly my mother has said she always wanted to adopt. I know that before I was born, she had a miscarriage. But growing up, she told us that she had always wanted to adopt children.

WHAT ABOUT GRANDPARENTS AND AUNTS AND UNCLES? WAS THERE ANY
PROBLEM IN TERMS OF THEIR ACCEPTANCE OF YOU AND YOUR SIBLINGS AS
MEMBERS OF THE FAMILY?

My mom's sister has two Korean adopted children, and I feel especially
close to them. They are younger, but they are my closest relatives. I have always felt extremely comfortable with them and their parents—my aunt and
uncle. My mother's side of the family has always been very loving, open, and
accepting. I am not close to my father's side of the family. I've never really
felt alienated, but I'm just not close to them.

WHAT ARE YOUR LONGER-TERM CAREER ASPIRATIONS?

At this point I am particularly interested in working with the child welfare system. I have seen so many horrendous things occurring in the foster
parents system, and I feel really fortunate to have been raised in a wonderful family with many advantages. I recognize those advantages and really
want to work and help children who are in the child welfare system.

WHAT ABOUT YOURSELF WHEN YOU WERE AN ADOLESCENT? DID YOU GO
THROUGH ANY COMPLICATED TIMES? A LOT OF ADOLESCENTS GO THROUGH
DRUG OR DRINKING PROBLEMS, ETC. WERE THERE ANY SUCH THINGS WITH
YOU OR YOUR SISTER?

When I was in high school I went through a rebellious phase. However,
it's hard to extract adoption issues from normal teenage rebellious behavior.
They were all entangled into a bundle of unhappiness. I experimented with
drinking late in high school, but I never touched drugs. High school was a
very difficult time for me and my whole family. I think I was angry at my
parents for adopting me and for making me feel different. High school was
very turbulent. My mom and I would really get into it, and we'd fight a lot—
about what, I can't remember. I was unhappy and depressed. I hated my
parents, the world, and I hated my life. Yet, I couldn't bring myself to rebel
too excessively. I always respected curfews, and I never did anything really
extreme. I guess I was afraid of pushing them too far. I had always been a
good kid, and I didn't want them to distrust me. I needed their acceptance
and love and approval more than I realized.

WOULD YOU HAVE PREFERRED TO HAVE BEEN ADOPTED BY A KOREAN FAM-
ILY?

Definitely not. I have enjoyed the privileges afforded to the white community, and I don't think I would have wanted to grow up in an Asian family. Asian culture can be very patriarchal, and Korean parents are supposedly *very* strict. My parents feel as "natural" as any biological parents could
feel.

DID YOU HAVE PROFESSIONAL HELP AT THAT TIME?

I've been on and off antidepressants since I was sixteen. A lot of it is chemical, but I think a lot of it has to do with my adoption. I refused to see a therapist though. It's funny—I have a bachelor and master's degree in psychology, yet I've always refused to see anyone to talk about adoption issues.

DID YOU TRY AND GET MORE INFORMATION ABOUT YOUR BIRTH PARENTS?

I started actively searching when I was sixteen.

WERE YOUR PARENTS HELPFUL WITH THAT?

They were. They were very supportive. When I was in college, I dated a Korean guy, and we went to Korea with his family for five weeks one summer, where we stayed with his grandparents and relatives. I was doing some searching on my own which was very, very frustrating because I didn't speak the language, and I was relying upon other people to help me. It was great because my mother was ready to fly over if I found anything. We talked on the phone all the time, so she was ready to come over if I needed her. The family I was traveling with was also supportive, but they were mostly interested in spending time with relatives. I had gone over there to do a search, but it turned into more of a family trip. I felt bad asking for a lot of help and ended up not focusing on my search as much as I had hoped. But overall, I never sensed anything but support from my parents.

DID YOU FIND ANYTHING?

I found the house where I was born. I went to visit and just looked around the area were I must have lived for a few weeks.

WHY WAS IT IMPORTANT TO YOU TO SEARCH?

I think mostly out of curiosity. I always just wanted to see pictures. And I've gone through different phases of being interested and then being disinterested. For the most part, I've always wondered if I have siblings. So I would want objective information. I don't even know if I was too interested in actually making personal contact. It was just more information gathering that I was interested in.

HOW ABOUT YOUR SISTER? DID SHE GO THROUGH SOMETHING LIKE THIS AS WELL?

Probably, but it wasn't too apparent to me. I'm sure she struggled with some issues. She and I haven't really talked that much about adoption issues. I guess there wasn't that much to talk about. It's not like we would sit around and say, "Let's talk about our adoptions!" Just recently she's come up to me with little epiphanies. The other day she came into my room and she's like, "I just realized my children will be first generation Korean Americans. I'm not! I'm not considered first generation! Whoa. I never thought about that." So she's had different thoughts that she's shared with me. But we've never really talked in-depth about those issues.

ARE YOU CLOSE IN OTHER WAYS?

We are. We don't see each other very often because she's in college in New Hampshire. During high school we were like regular siblings—fighting and me being the typical mean older sister. When I went to college, we became closer, and we continue to grow closer still.

HOW ABOUT YOUR YOUNGER BROTHER?

I left home when he was still very young. During that time it was really hard to establish any sort of concrete continuous relationship. That's also when I was going through an emotionally tough time. Today we're closer. I try to spend more time with him, and I love watching him grow up. We established our own relationship, and we do things like play Playstation together and go to the movies.

AND HOW ABOUT YOUR FATHER'S SON?

We never saw him while growing up because he was raised by his mother, so he felt like a stranger. He was a great deal older than me. He would visit us during the summer, so that was a treat, but I didn't really know him well. He moved back to the east coast for a few years when I was in middle school. High school is when I think I became more "interesting" to him. He began to talk to me more. It felt like he was a really good friend. Now we hang out a lot. He feels like an older brother to me because we've gotten so much closer.

I FORGOT TO ASK YOU, WHAT DOES YOUR FATHER DO FOR A LIVING?

He is the president of a business in the Washington, D.C., area.

DOES YOUR MOTHER WORK OUTSIDE THE HOUSE?

She is a marriage counselor/family therapist. She has been doing mental health work for over thirty years.

WE TOUCHED A LITTLE BIT EARLIER ON TRANSRACIAL ADOPTION. GIVEN CHOICES, GENERALLY DO YOU THINK THAT TRANSRACIAL ADOPTION IS A GOOD THING? DO YOU THINK, BY AND LARGE, SAME-RACE ADOPTION IS A BETTER VE-

HICLE FOR CHILDREN? WHAT DO YOU THINK ABOUT THAT WHOLE ISSUE? AS YOU KNOW, WITH BLACK/WHITE ADOPTIONS, THE NATIONAL ASSOCIATION OF BLACK SOCIAL WORKERS HAD CONDEMNED IT.

I believe there are inherent difficulties in transracial adoption, but I don't think they should ever prevent transracial adoptions from occurring. Children within same-race families go through their own difficulties and identity issues, so no one is immune to it. I think that transracial adoption is definitely a challenge with inevitable difficulties for both children and parents, but with strong families and a lot of work, you can transcend race and not focus so much on bloodlines. As long as there is an open dialogue within the home, I think transracial adoption can be really positive.

DID YOU KNOW THAT AS OF JANUARY 1997, A LAW WAS PASSED THAT SAYS THAT YOU CANNOT USE RACE AS A BASIS FOR MAKING A DECISION ABOUT ADOPTION? DO YOU GENERALLY AGREE WITH THAT, OR DO YOU THINK THAT RACE SHOULD BE USED AS A FACTOR IN WHETHER OR NOT A FAMILY CAN ADOPT?

For older children who are seeking placement, I think they should have some say as to what kind of family they'd like to be in. Other than that, I don't think race should be a factor.

AT WHAT AGE DO YOU THINK CHILDREN SHOULD HAVE SOME SAY?

I don't know. Once they are entering the pre-adolescent phase where identity is becoming a big issue. At an older age, kids already have some roots that are solidified, so that needs to be taken into consideration. Overall, I don't think race should be used as a basis for selecting adoptive homes. I think the most important thing is to examine the parents. Are they open-minded? Are they willing to face some of the challenges inherent in adoption? Are they willing to move to live in a more diverse area? Can they provide a loving and accepting home?

ONE OF THINGS THAT I LEARNED IN INTERVIEWING BLACK CHILDREN WHO WERE ADOPTED INTO WHITE FAMILIES WAS THEY RAN INTO QUITE A LOT OF FLACK FROM OTHER BLACK CHILDREN WHO CLAIMED THEY WERE NOT BLACK ENOUGH, DON'T TALK LIKE MANY OF US DO, DON'T LIKE THE SAME KIND OF MUSIC, WEAR THE SAME KIND OF CLOTHES. HAVE YOU RUN INTO PROBLEMS WITH KOREAN CHILDREN WHO LIVE IN KOREAN HOUSEHOLDS, THAT SOMEHOW YOU'RE DIFFERENT AND THAT YOU DON'T UNDERSTAND ABOUT BEING KOREAN?

Growing up I wasn't close to any other Korean children, so no. College was the first time I had Korean or Asian friends. I had several close Asian friends, but I always felt a little bit different. They wouldn't outwardly say anything, but they knew I was raised in a white American family, so they really didn't consider me Korean. They'd joke around and say, "Well, you're white anyway."

DID THAT BOTHER YOU?

Not really. It was sort of a running joke, and I agreed in some ways. I felt insecure because most of my Asian friends only hung out with Asians. I also heard a lot of derogatory comments about white people. In the back of my mind, I always wondered whether they would be comfortable if I brought them home to my family. Would they be racist towards my parents? How would they react to my parents?

AS YOU THINK ABOUT YOUR FUTURE AND YOU THINK ABOUT THE POSSIBILITY OF MARRIAGE AND SO ON, DO YOU THINK YOU'RE LIKELY TO MARRY SOMEONE OF KOREAN BACKGROUND OR IS THAT NOT A FACTOR?

In some ways, I've always felt a little bit displaced from Korean families. When I think about a future partner, I'd like to feel like I'm part of the family. I don't think I would intentionally seek out an Asian partner. Almost all of my previous boyfriends were white. I'd probably feel most comfortable in a white family.

ARE THERE ANY THINGS THAT YOU THINK YOUR PARENTS SHOULD HAVE DONE DIFFERENTLY THAN THEY DID AS YOU AND YOUR SISTER AND BROTHER WERE GROWING UP?

They really did a wonderful job of making me feel that I am a part of the family. They have always been as supportive as possible, and they have joined me in my ups and downs, which I am thankful for. Sometimes I've resented how much they've tried to bring in Korean culture, and then other times, I wish they had done more. Overall, I definitely think they did as much as they possibly could. I resisted anything Korean or Asian, but I knew that my parents would support me when I was ready to explore Korean culture. They really did everything to foster cultural awareness and make Korea feel like a special place. It was me who hated Korea and had no interest in learning about it. I'm incredibly grateful for everything my parents have done and have tried to do.

WHAT ADVICE WOULD YOU GIVE TO FAMILIES WHO WERE CONSIDERING ADOPTION ACROSS RACIAL LINES?

I definitely encourage transracial adoption because I think it opens many wonderful doors for both children and parents. But I would definitely advise parents to be prepared for struggles and issues that may not be so prevalent in same-race adoptions. For example, be prepared for when your child comes home crying because other children tease her about the way she looks. Another example—all a person has to do is to look at my family, and they know that I'm adopted. To me, it's private information, and when I go out in public, I feel like it's being broadcast everywhere. That used to bother me a lot. If I was out with my parents, and I saw another adoptive family I was interested, but then other times I just wanted to hide. It's issues like these that parents need to be aware of and prepared for.

Also, I think parents should realize that for many of us, identity formation takes a long time. For many of us, our identities are constantly changing as we encounter and deal with adoption issues. Even into adulthood, I'm still trying to figure out whether I'm American, Korean American, American Korean, etc. Right now, I don't identify with any of those labels. I think "Korean adoptee" more accurately describes how I feel. It's an ongoing process and doesn't necessarily end. So, I think parents need to be sensitive to that and understand that our identities are often very malleable.

IS THERE ANYTHING ELSE I SHOULD ASK YOU?

Overall, I think in general my experience is very common. I've been really fortunate to have such a wonderful family.

7

LISA LIM

GENDER:	Female
AGE AT TIME OF INTERVIEW:	24
RACE:	Korean
MARITAL STATUS:	Married
OCCUPATION:	

Lisa, twenty-four years old at the time of the interview, was adopted from Seoul, Korea, when she was three months old. When she turned three, her adoptive parents separated. Her father later remarried and remained in the same town, but she had "no contact with him at all" and to this day has no ties to him. Raised in New Jersey by her Caucasian mother with her older Caucasian brother, who is also adopted, Lisa had a "very confusing" time growing up in a multiracial household. Her mother also remarried when she was eight years old, adding to the family two stepsisters. Lisa describes her stepfather as more of a father to her than her adoptive father.

The Catholic schools Lisa attended were diverse, but there were no other Asian students. Her friends were mostly "black and Spanish kids." Growing up, Lisa remembers feeling that "deep down you always felt different, you never felt like you fit in. Your parents—you looked at them, and they're not like you." During her junior year in college, Lisa transferred to the Fashion

Institute of Technology in New York. For the first time in her life, she was exposed to other Asian and Asian Americans, and it was through her friends that she met her Korean husband, whom she married soon after.

At times her marriage has felt transracial because of the cultural differences between her and her husband. Though her family has never met her husband's family in Korea, Lisa travels to Korea often to visit her husband's family, who are very "accepting" of her. Because Korean adoptees are often perceived with disdain by the older generation, she can appreciate her in-laws' liberal and loving acceptance of her as their daughter-in-law. Since her marriage, she has learned a great deal about "Korean people and Korean culture and even the language." Yet, she has also noticed a discomfort when around Americans. When she is with her family, she feels Korean and "can speak for [her] husband and represent his culture." But when she is with her husband's family, she feels very American. Thus she has found herself "terribly in limbo."

Lisa first traveled to Korea in 1997 through the Korea Society. In 1999, Lisa returned to Korea and visited the agency through which she was adopted and learned that she had three older biological sisters. With only scant information about her birth parents, she was skeptical of ever finding them.

During her trips to Korea, Lisa has witnessed many negative stereotypes that are often experienced by Korean Americans, especially Korean adoptees. At times, her husband was been involved in physical altercations that arose from insults directed towards her. Yet she has still found a bond with the country and has been able to immerse herself into the culture.

With an associate's degree in fashion merchandising and a bachelor's degree in international trade and marketing, Lisa currently lives in Manhattan with her husband.

Since the interview, Lisa has been reunited with her birth family. In a post-interview, Lisa, now twenty-six years old, shared her experience of meeting her birth mother and four biological sisters. After her visit to Korea in 1999, Lisa contacted an organization that helps adoptees with birth family searches. With the help of her husband, Lisa was also able to contact her adoption agency in Korea and repeatedly ask for assistance in locating her birth family. After three years of her husband's persistence, and many phone calls later, the agency contacted her birth mother. In May 2002, she learned through an adoption search organization that a relative was trying to contact her. After an exchange of pictures, many phone calls, and DNA testing, she was able to verify that she had indeed found her biological mother.

In July 2002, Lisa traveled to Korea to meet her birth family. Though her biological father had passed away shortly after her birth, she was reunited with her four sisters and her biological mother. Her Korean family openly accepted Lisa, treating her with only love and affection. Through her husband, Lisa was able to communicate with her family. Through photos and frequent phone calls, she has maintained contact with her family and has had the opportunity to get to know each of her sisters, as well as her mother. She hopes that they will travel to the United States to meet her adoptive mother in New Jersey. To Lisa, her reunion with her Korean family was the "ideal" experience, and she encourages other adoptees to conduct their own searches.

WHAT IS YOUR NAME?

Lisa Lim.

WHAT IS THE ORIGIN OF FURCHAK, YOUR MAIDEN NAME?

My adoptive father was more Slavic, Czechoslovakian.

HOW OLD ARE YOU?

I'm twenty-four.

WHERE WERE YOU BORN?

I was born in the northern part of Seoul.

WERE YOU BORN IN A HOSPITAL?

Actually, a midwife clinic. Back then, a midwife clinic was very modern. It's like a hospital for them, but most people in the late seventies were still born at home.

DO YOU KNOW THE NAME THAT YOU WERE BORN WITH?

Korean Social Services gave me the name Sung Choon Hyang. It's not like my parents gave it to me or anything; it's just for identification purposes. That name is really famous in Korea. It's embarrassing because no one believes me, that my name is Sung Choon Hyang. You ask anybody on the street, and everybody knows who this is. It was like a character in a love story like Romeo and Juliet. It's like a folk tale.

So it was very deliberate?

Yeah. It's kind of weird. Everyone remembers my Korean name because it's kind of stupid. Like it's not really a name because it's obviously just how the agency names everything.

What agency were you adopted through in Korea?

I was adopted through Korean Social Services in Korea, and then in the United States it was Welcome House in Pennsylvania.

How old were you when you were adopted?

My mom knew about me in the states when I was a week old, but the paperwork took time. I was born in February of '77, and I came to the United States to JFK in New York in May of 1977—so three months. But they knew about me almost immediately.

What are the ethnicities of your adoptive parents?

My adoptive dad is Czech, and my mom is Danish and Polish. They're third or fourth generation.

Do you have any brothers or sisters?

I have one older brother who is six years older than me.

And was he adopted?

Yes, he was adopted and he's white. He blends in with blond hair, blue eyes. Back then, they tried to match up children with the characteristics of the parents. My mom has blond hair, and the child had blond hair and fair skin. The reason that they adopted me is that they wanted another child. They wanted another white baby, but white babies are prime, and there's really a long waiting list. So that's why they looked overseas. They wanted another child, but they didn't want to wait three or four years. Back then in the 70s, children from Central America were an option, but you had to go to their village and pick up the child. For working parents, who has time to go to a village and pick out a child? So back then, what was really big was Korea. The Korean baby comes to you, and you pick him or her up at the airport. So that's what they did.

Growing up, what kind of relationship did you have with your brother?

Oh, it was pretty bad. I don't talk to him. I only see him once a year.

HOW OLD WAS HE WHEN HE WAS ADOPTED?

I think he was less than a year.

DOES HE HAVE ANY INFORMATION ABOUT HIS BIRTH PARENTS?

Yeah. He was born in New Jersey, just four or five towns over from where my parents grew up. The adoption agency told my brother that his mother was fourteen and his father was sixteen when he was born in 1971. We used to joke around with him when he was a teenager, that when he is in his early twenties, he could date his mother. He could meet her in a bar. She was just fourteen years old. But he's got a lot of emotional problems, and who knows—maybe there were some drug problems from his mother.

HAS HE EVER BEEN INTERESTED IN SEARCHING?

No.

WERE YOU ABLE TO TALK OPENLY WITH HIM ABOUT HIS ADOPTION?

Oh, yeah, about adoption and stuff like that when we were young. Like I said, now he's gotten too weird. He's like a white supremacist and very scary.

THAT'S INTERESTING, GIVEN THAT HE GREW UP IN A MULTICULTURAL HOUSE.

His wife is Puerto Rican, but he'll say she's a "watered down" Puerto Rican. She's very Americanized. He's got a very mixed family, but he's still white supremacist. It's just weird.

WAS HE ALWAYS LIKE THIS? OR DID THAT SLOWLY EMERGE?

That emerged in his early twenties, and now he's thirty. So we really don't see eye to eye on too many things.

I CAN IMAGINE. HOW DO YOUR PARENTS FEEL ABOUT THAT?

Well, they kind of avoid him too. It's difficult. We see him on holidays.

WHAT WAS IT LIKE GROWING UP IN A TRANSRACIAL HOUSEHOLD?

Very confusing. Incredibly. I mean, I wouldn't trade those days with anyone. It was really bad. I had to go through a lot of therapy, a lot of light drugs to search out what was going on. I always thought I was white like everyone. Fair skinned, big boobs, blond hair—I totally thought I was white. I wore my hair like that, blue eye shadow and pink lipstick. But obviously, you know you're not white. You know you're Korean, but you have no role model to show you how to be Korean or what's the Korean style.

Like you don't have someone to show you how to put makeup on Asian eyes.

And your breasts just never develop like a big blond. But then you go back to Korea, and you can't even buy a bra bigger than a B. Everything is padded, and you're ok, you're normal.

Going back to siblings. Do you know if you have any siblings born to your birth parents?

The information I got from KSS was that I had three older sisters at the time of my birth in '77. So I was the fourth girl. That was probably very devastating for them. I mean it's not like China where you have to have a boy, but at the same time—four girls?

Were they placed for adoption?

I don't know. I only know that at the time of my birth, there were three girls. I have no idea what happened to the other three. And I don't know their ages or anything like that.

Did you learn more about your biological parents?

I learned that my father was a civil servant. That was a fairly decent job at the time. It wasn't high class, but they weren't poor. He was thirty-six and my mother was thirty-two in '77. She was a housewife. That was very typical. They gave me my birth weight, and my height and my weight was above normal, so that meant I was healthy. My mom did eat well. I did visit the area where I was born, and that was interesting. It was very emotional because I would look up and see mountains and think maybe these were the mountains my parents looked at. And then my husband was with me, and then we would go there. We were going around asking the elderly people who lived there if they know anything about these three girls and other information. Some of these people probably lived there for thirty to fifty years.

Was anyone able to remember?

No, no, they weren't. But it was still so emotional to go with my husband.

Going back to your adoptive parents, can you tell me a little more about them, their schooling, their work and anything that you'd like to share about them?

My parents separated when I was really young. I was only like two or three. And I never remember my father living in the house. They officially divorced when I was five or six. He lived in the same town, and then he

remarried. It was weird because he lived in the same town, and I never saw
him. He paid child support, and he paid for my college, but I have no contact with him at all.

DOES YOUR BROTHER HAVE CONTACT WITH HIM?

No.

DID HE HAVE CHILDREN AFTER HE REMARRIED?

Nope. They think he couldn't. My mom says they think he couldn't have
children because I think he had polio when he was younger. So I was with
my mom, and my mom remarried when I was eight. So my stepfather and
my mom raised me. My stepfather is great. He's got two daughters of his
own. So I have one brother who's six years older and two stepsisters.

AND THEY ARE OLDER?

They are about the same age as I am. One of them is three years younger.

WAS YOUR STEPFATHER MORE A FATHER FOR YOU?

Definitely. I was eight years old when they got married.

YOU SAID YOU HAVEN'T SPOKEN TO YOUR FATHER IN FIFTEEN YEARS?

At least fifteen. He didn't come to my graduation. He never knew about
my wedding. Nothing.

DO YOU FORESEE ESTABLISHING OR REESTABLISHING ANY SORT OF RELA-
TIONSHIP WITH HIM?

No, unless he dies and gives me something in his will!

SO HE'S REALLY MADE NO EFFORT WHATSOEVER TO BE A PARENT?

No—and I don't really care about him. I don't even call him my father. I
call him by his first name, Paul. He did nothing to be a father to me.

ARE YOUR PARENTS INTO MULTICULTURAL ISSUES?

Well, now they are. Now I'm training them. Since I've gotten married to
Won Yung, I've changed. I'm not changing them, but I'm educating them
about Korean culture. I tell them when we have children, they're going to
be half American and half Korean.

WHEN YOU TALK TO YOUR PARENTS ABOUT KOREAN CULTURE, IS IT MORE BECAUSE IT IS YOUR HUSBAND'S CULTURE OR DO YOU ATTRIBUTE IT TO YOUR OWN HERITAGE?

Both. Yes, we're culturally different. I'm American 100 percent and he's definitely native Korean. The thing is that I don't mind learning, and I'm open-minded to his culture because it is inevitably my own.

DO YOU FEEL LIKE YOU'RE IN A MULTIRACIAL OR BIRACIAL COUPLE?

Sometimes. Sometimes I feel like we're the same, but I'd say sixty percent of the time, we're definitely different. It comes up everywhere.

IF HE WASN'T KOREAN, WOULD YOU BE AS INTERESTED IN LEARNING?

No, definitely not.

DID YOUR PARENTS HAVE ANY ASIAN FRIENDS?

No. They didn't even eat Chinese food. We never even had take-out. They didn't know anybody.

HAS ANYONE IN YOUR FAMILY BEEN TO KOREA?

No. I've been trying to get them to. The only places internationally that they go is the Virgin Islands and Aruba. They will not go. That's very big for them—they don't want to feel uncomfortable.

HOW DOES THAT MAKE YOU FEEL?

Well, it's kind of sad because we've been married two and a half years, and our families have never met. They have never talked on the phone.

THAT MUST BE REALLY DIFFICULT.

My in-laws are much older, and my parents are in their mid-fifties. There's just no way that at this age they're going to learn each other's language. I talk to my mom a lot about going, but she says she doesn't have to go to Korea to learn Korean culture, that she can learn Korean culture through me. She's just hoping that his parents will come here. Eventually they'll be granted a tourist visa.

ARE YOU LEARNING KOREAN?

I've really tried. I've taken a class at the Korean Society. And I mean I think I've definitely improved in the last three years.

ARE YOU ABLE TO COMMUNICATE AT ALL WITH YOUR IN-LAWS?

Not really, but I mean in person we're so much better. We really communicate with facial and body language, and we do much better in person.

HOW DID YOUR PARENTS FEEL ABOUT YOUR MARRYING A KOREAN MAN?

They didn't care. I mean as long as he loved me, they didn't care what color he was or anything.

WHAT ABOUT HIS PARENTS? WAS IT AN ISSUE THAT YOU ARE AMERICAN?

I thought it was. I was actually very nervous, not because I am American, but that I'm an adoptee. Adoptees don't have a very good rap over there.

HOW ARE KOREAN ADOPTEES PERCEIVED OVER THERE?

Over there, pretty bad. It's not good at all. It's really debilitating. It's almost like this huge handicap that you have no control over. You have black hair, chinky eyes—you cannot change that. You cannot change that you're adopted. It's something that really pisses me off. The longest I've been there is three months, and to me that's a long time living in a Korean house. It is very hard. It's like a love-hate relationship because I love the country, and I feel like there is a bond.

BUT YOU FEEL REJECTED?

Totally. They look at Korean adoptees like they're ashamed of how many babies left, and they look at you like you're kind of pathetic and poor, like "Are you ok?"

SO WE'RE SEEN AS A PITY CASE?

Yeah. And they yell at me and are really nasty to me because I don't speak Korean. "What the hell is wrong with you?" And then they ask, "Are you Chinese?" Sometimes it's just easier to say you're Chinese, say you're Japanese, because otherwise if you say you're Korean, there're like twenty more questions. Then finally you say you're adopted and then they go "ooh."

When I'm with my husband, all we speak is English, so we'll be on the bus or subway and they look at us really obnoxiously. My husband got in a couple of fights because these snot-nosed high school kids looked at us like we were being elitist—that we were being snobby because we would speak in English. Everyone in Korea wants to learn English. So they looked at us like, "What the hell? Why aren't you speaking Korean? Who the hell do you think you are?" He got in a couple of fights.

IS HIS EXTENDED FAMILY OR ANY OF HIS FRIENDS SUPPORTIVE OF YOUR RE-
LATIONSHIP?

Oh, yeah, they're really cool. Actually it's weird because I met all of his
extended family this last September through November. Just the immediate family knows I'm adopted—his brothers and his parents. It really
doesn't personally offend me that they didn't tell his aunts and uncles and
his cousins that I was an adoptee. They just know I'm a Korean American.
My in-laws and my husband said they're actually trying to protect my image. They're trying to make me look better. If they're honest and they say,
"Oh, our daughter-in-law is a Korean adoptee," they would totally look at
me differently. They're trying to protect my image and make me look the
best I can.

I WOULD IMAGINE IT'S AN AWKWARD SITUATION FOR THEM.

Well, yeah. My in-laws are great. It's a blessing how wonderful they are.
The first time I went over there was when we started dating in '98. In January of '99, I went to Korea by myself. I was very nervous. I can't speak the
language, I'm marrying their son, and I'm by myself totally. I was a nervous
wreck because I was going to be living with them, and I was going to the
agency. That was a whole other emotional trauma. I was a basket case on
the twenty-hour flight. I was so emotional. I was nervous, but they turned
out to be so wonderful. They gave me a fork to eat with. We couldn't communicate, but my mother-in-law would take my hand, and we would just
hold hands. She wanted to buy me food. She thinks all Americans eat ham-
burgers and pizza, so she wanted to find a Pizza Hut or a McDonald's because she wanted me to eat more. I thought it was so sweet that she cared.
And when I was there, I showed her my adoption paperwork, and she was
crying, and then she gestured, "I'm your Korean mom."

HOW WONDERFUL.

They were wonderful. They were so accepting of me; it was just really
good.

WHY DID YOUR HUSBAND DECIDE TO MOVE TO THE U.S.?

He came to this country to study demolition architecture—like blow up
buildings. But then he found out that it was impossible because it is like a
family-run business in this country. He could take architecture. Then we
started dating, and it took him a while to learn English. I went to Fashion
Institute of Technology in New York as a junior. The whole college is
freakin' Asian. I was so taken aback. The third year in college was the first
time in my life that I dealt with Asian people.

WHAT WAS THAT LIKE?

Very scary because they were bonding with you. They were, "Oh, you're Korean—let's bond." It was so strange.

WHEN DID YOU TELL YOUR HUSBAND THAT YOU WERE ADOPTED?

He knew right away. I think he just knew. Anyway, he came up to me and he wanted to learn English, and he was so cute. We exchanged phone numbers, and I called him. His looks must have really just captivated me because otherwise I would have been like, "Do I want to date another native Korean?"

DO YOU FEEL PRETTY CLOSE TO THE WHOLE FAMILY?

Yeah. They see me as very refreshing and very different because Korean women—Korean people, in general—are very reserved with their emotions. But for me, my face says everything. I'm not an actress. So if I'm happy or sad, you see it; whereas Korean people are really more solemn. They hold more things in. I think I'm refreshing because I'm so expressive, I'm outgoing. Korean girls are totally different.

CAN YOU TELL ME ABOUT HOW YOUR IDENTITY HAS CHANGED OVER THE YEARS?

I've changed from when I got married to Won Yung. The more I know about Korean people and Korean culture and even the language, the more I feel uncomfortable with Americans. Particularly with my own family, with my own parents. I feel Korean, and I can speak for my husband and represent his culture.

HAS IT BEEN POSITIVE OR HAS IT BEEN MORE CONFUSING?

It's hard because when I'm with American people, I feel very Korean, even with my own family; but when I'm with Korean people, I feel very American because I'm never going to be up to snuff with the language.

SO YOU ARE SOMEWHERE IN LIMBO BETWEEN THE TWO CULTURES?

Terribly in limbo.

WHAT WAS IT LIKE FOR YOU GROWING UP? WERE THERE OTHER ASIANS IN YOUR PAROCHIAL SCHOOL?

No. I didn't know anything about Asian culture, nothing. Didn't have any chopsticks, never tried. I really thought all of us are the same—all chinky eyes. It's really bad now being around my husband because I've adopted some of his prejudices against Asians. Like I said before, I thought we were all the same before. But Korean young people my husband's age have prejudices against Japanese and Chinese. My husband never experienced colonization; he's never experienced war. He has prejudices that were passed on. But you know what? I feel some of his prejudices, and I totally see it in his eyes. Now I see Chinese people as bad, not all, of course, but a lot of Chinese people. I think they're dirty, they're nasty, their language bothers the shit out of me. When I hear their language, it's like nails on a chalkboard. Just the sound of Cantonese and Mandarin drives me crazy. When I'm in Chinatown, I feel so separate from them. I put them below me, like they're Chinese. And Japanese, I just see them as weird and morphed looking. Some of them are a little bit weird looking. Their clothing and facial features are totally different than Korean. Chinese—I really feel that they're dirty. But Japanese, I don't feel that. I just feel like they've got a whole different attitude. It is because of my husband, I think, that I feel that.

HAVE YOU NOTICED SOME COMMONALITIES AMONG OTHER KOREAN ADOPTEES OR ADOPTEES IN GENERAL? ARE THERE THINGS WE ALL HAVE IN COMMON?

I've met a lot of Korean adoptees. I think that all of us, whether they want to admit it or not, have felt this loneliness and this feeling of not fitting in. I've met other ones that always said, "Oh, no, no. I've always felt like I fit in." Maybe it was in Minnesota white world or something. No, I think deep down you always felt different, you never felt like you fit in. I'm sure there were points where you felt lonely. Your parents—you looked at them, and they're not like you. I think for all Korean adoptees, or for all adoptees who are a different race than their parents, I think they always feel different. You always feel like you don't fit in, especially during the preteen years. You want to fit in, and you keep asking yourself, "Who are you? What is your nationality?"

WHEN DID YOU FIRST START TALKING ABOUT YOUR ADOPTION?

Oh, I've always known. There was never a point where my parents sat me down. My brother and I have always known. But my brother never had this whole identity thing because he's white and my parents are white.

HOW DID YOUR PARENTS HANDLE THINGS WHEN YOU WENT THROUGH DIFFICULT PERIODS?

In their generation and the time when I grew up, they just said, "Love your child and they'll be fine." And then when I was seventeen, I think that was a little too late. I did go to a culture camp, a Korean one, and it was really hard because I was the oldest kid there, I was seventeen. The counselors were younger than me and I was thinking, "Who the hell are they to tell me what to do?" I was bored out of my mind. I got into drugs a lot then. One of the counselors was actually on parole—he was a Korean adoptee. I did acid and weed in the woods and got kicked out of the camp. My mom's reaction was, "The only time I reached out to your Korean culture and helped you out, you got kicked out." I was just so bored and so out of sync with everyone. Like I said, at seventeen I was a little too old for it.

YOU WERE PROBABLY RELIEVED TO GET KICKED OUT, WEREN'T YOU?

I just felt they were trying to tell me what to do. I was thinking about college and graduating, and they're trying to hold hands and do a circle, and I was really not into that. That's why I got into drugs.

IF YOU HAVE CHILDREN, HOW DO YOU THINK YOU MIGHT RAISE THEM. DO YOU THINK YOU WOULD EVER ADOPT?

No. I just want my own children. I've always wanted to be a mom. I've always wanted to have my own children, and it has to have something to do with blood, something I can create, something I can have—a Korean child. They're going to be one hundred percent Korean.

AND THEY'LL LOOK LIKE YOU

Yeah, and it's so strange. Deep down I never wanted mixed children. I never wanted white and Asian. Now I know I really always wanted a 100 percent Korean child.

WHAT DO YOU THINK IT WILL BE LIKE? DO YOU THINK YOU WILL RAISE YOUR CHILDREN TO BE MORE KOREAN?

Oh, they're going to be totally Americanized. They're going to have to learn both languages. And that's why I'm trying to kick myself into trying to learn and my aspirations for learning the language aren't that high. I want to be able to listen and understand.

THAT'S A BIG ACCOMPLISHMENT, ESPECIALLY LEARNING THIS LATE IN LIFE.

Well, they have to speak with both sets of grandparents.

I WOULD LIKE TO GO BACK AND ASK YOU SOME QUESTIONS ABOUT YOUR SCHOOL. GROWING UP, WERE YOU TEASED FOR BEING DIFFERENT, FOR BEING ASIAN?

Oh, totally. A lot of times. "You're chinky." All the usual things. Even to this day, it's so stupid, you would think that when you're an adult it would stop but it doesn't. To this day I live in Harlem, and even these stupid little black kids would be like, "Oh, chinky." And even hoodlums on the street, so cliché—and I'm thinking, can't you be a little more original?

DO YOU THINK YOU'LL EVER SEARCH FOR YOUR BIRTH PARENTS?

I have my information on a website, and I think it's been in one of the newspapers. But it's not an active search. I'm a little bit more interested in my sisters than my parents because there're three of them, and they are older than me. That could be kind of cool.

IF YOU DID FIND YOUR BIOLOGICAL PARENTS, WOULD YOU ACTUALLY MEET THEM?

I don't know. I think I would be scared to death. I don't hold any resentment because I've learned a lot about Korean culture. I was always upset, like "Why don't Korean people adopt their own children?" And it's because Confucianism is very in touch with bloodlines, and they would never adopt a child outside their blood.

I DON'T KNOW IF YOU'RE AWARE OF THIS BUT IN 1971 THE PRESIDENT OF THE NATIONAL ASSOCIATION OF BLACK SOCIAL WORKERS SAID, "BLACK CHILDREN BELONG PHYSICALLY, PSYCHOLOGICALLY, AND CULTURALLY IN BLACK FAMILIES IN ORDER THAT THEY RECEIVE THE TOTAL SENSE OF THEMSELVES AND DEVELOP A SOUND PROJECTION OF THEIR FUTURE.
WHAT ARE YOUR THOUGHTS ABOUT THAT?

Several years ago, a Hispanic couple adopted or was fostering black children. It was this big thing about black children are being robbed of their roots because of a Hispanic family. I was so upset because I was thinking, "Why is there an Al Sharpton for these black children to speak for them, but why isn't there anyone speaking up for Asian children?" It's like society thinks that Asians are white. They're both of the same skin tone, they just mesh together perfectly fine. I think that's so unfair. I was totally robbed of my culture. Why isn't there anyone standing up?

DO YOU THINK GROWING UP IN A MULTICULTURAL HOUSEHOLD HELPED YOU HANDLE THE RACISM THAT IS STILL PRESENT TODAY?

I guess so. I mean my mom doesn't know where I'm coming from when I'm hired because of affirmative action reasons. She doesn't understand. She doesn't understand the prejudices, but I have to admit though, with Asian people there are a lot of positive stereotypes. I mean we're the model minority. We're smart; we're supposed to be hard workers. We're not known to be drug dealers or into gangs.

HOW WOULD YOU DEFINE YOUR RACIAL IDENTITY TODAY?

Korean, Korean American. But I think I know more now what it really means to be Korean.

SO YOU CAN APPRECIATE IT IN A WAY MOST KOREAN AMERICANS OR KOREAN ADOPTEES CAN'T?

Right. Like I know what it means besides the color of skin and my blood. I know the culture more.

BUT YOU FEEL ACCEPTED BY THE WHITE AND ASIAN COMMUNITIES?

Yeah. I feel totally accepted by the white community because my family is white. I know how they think. When I see white people in Korea or white people in a Korean restaurant, I kind of want to go over and say, "I know what you're feeling. Don't you feel a little weird?" I feel the same way even though I blend in.

DO YOU THINK THERE'S MORE PRESSURE PLACED UPON TRANSRACIAL ADOPTEES TO REALLY FORMULATE AND SOLIDIFY THEIR IDENTITIES THAN NON-ADOPTEE KIDS?

Probably, just because it's in their face more.

IN SELECTING AN ADOPTIVE OR FOSTER HOME WHAT DO YOU THINK WOULD BE THE BEST SITUATION FOR A CHILD OF COLOR?

Even though I had a lot of problems growing up, I really don't think it's bad to be in a multicultural foster family situation. It's like that old saying in the seventies: "If you just give your child love then everything will be fine." And really with enough therapy, everything will be ok. I don't think it's bad that I had the problems, because I think the problems would have come up anyway.

DO YOU THINK THEY ARE INEVITABLE IN EVERY SITUATION? FOR MOST ADOPTEES?

You mean identity issues? I think so.

HOW MUCH OF A TRANSRACIAL ADOPTEE'S HERITAGE SHOULD BE BROUGHT INTO THEIR LIFE BY THEIR PARENTS?

I think that's really important. I think it should be incorporated.

IF YOU HAD BEEN OLDER WHEN YOU WERE ADOPTED, DO YOU THINK IT WOULD HAVE BEEN BETTER IF YOU WERE ADOPTED INTO A KOREAN FAMILY OR KOREAN AMERICAN FAMILY?

I don't think it would have mattered. I had no problem with being adopted by a white family.

SO ARE YOU GLAD THAT YOU ARE ADOPTED?

Oh, of course. I think I have way more opportunities than if I were a Korean person and certainly growing up in Korea.

Women are secretaries; they're hostesses; they're showroom girls like for Samsung electronics. They are not CEOs; they are not managers. I have a problem with that. I think it's horrible.

WHAT WAS THE MOST ENJOYABLE PART OF GROWING UP ADOPTED OR WITHIN A TRANSRACIAL FAMILY.

I think I'm a more well-rounded person all in all, even though I have so many problems being in two different cultures. I think in the long run it was better because I can see more than one side of things.

DO YOU HAVE ANY SUGGESTIONS OR ADVICE THAT YOU WOULD GIVE TO PARENTS WHO ARE THINKING OF ADOPTING?

Just expose them to whatever culture they are.

DO YOU THINK IT IS POSSIBLE FOR TRANSRACIAL ADOPTEES TO COME TO SOME CONCLUSION AS TO WHO THEY REALLY ARE AND WHAT THEIR IDENTITIES ARE?

I think eventually. It just comes with age. No matter who you are, whether you are adopted or not, you just get more comfortable in your skin, and you get more comfortable with what your place in society is and how society looks at you. But that comes to anybody. No matter where you came from, whether you're adopted or not adopted.

ARE THERE ANY OTHER IMPORTANT ASPECTS OF ADOPTION THAT YOU'D LIKE TO SHARE, OR IS THERE ANYTHING THAT I FORGOT TO ASK YOU ABOUT YOUR EXPERIENCE?

No.

———— ⚬⚬⚬ ————

Several months later, Lisa called Heather to tell her she had found her birth mother. The following describes Lisa's reunion with her birth family.

———— ⚬⚬⚬ ————

How did you find your birth mother?

I think I told you earlier that in 1999 I originally went to the agency (Korean Social Services) and just inquired about opening up my file. They just told us the basics, like I have older sisters and my parents were this age, and I was born at this midwife clinic, but the midwife clinic had shut down. They didn't tell me the family name, they just told me the ages of my parents and what they did at that time. So I was like a devil's advocate. "How do I know this is even my story because they could pull any file?" I took all this information and I went to GOAL (The Global Overseas Adoption Link), and they helped me search. They put it in some newspapers. And then two or three years went by, and I never really thought about it again. Won Yung, my husband, kept calling them, and just kind of inquiring every six months.

Then out of the blue, in May of 2002, last year, someone emailed me and called me saying that we think that a relative is trying to contact you, so how do you want to handle this? Can we give them your phone number, or do you want to call them? They wanted to really play it by ear. So we got the phone number and Won Yung called, and it turned out to be my brother-in-law. What happened was that Korean Social Services contacted my birth mom. They only moved one time since my birth. Korean Social Services called them. My birth mom never told my sisters. My mom said that I died at birth. My older sister is eight years older than me, and she remembers mom being pregnant, but they just thought I was stillborn. So the only people who knew of my existence were my mom and my maternal grandmother. My birth father died ten days after I was born. So my mom has like three girls at home, I'm the number four girl, the father just died after I was born, and it was just too much to handle. She was a housewife; she never made her own money, so she is kind of like freaking out now. He died of kidney failure.

So Korean Social Services called my mom. I really give her a lot of credit because she could have easily said, "I don't want to revisit that chapter in my life. I don't want to deal with it; good-bye. I don't know what you are talking about." But she didn't. She said, "Oh, my God," and she had to tell my sisters. They didn't know of my existence until May of 2002. They thought I died at birth.

Do you know how your sisters responded?

They were shocked. They are still in shock, I think. My oldest sister is eight years older and at eight years old you have a pretty good memory. Also, I have a younger half sister that is three years younger than me. They didn't want to tell me that she existed because they thought that I would be really angry. We have the same mother and father, the four girls, me and my three older sisters.

DID YOUR MOM REMARRY?

No, she didn't. She owned a deli after my father died, and she had to make money. She had a regular customer who she got to be friendly with and with whom she thought she could have a relationship. She got pregnant, and he turned out to be, in translation, a bum. He wanted to give my half-sister up for adoption. He didn't want anything to do with this family. I was told my grandmother wanted my mom to get pregnant. She thought, "You know, this guy doesn't want to be attached to you because you have three other daughters by another man. Maybe if you have a child with him, he'll feel more connected to you." My mom was like, "You know I can't give this child up. I already gave up one child; I can't do it again. No matter what, I have to keep her." So all of them grew up together. When I found them, I only knew of the three older sisters. I didn't know that I had a half-sister, and they didn't want to tell me because they were afraid that I would be angry.

We did DNA testing, and GOAL paid for the DNA test. They sent me some cotton swabs, and I had to put them in my cheek, and then I mailed them back to Korea. My mom did the same thing, and then they went to the Korean lab. I told Won Yung that if the DNA test said that I wasn't family, I couldn't look anymore. This is too difficult. This is it. We were scared about doing a DNA testing. We had swapped pictures back and forth, and there are so many things that are very similar. Me and my second sister, she's the one who's six years older than me, we are like twins. She and I look exactly like our father who died, and my others sisters look like my mom. She was always the sister who looked like she didn't fit in, but now that I'm around, she and I look like twins.

My first sister and my third look totally like my mom. Apparently I look exactly like the father. It is just interesting, like how even if our faces don't match, our body type is the same, our feet, our neck, everything about us is exactly the same. When I went to Korea and saw them face-to-face, it was so scary. We have the same nose, same teeth, same hands. We wear the same size. It is pretty astonishing.

WHEN DID YOU FIRST MEET THEM?

In July/August I went there for three weeks. It was very emotional that first day, seeing them face-to-face. Every time I had talked to her on the phone, my mom was like, "Oh, I'm sorry; I'm sorry." It's really very hard. I really don't hold any grudges, and I told her that I didn't have any grudge against her. I had a good life here. I understand a lot more of what happened. I am not angry, I just don't understand. I'll never understand. No matter how poor you are, "How do you do this? Didn't you have more family members?" I mean I met my uncles, my mother's two brothers. "You had family, and no one helped you? I don't understand."

I THINK THE CULTURAL GAP MAKES IT REALLY DIFFICULT.

I am kind of angry because I can't speak Korean, and I don't know Korean culture. All those things you can get back—I can study harder at learning Korean, but I am still like, "I'm never going to get that back." In a sense, I'm angry a little bit. I don't judge her, but I don't understand it at the same time. At the other hand, I'm a different person because of it. Because I grew up here, I am who I am. I really wouldn't have had the opportunities that I've had. So there are definitely positives and negatives.

HOW DID YOUR ADOPTIVE PARENTS REACT?

My mom was a basket case. She was like, "How do you know this woman was your mother? What's going on?" She was very skeptical about it. She was just so concerned. She didn't want anything to hurt my feelings, like if the DNA testing didn't work. And she also felt threatened. I know she was crying a lot, and she was like, "I hope I did a good job." It was kind of weird to hear that. It was like, "Was I on loan?" She feels threatened and at the same time protective of me.

DOES YOUR ADOPTIVE FATHER KNOW THAT THIS IS GOING ON?

No. I haven't talked to him in years. So it's just my mom and my stepfather.

DO YOU THINK YOUR ADOPTIVE MOTHER WILL EVER GO TO KOREA?

No, she won't go. It's too far. She's got some back problems that she can't be on a plane that long.

WOULD YOU LIKE HER TO MEET YOUR BIRTH MOTHER?

Oh, yes. She wants to, but only if she comes here. It is so one-sided.

SHE WAS PROBABLY STILL IN SHOCK.

Yes, but my sisters have been so great. They are totally open armed. They want to get to know me, and they are just so excited that they have another sister.

How often do you keep in contact with them?

About once a week.

How has all this changed who you are? How you identify your-self?

I know my birth family now, and I have roots and medical history. It's silly, but as an adoptee you always felt like no one is connected to you biologically. You always felt like you were alone in this country. Of course you have your family, but in a sense you are alone. I always felt like you're an immaculate conception. You're just here; you don't have any roots. So now that I have like medical history, it is just weird. It is kind of nice.

Do you feel more Korean because of this?

No. When I am with all of them and with Won Yung, I feel so American; I feel so different. When I'm with other Americans in this country, Caucasians or anything, I feel very Korean. I even feel there is more a separation between my adoptive mom in New Jersey. Sometimes I feel like we are really different. We're the same, but we are different because I'm learning more and more about Korean Culture.

Have your friends been supportive in the U.S.? How have they reacted to this?

It is really sad, but my friends and co-workers have been more excited about the whole birth family thing than my actual family. Don't get me wrong, my mom in New Jersey has been really excited and supportive, but my extended family in New Jersey has not.

Why do you think that is?

It is not that they're not supportive; they're not excited. They're just like "Oh, ok," and they're not like "Oh, wow, you went to Korea. I want to see pictures," and they don't ask me questions. It's not a big thing. And the picture that I sent them with all of us—my family, even my mom—no one knew which one was me. Makes me feel more like I am not part of you guys.

Is there anything else you would like to learn about your sisters or birth mother? Do you have any lingering questions?

I'm upset that I've lost so much by growing up here, in a sense. But on the other end, I've got my whole lifetime to get to know them. Actually, if you look at it that way, it is not that long that I've been separated, so I am grateful for that.

8

TONY*

GENDER:	Male
AGE AT TIME OF INTERVIEW:	31
RACE:	Korean
MARITAL STATUS:	Single
OCCUPATION:	Student

Tony was adopted from Seoul, Korea, by Caucasian parents when he was five years old. His parents had two biological children, both of whom were substantially older than Tony. Even before their marriage, his parents had both wanted to adopt. Though adopted at age five, Tony has no recollection of his experience in Korea.

While Tony was not treated differently than his siblings, he feels that the multicultural aspect of the family was overlooked or ignored. He reports that he was "pointed out" and "always treated completely differently" within his predominately white neighborhood and never felt as if he fit in. He recalls being called "chink" and being asked, "Why don't you open your eyes." But, he felt loved by his parents and his extended family.

---

*Identifying information about this participant has been omitted or changed.

Raised in Nebraska, he was heavily involved with church activities during his high school years. Most of his friends were white, and they never talked about his adoption with him. After attending a Christian college for a few years, changing majors, and then transferring to a college in Nebraska, Tony chose an applied science field. It was at this time that he began to think about his adoption.

Today, as a thirty-one-year-old Asian male, Tony describes the stereotypes he has encountered. Primarily, he refers to the "desexualization or the emasculation of the Asian male," a cultural dynamic that he has noticed in many other Asian men during his travels. At one point he moved to Seattle where he took a few Korean language classes. He noticed that Korean came easier to him than others and was told he had a perfect accent.

Tony describes his current relationship with his parents as "distant." Struggling with abandonment issues and other emotions related to his adoption, he has become disconnected from his family. While he describes himself as Korean American and "culturally American," he feels equally accepted by the white and Asian community. Yet, he still feels displaced from both communities and considers himself the "missing sock in the dryer. [He doesn't] have a match anywhere."

Tony has considered the prospect of adopting, but he is concerned because he feels as if he's "the top of the generational tree because [he's] the one who gets to start over." From his own experience, he describes adoptive children as lonely deep inside, and although they want to be close, they cannot. He encourages adoptive parents to work towards learning their child's language and culture, and even moving to a place where the culture is accepted. To overcome cultural barriers, Tony feels that the media should "give different perspectives of those races and heritages that aren't represented" in the media.

WHAT YEAR WERE YOU BORN?

1972.

WHERE WERE YOU BORN?

Seoul, Korea.

HOW OLD WERE YOU WHEN YOU WERE ADOPTED?

Five.

DO YOU KNOW WHERE YOU WERE LIVING UP TO THE POINT WHEN YOU WERE ADOPTED?

Supposedly Cha Chon Orphanage.

DO YOU HAVE ANY MEMORIES ABOUT THAT?

No.

CAN YOU TELL ME A LITTLE ABOUT YOUR ADOPTIVE PARENTS?

Middle American, Christian family.

ARE THEY BOTH CAUCASIAN?

Yes.

DO YOU HAVE ANY BROTHERS OR SISTERS?

Yes, a brother and a sister. They are both older.

AND NEITHER OF THEM ARE ADOPTED, IS THAT CORRECT?

Yes.

GROWING UP, WHAT KIND OF RELATIONSHIP DID YOU HAVE WITH YOUR BROTHER AND SISTER?

It seemed to be ok. It was friendly.

DID YOU EVER TALK OPENLY WITH THEM ABOUT YOUR ADOPTION?

Not really.

BECAUSE THEY WERE YOUR PARENTS' BIOLOGICAL CHILDREN, DID YOU EVER PERCEIVE ANY DIFFERENCES IN THE WAY YOU WERE TREATED?

No, not really. Not within the family.

CAN YOU TELL ME A LITTLE BIT MORE ABOUT WHAT IT WAS LIKE GROWING UP IN A MULTICULTURAL HOUSEHOLD?

When you are inside your own skin, you know, you understand it, but you can't necessarily describe it. I guess I had always thought that it didn't matter. When I was younger, it was treated like it didn't matter by my family.

SOME PEOPLE THINK IT IS GOOD THAT IT DOESN'T MATTER, BUT SOME PEOPLE THINK THAT IT IS BEING OVERLOOKED.

I would say that it is being overlooked. It is probably more important to develop, instead of having no identity at all, which is what I sort of felt growing up. I think it would have been helpful to at least know about my cultural heritage so I can have maybe a sense of pride and empowerment, so that I can associate myself with these types of people. Korea is a great nation, but I didn't know that when I was a kid. And I would never have thought that. When you are treated like you are, growing up in a predominantly white neighborhood and/or community, you are always different. You are always pointed out, or you are always treated completely differently. Regardless, you are treated differently. And you never feel like you fit in.

DO YOU THINK IT'S A BY-PRODUCT OF HOW PARENTS IN THE '70S WERE TAUGHT TO RAISE TRANSRACIAL ADOPTEES? THEY WERE TOLD, "OK, JUST TREAT THEM LIKE THEY'RE WHITE AMERICANS."

I think it is the whole idea of assimilation and acculturation. The focus is making sure you instill the culture of America.

CAN YOU TELL ME MORE ABOUT YOUR PARENTS' BACKGROUND, WHAT KIND OF EDUCATION THEY HAVE, WHAT KIND OF WORK THEY DO?

Both of them went to a Christian college. My father is a pastor, a minister, and my mother is an office manager.

WHERE WERE YOU RAISED?

In the Mountain region.

DO YOU KNOW WHY YOUR PARENTS DECIDED TO ADOPT?

They had told me that they always wanted to adopt. Before my mom and dad got married, they said that they wanted to adopt, so when they got together the obvious thing to do was to adopt.

DO YOU KNOW IF THEY SPECIFICALLY WANTED TO ADOPT FROM KOREA?

I don't think they cared.

SO IT WAS JUST THE IDEA OF ADOPTION?

I think it was the idea, probably the idea of romanticizing it, to a certain extent.

DO YOU KNOW IF YOUR PARENTS RECEIVED POSITIVE SUPPORT FROM EITHER THEIR FRIENDS OR THEIR EXTENDED FAMILY?

Yes, I think they had tons of support from everybody.

DID YOUR PARENTS OR SIBLINGS HAVE ANY FRIENDS WHO ARE KOREAN OR KOREAN AMERICAN?

Not really.

ARE YOU CURRENTLY MARRIED?

No.

IF THAT IS SOMETHING IN YOUR FUTURE, IS IT IMPORTANT FOR YOU TO
MARRY OR BE WITH SOMEONE WHO HAS A SIMILAR RACIAL BACKGROUND?

No, it's not so much important that they have the background, but it is
important that they have an open mind, the same mentality, even some of
the same experiences, if possible.

WHAT ARE YOUR EXPERIENCES OR THOUGHTS REGARDING INTERRACIAL
DATING OR MARRIAGE?

I think it is great. I do have some problems with doing it to romanticize
the idea, or because of some stereotypes, or because it's cool. That's when I
think it is inappropriate to have that relationship. On the other hand, everyone does things for their own reasons.

I DEFINITELY KNOW WHAT YOU MEAN. I THINK SOME PEOPLE DO IT BE-
CAUSE IT IS FASHIONABLE. THEY'RE MAKING A STATEMENT MORE TO THE
WORLD RATHER THAN TO THEMSELVES.

I lived in San Francisco for a little while, and it is very fashionable for a
Caucasian girl to be dating an Asian man. It's weird.

REALLY? ON THE EAST COAST YOU DON'T SEE THAT.

It would be the only place that would be fashionable. You've heard about
the Jewish community and the Asian community being connected in a so-
ciological way. Getting together because economically or sociologically they
are similar. I would say that the hyper-sexualization of the Asian female is
really frustrating because men of every color are going after the Asian girl,
and she can pick and choose. I think sometimes she forgets that she has a
lot of similarities with the Asian men.

DO YOU THINK ASIAN MEN HAVE FOUND A PLACE IN THIS CULTURE?

If you're an Asian in San Francisco, you're hooked up; you're fine—if
you're not gay. I travel all the time, so I'm able to meet a lot of different
people from different places, and I would say that Asian men are all the
same. We have all gone through the same crap; we all deal with the same
stuff, especially when it comes to dating and to pop culture because we are
not really represented at all in the media. It is a very difficult thing when
you notice that everyone looks at you as something that doesn't matter at

all. The desexualization or the emasculation of the Asian male, which is that they can't have sex.

THEY'RE SEEN AS ASEXUAL.

Yes, asexual being. That's right. And it is perpetuated.

HAVE YOU EVER DATED SOMEONE FROM KOREA?

I have never dated a Korean. But I am currently dating a Chinese American.

WHAT IS THAT EXPERIENCE LIKE?

It's all about identifying and about being able to say, "Wow, you understand me." And I don't have to explain myself anymore, and that's the thing. That is an advantage. Another thing that is nice is that she grew up in a predominantly white environment. So in fact, I am the first Asian man she's dated, and she's the first Asian female I've dated. And it is really good.

IN SOME WAYS DOES IT FEEL LIKE A TRANSRACIAL DATING SITUATION, OR INTERRACIAL SITUATION?

Sure. I'm sure it feels that for both of us.

SOME ADOPTEES WHO HAVE DATED PEOPLE WITHIN THEIR RACIAL OR ETHNIC BACKGROUND, SUCH AS KOREAN ADOPTEES WHO DATE KOREAN AMERICANS, FEEL LIKE THEY'RE IN AN INTERRACIAL RELATIONSHIP.

Absolutely. Honestly, if I dated a Korean who spoke Korean and had a Korean family it would be a completely interracial experience at that point.

DO YOU HAVE ANY CHILDREN?

No.

WOULD YOU EVER LIKE TO HAVE KIDS?

Sure.

WOULD YOU EVER CONSIDER ADOPTING?

Possibly. My biggest suggestion is adopt as close to your race and skin color as possible.

SO YOU PROBABLY WOULDN'T GO OUT AND ADOPT A KID FROM, SAY, RUSSIA?

That wouldn't be my focus. On the other hand, if the opportunity presented itself, then sure.

IF YOU DID HAVE KIDS, WHETHER THEY ARE ADOPTED OR NOT, DO YOU THINK IT WOULD BE IMPORTANT FOR YOU THAT THEY ARE EXPOSED TO KOREAN CULTURE OR THAT THEY LEARNED TO APPRECIATE THEIR HERITAGE?

That's tough. Because sometimes I feel like I'm kind of the top of the generational tree because I'm the one who gets to start over. So I don't know if I could give them that to the same depth as someone who grew up in that environment could.

IT'S A TOUGH QUESTION.

It's like you want to, but is it possible to teach something that you don't know yourself?

IT'S ALMOST TRANSPARENT TO THEM IF YOU'RE TRYING TO TEACH SOMETHING TO THEM THAT YOU REALLY AREN'T GROUNDED IN YOURSELF.

I guess kids would need some kind of a grounding identity to work with, to feel comfortable and secure in. I don't know if I would give them that.

IT IS ALSO VERY POSSIBLE THAT BY THE TIME YOU HAVE KIDS, THERE WILL BE OTHER IMPORTANT ASPECTS OF YOURSELF THAT YOU WOULD WANT TO GIVE THEM RATHER THAN FOCUSING ON KOREAN HERITAGE. . . . CAN YOU TELL ME ABOUT YOUR EDUCATION?

I have an engineering degree.

IS IT A GRADUATE DEGREE OR UNDERGRADUATE?

Undergraduate.

WHAT REGION DID YOU GO TO COLLEGE IN?

The Mountain region.

PRIOR TO COLLEGE, WERE THE SCHOOLS THAT YOU ATTENDED PREDOMINANTLY CAUCASIAN?

Oh, yes.

CAN YOU TELL ME ABOUT YOUR FRIENDS PRIOR TO COLLEGE? DID YOU KNOW ANY ASIAN KIDS?

I did, but I looked upon them with the same disdain that I looked upon myself. I saw them, and of course wanted to avoid anything that I didn't like.

THE ASIAN KIDS THAT YOU KNEW—WERE THEY ASIAN AMERICAN?

One kid was adopted. He was a freak. What I mean by that is that my perception of him was that he was a freak. So I stayed away. I was probably perceived as a freak, too, but differently.

So is it safe to say that most of your friends were white?

Yes.

Were you ever teased when you were younger?

Yes.

What kind of teasing?

Oh, the usual "chink," and "Why don't you open your eyes?" I had kind of a flat nose, I guess, so that was a big one—"flat nose."

Were you ever embarrassed to go out with your family because you knew that people looked at you and probably could tell that you were adopted?

Yes. I would just ignore it, but it was irritating. I remember one time that during a soccer game I told my dad that I didn't want him to show up, I didn't want him to be there. I was embarrassed.

Was there a time when you started asking questions about your adoption when you were younger?

Yes. I would say it would have been around ten years old when I asked some questions about it.

And you really don't have any recollection prior to when you came over here?

No. None.

Do you wish that you did?

Yes. I did. Three or four years ago I probably thought it would be really nice to know what happened. But now that I think about it, I think that it is a sort of protection from myself—whatever traumas I went through, maybe it is best left in the past and never brought up again. However, it is all those emotions. There is the whole abandonment issue and all that stuff that I can never get past without exploring what happened.

When you were growing up, did your family do anything to recognize Korean culture?

Yes. One way was they met some woman from Korea. I think she was a missionary or friend of a missionary, and they had her come over and talk to me, but I was not interested.

I think my parents did something similar with me. Their friend introduced my family to a Korean woman, and I was like "Uh, ok. Hi."

Exactly. You do what you have to do, but there was no real interest in it. I did not have interest in meeting anyone as a kid.

Was there any point, growing up, when you had any behavioral problems that you could attribute to adoption issues?

I think my biggest behavioral problem was aloofness. I would just stay emotionally aloof from everyone, just protecting myself from everyone, and being completely noncommittal about things that touch me emotionally.

Tell me a little bit about your extended family.

They're all Christian in the bubble of religion. They're all seemingly genuine individuals, and they are loving and they do care.

You alluded to some differences in the way you felt you were treated compared to your brother and sister?

I was probably treated better than my brother and sister. When I was in high school and college, I started feeling like my mother cared more about my brother.

Do you think your brother and sister ever resented you coming to the family when they were younger?

I don't think so. I don't think they were close enough to be resenting it too much because it was a decision they asked the kids about. There was no resentment that I saw, and there was definitely no overt resentment.

Have you ever received any sort of mental health treatment?

I have and haven't at the same time. I would say it's more counseling that my parents wanted me to have when I was in high school, when they just were pretty much exasperated with my attitude towards them. They gave me some counseling from a trained therapist. I was not interested. Any authority-type figure, I just don't like, I don't respect. I don't trust anyone. When I was in California, I did go to an official therapist for a couple times, but she was freakier than I was, so it didn't help me much. She told me I was normal, and I was like "Well, I'm putting on a complete show for you then." I don't think she had any idea. On the outside, I think we are really good at being a chameleon and just being whoever we need to be at the time. It is a huge and perfect skill in the business world, but it's a very annoying one because it is a very lonely life.

WAS THERE A POINT IN YOUR LIFE WHEN ADOPTION ISSUES BECAME A FO-
CAL POINT OF YOUR EVERYDAY IDENTITY?

In college and after I went to the Christian college, and then went back
to school in the Mountain region. That's where it really became apparent.

WAS YOUR COLLEGE FAIRLY DIVERSE OR WAS IT STILL PRETTY HOMOGE-
NOUS?

It was diverse in a segregated way. All the Indians hung out together; all
the Asians hung out together.

HAVE YOU EVER BEEN BACK TO KOREA?

I have not.

IS THAT SOMETHING THAT YOU THINK YOU WOULD LIKE TO DO?

Someday. I want to go back to visit the orphanage, but I don't know what
I would do. I've met people who are either from there or have family there,
so I have connections if I needed them. But I've also heard horror stories
that if you're Korean looking but don't speak Korean, they hate you even
more.

I'VE HEARD STORIES LIKE THAT TOO, THAT ADOPTEES ARE NOT NECESSAR-
ILY WELCOMED.

Yeah. We're the bastard children.

WE PUT THEM TO SHAME. I THINK A LOT OF THEM FEEL EMBARRASSED
ABOUT IT. AND SO THEY JUST TURN THAT TO RESENTMENT. IF YOU DO GO TO
KOREA, DO YOU THINK THAT YOUR PARENTS WOULD GO WITH YOU OR WOULD
YOUR GIRLFRIEND?

At first, I thought it would be ok for my parents to go. But the more I
think about it, I don't want them to go. I almost would want to go by myself.

HAVE YOUR PARENTS EXPRESSED INTEREST IN GOING?

Yes. They would be interested.

HAVE YOU EVER BEEN INTERESTED IN DOING A BIRTH PARENT SEARCH?

No official interest. Maybe.

DO YOU KNOW ANYTHING ABOUT THEM?

A little bit. I would do it once I commit to it, but I haven't committed
to it.

IT IS ALSO VERY DRAINING AND VERY EMOTIONAL AND NOT SOMETHING YOU CAN JUST SIT DOWN AND DO AND WALK AWAY FROM.

Like, can I take six months off and do that?

IF YOU WERE TO HAVE ACCESS TO ANY INFORMATION, WHAT KIND OF INFORMATION WOULD YOU WANT?

I haven't even thought of what level of information I would want. I don't even know. The medical thing doesn't really matter to me.

IF YOU WERE TO DO A SEARCH, HYPOTHETICALLY, WOULD YOUR ADOPTIVE PARENTS FEEL COMFORTABLE, WOULD THEY BE SUPPORTIVE?

I don't know. Maybe. I don't know if I would tell them.

DID THEY EVER TALK TO YOU ABOUT LOOKING FOR THEM WHEN YOU WERE YOUNGER?

Not that I remember.

HOW WOULD YOU DESCRIBE YOUR RELATIONSHIP WITH YOUR PARENTS TODAY?

Definitely distant. I hardly even like to call them. It is very difficult because I love my niece and nephew, but I don't want to talk to the rest of the family. I just don't want to talk to them. I think it is part of the abandonment issue. There is so much emotional baggage there that I'm dealing with.

CAN YOU TALK TO YOUR GIRLFRIEND OR YOUR FRIENDS ABOUT ADOPTION ISSUES?

Absolutely. My girlfriend especially. I can talk to my friend in Japan and both my best friends.

HAVE YOU MET YOUR GIRLFRIEND'S PARENTS?

I have, yes.

ARE THEY WELCOMING?

They welcomed me a little more than they welcomed the past four Caucasian boyfriends who she's brought home. They are glad that I'm Asian, even though I'm really white, right?

IN 1971, THE PRESIDENT OF THE NATIONAL ASSOCIATION OF BLACK SOCIAL WORKERS CAME OUT WITH A STATEMENT: "BLACK CHILDREN BELONG

PHYSICALLY, PSYCHOLOGICALLY, AND CULTURALLY IN BLACK FAMILIES IN OR-
DER THAT THEY RECEIVE THE TOTAL SENSE OF THEMSELVES AND DEVELOP A
SOUND PROJECTION OF THEIR FUTURE." WHAT ARE YOUR THOUGHTS ON THAT?

It's like if you don't know your past, you don't know your future. Same
concept.

THEY MAKE IT SEEM LIKE IT'S A FORM OF GENOCIDE. IF YOU STICK BLACK
KIDS IN WHITE FAMILIES, THEY ARE GOING TO LOSE EVERYTHING.

I definitely would disagree with that. To be dogmatic about that idea
would be to lose sight of America as a whole, the whole concept of what
America could truly be. The culture of America should be the number one
culture.

I THINK A LOT OF PEOPLE STILL AGREE WITH THAT STATEMENT. UP UNTIL
NOW IT HAS BEEN LARGELY A BLACK-WHITE ISSUE, BUT THERE ARE SO MANY
MORE FAMILIES WITH KIDS FROM ASIA OR EASTERN EUROPE OR SOUTH
AMERICA. WE'RE FORCING THEM TO LOOK AT IT FROM DIFFERENT ANGLES.
TELL ME ABOUT SOME OF THE IDENTITY ISSUES THAT YOU'VE GONE
THROUGH AND HOW YOU'VE DEALT WITH THEM?

The biggest thing is learning to accept myself. That's the hardest thing—
for me to say "I am who I am, and I'm not going to change."

HOW WOULD YOU DESCRIBE YOUR RACIAL IDENTITY TODAY?

I definitely think of myself as Korean American, but I do consider myself
culturally American, period.

DO YOU THINK YOUR SELF-ESTEEM HAS SUFFERED BECAUSE OF ADOPTION
ISSUES?

Absolutely.

HAS IT GOTTEN BETTER SINCE LEAVING HOME?

Yes. I would say leaving home is what propelled my interest into knowing myself and learning about myself.

DO YOU FEEL ACCEPTED LARGELY BY THE WHITE COMMUNITY OR THE
ASIAN COMMUNITY?

No. I feel about as accepted there as I feel by the white community. I
consider myself the missing sock in the dryer. I don't have a match anywhere.

IN TERMS OF SELECTING ADOPTIVE HOMES, WHAT DO YOU THINK IS IN THE BEST INTEREST OF A MINORITY OR BIRACIAL OR TRANSRACIAL CHILD?

Well, I think any place where you have a loving family is still going to be better. I don't care what color they are as long as you have a loving family. That is better than what you would probably get.

DO YOU THINK THAT ADOPTIVE PARENTS SHOULD INCORPORATE THEIR CHILD'S HERITAGE INTO THE FAMILY?

Definitely. No matter how hard it is. If you are going to make the decision to bring over a child and raise a child, then you are going to have to bring in the heritage.

THIS NEXT QUESTION IS SORT OF UNFAIR, BUT I'M GOING TO POSE IT ANYWAY. IF YOU HAD BEEN OLDER WHEN YOU WERE ADOPTED, DO YOU THINK IT WOULD HAVE BEEN BETTER FOR YOU TO BE BROUGHT UP IN A FAMILY THAT WAS KOREAN OR ASIAN?

No. Well, I guess if I could continue to speak the language, then I guess maybe that would have worked.

WHAT DO YOU THINK WAS THE HARDEST PART OF GROWING UP IN A MULTICULTURAL FAMILY, AND WHAT WAS THE MOST ENJOYABLE PART?

The hardest part of the multicultural family is just never feeling truly a part of anything—part of the family or not part of the family. The best part is the exposure to experiences that you'd never have if you weren't a part of the family, even if they are bad.

OVERALL, ARE YOU GLAD THAT YOU WERE ADOPTED?

Yes. Again, I had no choice.

DO YOU HAVE ANY OTHER SUGGESTIONS OR ADVICE THAT YOU WOULD GIVE TO PARENTS WHO ARE NOW THINKING OF ADOPTING TRANSRACIALLY?

If you are going to take that responsibility on, make sure you work as hard as you can to learn the language, the culture. If you can, move to somewhere that the culture is accepted. Don't take it too lightly. A child will always want to be included and always want to feel like they are loved and always want to do the best thing, and the right thing, and make their parents happy. Don't be fooled. Deep inside, we're lonely; we want to be close but we can't. There are so many things that we want, but we are not what we pretend to be, and we are really good at the pretending.

I think I have a unique aspect because I was brought over at age five. Maybe those traumatic experiences, those experiences of being in an orphanage and seeing people and developing a bond and then losing that over and over again, maybe that is what makes me the way I am today and makes me think that it is not the best thing in the world. But for those others who were babies, maybe it is ok. I would say that if you're going to do it, do it as early as you can. Have the child as early as possible.

ARE THERE ANY OTHER THINGS I FORGOT TO ASK YOU CONCERNING WHAT YOUR EXPERIENCE HAS BEEN OR ANYTHING ELSE YOU'D LIKE TO SHARE?

I guess we need to change the media to understand and give different perspectives of those races and heritages that aren't represented, that don't have any place in the media.

WE HAVE A LONG WAY TO GO, BUT I THINK WE'LL GET THERE.

I absolutely know we will. But I tell you it is hard. Have you been to places in the South where you know you are being looked on, and you just know you are in the wrong place?

YEAH. "WHAT ARE YOU?" AND "WHERE ARE YOU FROM?" "VIRGINIA," I'LL SAY. "NO, WHERE ARE YOU *REALLY* FROM?"

That's my favorite question, *where* are you from?

DOING THESE INTERVIEWS IS THE FIRST TIME I HAVE SPOKEN TO OTHER ADOPTEES ABOUT ADOPTION ISSUES. IT'S FUNNY BECAUSE I CAN SAY SOMETHING, AND I DON'T HAVE TO EXPLAIN WHY OR JUSTIFY ANYTHING. YOU GUYS TOTALLY UNDERSTAND.

9

CHRIS DUM

GENDER:	Male
AGE AT TIME OF INTERVIEW:	20
RACE:	Korean
MARITAL STATUS:	Single
OCCUPATION:	Student

"My parents always say that they see a lot of them in me."

Born in Korea, Chris was adopted by Caucasian parents when he was only a few months old. At the time of the interview, Chris was a twenty-year-old junior at American University studying law and society.

In many ways, Chris's story represents the positive side of transracial adoption. As an only child, he spent a lot of time with his parents, who are both professors. When asked about adoption issues, Chris could not recall any times in his life where adoption was a big part of his life. He didn't go through many of the identity crises or issues that many other transracial adoptees experience throughout their upbringing. In describing his relationship with his parents, he said, "Our relationship is awesome. I love them a lot, and we do a lot of things together."

Chris's parents were very open to talking about his adoption. Each year, they celebrated the day that he arrived in the United States and introduced him to Korean toys and other artifacts. He also described his friends as very accepting of him. Today, he describes his identity as Korean, but he tells people that he's "very Americanized in terms of culture." He suggests that adoptive parents allow children to have good experiences and advises parents that from a child's perspective, "you are just a person who is trying to live and have a happy life."

WHAT IS YOUR FULL NAME?

My full name is Christopher Philip Dum.

HOW OLD ARE YOU?

Twenty.

WHERE WERE YOU BORN?

I was born in Seoul, Korea.

HOW OLD WERE YOU WHEN YOU WERE ADOPTED?

Less than one year. Probably a month or two.

DID YOU PARENTS GO OVER TO KOREA TO PICK YOU UP, OR DID YOU FLY HERE AND THEY MET YOU?

I did the big trip to JFK.

ARE BOTH OF YOUR PARENTS CAUCASIAN?

Yes.

DO YOU HAVE ANY SIBLINGS?

No, I am the only child.

DO YOU WISH YOU HAD SIBLINGS?

Sometimes. Actually when I was younger, I used to tell people that I had siblings because all my friends did. I used to tell everybody I had a sister, and they'd ask, "Where is she?" I'd say, "She's not here." Eventually the truth came out.

CAN YOU TELL ME MORE ABOUT YOUR PARENTS—WHAT KIND OF WORK THEY DO, WHERE THEY'RE FROM.

My parents were both born in eastern Pennsylvania. They are both professors of neurophysiology at the University of Pittsburgh, so they have been working together for seventeen years. They used to live in Washington, D.C., then they moved to New York, and they adopted me sometime when they were in Syracuse.

DO YOU KNOW WHAT INFLUENCED YOUR PARENTS' DECISION TO ADOPT?

They couldn't have kids.

DO YOUR PARENTS CURRENTLY HAVE ANY FRIENDS WHO ARE KOREAN AMERICAN?

They must. A lot of work that they do brings them into contact with people from different countries. We lived in Japan for two months, so they have a lot of interaction with Japanese people. I'm guessing with Koreans too.

DID YOUR PARENTS EVER BELONG TO SOME KIND OF PARENTING GROUP OR SUPPORT GROUP FOR ADOPTIVE PARENTS?

They must have back in Syracuse. I remember going as a kid to get-togethers with other Korean families and stuff like that.

WOULD YOU LIKE TO HAVE KIDS?

Yes.

WOULD YOU CONSIDER ADOPTING?

I would if I couldn't have kids, but if I could have my own, I would.

WOULD IT BE IMPORTANT TO YOU TO EXPOSE YOUR KIDS TO KOREAN CULTURE?

I probably would because they would probably end up asking at some point.

WHAT YEAR ARE YOU AT AMERICAN UNIVERSITY?

I'm a junior.

WHAT ARE YOU MAJORING IN?

I'm a double major in law and society, and psychology.

Were all of your friends Caucasian?

I had a few African American friends, and I had a Jewish and Indian friend. I tried to be ethno-friendly.

Do remember ever being teased in school for being Korean or different?

Not for being Korean, more because of my last name. It used to be something like Dumin—it's German—and then it got shortened in the civil war somehow. I don't think I have any emotional scars from teasing.

Did other kids ever ask you about your family and why you didn't look like your parents?

A lot of people never saw my parents together. My dad is like 6'5" and they were like, "Wow, your dad is really, really tall!" And maybe on the inside they wondered why I wasn't tall. My roommate didn't even know I was adopted. She was weirded out by realizing it. Some people don't even ask.

Tell me more about your childhood, like when you first started talking about your adoption, or some of the issues that may have come up or some of the questions that you may have asked.

I can't quite pinpoint any age, but I remember from a very young age my parents would get Asian stuff to put around the house, like a South Korean flag, and they would buy some Korean toys and say the kids in Korea would play with these. I was like, "These are really stupid. I want to go play soccer." And we had this workbook that we used to fill out every Sunday. Words and stuff like that to get bad feelings out and stuff like that. I never felt too bad about it. I remember getting together with those other adopted kids a lot and having group get-togethers and doing things that involved us in Korean culture. The parents were more involved in exposing their kids to Korean culture than my parents. There's Korean culture and there's American culture as well, but I didn't want it to pass me by. I didn't want to be too different, so I thought it would be best to just sort of assimilate myself.

Do you remember if your family did anything to celebrate Korean holidays?

We had this thing called airplane day when I was a little kid. I think the 20th of October is the day that they went to pick me up so we'd always get a cake and a present and we'd sit there and talk. We put a candle on the cake and talked and said things that we would want to say to my birth parents. So that was a pretty cool thing to do. Pretty emotional.

DID YOU HAVE ANY ROLE MODELS OR PEOPLE YOU ADMIRED WHO ARE KO-REAN?

I did martial arts for a while, and I looked up to the master of my Tae Kwon Do school, but not really. I remember during the World Cup I would follow the Korean soccer team because I thought it was cool when they did well, but it wasn't like they were role models or anything. I don't really know that many Korean celebrities or anything.

WHEN YOU WERE GROWING UP, DID YOU HAVE ANY UNUSUAL BEHAVIORAL ISSUES OR PROBLEMS THAT WERE UNIQUE?

Nothing you could attribute to adoption issues. No serious emotional disorders.

GROWING UP, DID YOU FEEL LIKE YOUR GRANDPARENTS TREATED YOU AS THEIR OTHER GRANDCHILDREN?

Yes, definitely. I remember my grandparents being very nice to me. I have very fond memories. I'm the oldest grandchild on my mother's side, so I got a lot of interaction. That was really important.

MOVING ON TO YOUR ADOLESCENCE. DID YOU GO THROUGH ANY MAJOR IS-SUES OR ANYTHING SIGNIFICANT?

I don't think I had any crises. I did the whole straight edge movement and vegetarian movement for a while, but that didn't really last. I think my parents were glad when that phase dissipated.

DID YOU REBEL AGAINST YOUR PARENTS IN SOME WAY?

I don't think more than the average kid. I don't think I had adolescent issues.

WAS THERE ANY POINT IN YOUR LIFE WHEN ADOPTION HAS BECOME A CEN-TRAL PART OF YOUR IDENTITY, OR WHEN YOU'VE STARTED THINKING MORE ABOUT YOUR ADOPTION?

I'm thinking about it less as I get older. I'd say maybe in middle school it might have been more important. In middle school and the beginning of high school especially when every person is trying to impress everybody else. My friends were very accepting. They didn't really make a big deal about how I looked, so it really didn't come up too much.

WAS THERE A TIME WHEN YOU TRIED TO MAKE YOURSELF LOOK MORE WHITE?

I dyed my hair a lot in high school because I was in a band and that was the cool thing to do then. But it wasn't a rebellious thing. I didn't really rebel against my Asianness.

WHAT WAS IT LIKE LIVING IN JAPAN WHEN YOU WERE YOUNGER?

Living in Japan was a really good experience. I went over there when I was in second grade. My parents were working with an exchange program for scientists. We lived in Tokyo and Kyoto and split time there each month. I went to an American school, actually. There were a few Asian kids in that school as well. It was really cool. I made some really good friends who had been there for a while actually, so I remember going to different parts of Japan.

WHAT WAS IT LIKE BEING AROUND OTHER ASIAN PEOPLE?

They all thought I was Japanese. You know all Asian people really don't look the same, you can tell from their facial features. Some people would say things to me, and I would have no clue about what they were saying.

DID IT BOTHER YOU?

I think my mom said it kind of freaked me out. I couldn't really interact with them, and people were asking me all these questions.

DO YOU THINK YOU WILL EVER SEARCH FOR YOUR BIRTH PARENTS?

I haven't tried to. I think my parents have their names somewhere. I know they both worked in a factory.

IS THERE ANYTHING THAT YOU WOULD SPECIFICALLY WANT TO KNOW ABOUT YOUR BIRTH PARENTS IF YOU HAD THE OPPORTUNITY TO MEET THEM?

I think one cliché question would be "Why put me up for adoption?" But it seems to me it's a probably pretty obvious answer. It was probably a pretty caring thing to do. There is no anger or resentment towards them. I would like to know about their personalities, maybe some health questions. Just interacting with them and seeing what they're like would be interesting. I'm at the point of maturity where I could handle that. There is no anger.

WOULD YOUR PARENTS BE SUPPORTIVE IF YOU LOOKED FOR THEM?

Yes, they would be.

DO YOU THINK THEY WOULD GO TO KOREA?

They would. They would want to. But I think they would be comfortable, too, with me going alone. They've been such a big part of my life, and they are so wonderful; I wouldn't want to leave them out.

BEING ADOPTED, THERE OBVIOUSLY ISN'T ANYONE WHO LOOKS LIKE YOU GENETICALLY. IS THAT AN EXPERIENCE THAT YOU WOULD SAY IS SIGNIFICANTLY DIFFICULT? DOES IT BOTHER YOU AT ALL?

I don't think it has bothered me that much. I think other people are more affected by it than me.

GOING BACK TO YOUR PARENTS, CAN YOU TELL ME MORE ABOUT YOUR CUR-RENT RELATIONSHIP WITH THEM?

They are very supportive in whatever I like to do. They've really done a good job. We're fortunate because we're fairly well off, I guess, so that has been a comfort in growing up that I wouldn't have had if I had stayed in Korea. Our relationship is awesome. I love them a lot, and we do a lot of things together. Growing up they tried to make me a pretty active kid. My dad was coach of my soccer team, and we'd go hiking a lot and go on lots of trips. We'd go camping and backpacking and mountain biking together. They are pretty active. They're getting up there, but they're strong.

HAVE YOU EVER FELT PRESSURED TO JOIN A SOCIAL GROUP OR CLUB JUST BECAUSE YOU'RE KOREAN?

When I was younger, it sort of annoyed me that I had to go to all these Korean things because I felt that we didn't really have anything in common except for being Korean. I didn't feel that we had to hang out just because of that.

THERE IS A QUOTE THAT I WOULD LIKE TO READ TO YOU AND GET YOUR RE-ACTION. IN 1971 THE PRESIDENT OF THE NATIONAL ASSOCIATION OF BLACK SOCIAL WORKERS SAID, "BLACK CHILDREN BELONG PHYSICALLY, PSYCHOLOG-ICALLY, AND CULTURALLY IN BLACK FAMILIES IN ORDER THAT THEY RECEIVE THE TOTAL SENSE OF THEMSELVES AND DEVELOP A SOUND PROJECTION OF THEIR FUTURE." WHAT ARE YOUR THOUGHTS ON THAT IN LIGHT OF YOUR OWN EXPERIENCE?

There is definitely a difference, I think, between growing up as an Asian child and growing up as a black child, in this country particularly. I'm not really quite sure of the validity of that quote. Personally, I think, of course, parents who are the same ethnicity as their child might be able to offer some wisdom or experiences to that child's upbringing, but I don't think it is a necessity or that it should block anyone from adopting a black kid or an Asian kid.

HAVE YOU EVER EXPERIENCED ANY PREJUDICES OR RACISM?

I was in a fight with some kid and he said, "Oh you're just here because your parents didn't want you." And that was a time that really upset me. I think that was the only time. I am surprised at how little discrimination and prejudice that I faced. So I guess I was lucky in that respect, because there are probably a lot of people who did face it. For me it is not a big deal.

WAS THERE ANY TIME WHEN YOU WENT THROUGH A SORT OF IDENTITY CRISIS OR YOU WEREN'T SURE WHO YOU WERE, WHO YOU IDENTIFIED WITH?

I don't think so. Not that I can think of.

HOW WOULD YOU DEFINE YOUR RACIAL IDENTITY TODAY?

I would consider myself Korean, but I always tell people I am very Americanized in terms of culture. I guess that is the most honest thing I could say.

IS THERE A SPECIFIC REASON WHY YOU WOULDN'T SAY KOREAN AMERICAN?

It's always up in the air about what is politically correct—what people like to be called. My Indian friend—I don't call him Indian American. I'm not really sure. I would say Korean American, but I think Korean Americanized sums it up better for me. I was born in Korea, I look Korean, but my mannerisms are very American, and there's not much more that's Korean. There may be more deep down somewhere.

DO YOU THINK THERE'S MORE PRESSURE PUT ON TRANSRACIAL ADOPTEES BY SOCIETY AND THEIR FAMILIES TO DEVELOP THEIR IDENTITY EARLIER ON? A LOT OF ADOPTIVE PARENTS WANT THEIR KIDS TO BE EMOTIONALLY WELL OFF, SO THEY REALLY TRY TO WORK WITH CULTURAL ISSUES AND HELP THEM FIND THEIR IDENTITY.

I think my parents might have worried about that. I don't know if I did. Most of my concentration was on making myself happy. My parents and I share a lot of similar interests and respect, so a lot of the time I was trying to please them. The accomplishments that I celebrated are the same ones that they would too.

IN CHOOSING HOMES FOR CHILDREN, WHAT DO YOU THINK IS IN THE BEST INTEREST OF THE CHILD WHO ISN'T CAUCASIAN?

I would say the best interest is the family that loves them. Care and dedication in parents is the most important thing, regardless of what they look like. You hear so many horror stories about foster parents and people really misusing kids that they have adopted or they're taking care of. So I feel that if the parents love the child, no matter who they are—gay, straight, white, black—no matter what the child is, the most important point is just that the parents have sound minds.

DO YOU THINK IT IS IMPORTANT FOR THE PARENTS TO INCORPORATE THE CHILD'S HERITAGE INTO THEIR LIFE WHILE THEY ARE GROWING UP?

I think it is important to attempt to but not to be forced upon the child. That could create some issues. I think they should definitely attempt to. I am sure there are some kids like me whose parents tried and they grew out of it, and I'm sure there are others where it became a very large part of their lives. And that is fine.

WAS THERE A DIFFICULT PART ABOUT GROWING UP IN A MULTICULTURAL FAMILY AT ALL?

Maybe looking at pictures. It must have been kind of weird when I was little being the "Korean kid."

THIS IS SORT OF AN UNFAIR QUESTION, BUT ARE YOU GLAD THAT YOU WERE ADOPTED?

I think so. If I could look at both lives, I think what I would have in Korea would definitely not be anywhere close to what I'm experiencing now. There are a lot of things that I take for granted. When I think back, things could be a lot worse. So I'm glad.

DO YOU HAVE ANY SUGGESTIONS OR ADVICE THAT YOU WOULD GIVE THE PARENTS WHO ARE THINKING OF ADOPTING FROM OVERSEAS OR TRANSRACIALLY?

The most important thing is just staying active with your child. It doesn't matter if it is with their culture. Let your child have experiences. You are adopted, but at the same time, you are just a person who is trying to live and have a happy life. If you want to adopt and you want to nurture and raise a kid and take on that responsibility, then more power to you.

ARE THERE ANY OTHER ASPECTS OF YOUR ADOPTION OR LIFE THAT YOU WOULD LIKE TO SHARE, THAT YOU THINK IS IMPORTANT?

My parents always say that they see a lot of them in me.

10

BENJAMIN NGUYEN WEXLER

GENDER:	Male
RACE:	Vietnamese
AGE AT TIME OF INTERVIEW:	27
MARITAL STATUS:	Single
OCCUPATION:	Works for a senator

Born towards the end of 1973, Nu was adopted from Vietnam by a Spanish family in Miami when he was a year and a half old. Having spent the first year of his life in a French orphanage in Vietnam, he arrived in the United States with a "large, distended stomach from malnourishment" and was very sick. Afraid he was going to die, the family who adopted Nu returned him to the adoption agency, and he was again placed for adoption. Almost immediately, he was adopted by Caucasian parents. Because his exact age was unknown, his father, a radiologist, had to estimate his approximate date of birth by using x-rays of his wrist.

Raised with his younger non-adopted brother and sister, his family lived in Florida until he turned eleven. He described the rural area of Florida where he lived as "very white and homogenous." His family later moved to North Carolina where he spent the rest of his childhood. Having grown up in the South, Nu felt that his "connection with the South is probably about equal to [his] connection to Vietnam." Though his ethnic origin is unclear, Nu was told that his birth father might have been an American serviceman during the Vietnam War. Nu was part of a U.S. government program called "Operation Babylift," which flew thousands of Vietnamese orphans to the United States following the fall of Saigon. Due to his childhood fear of flying, his family believes he may have been on one particular plane that was evacuating hundreds of children out of Vietnam. Shortly after takeoff, the plane crashed and killed many babies and children who were on their way towards being adopted.

Nu's parents were always open to talking about adoption issues, and "would go out of their way to say little things like 'you were chosen.'" His father was Jewish and his mother was raised Baptist, so growing up, he "tried to split the differences between the two religions." Still, he expressed a disconnect with Judaism "because everything is genetic . . . [he] never really could relate to that because so much of it is passed on through blood lines." He described his mother's extended family as "very, very conservative" and having "always seen [him] as white." His grandparents were opposed to interracial dating, but still considered him the exception from their racial ideology. Nu was very close to his siblings and enjoyed talking to them about nature versus nurture issues and how it manifested in their family. When Nu was thirteen, his adoptive father passed away from cancer. His mother remarried when he was older, and he still remains close to his immediate family.

After high school, Nu attended the University of South Carolina, where he received his bachelor's degree in Government and International Studies. He then worked on several political campaigns and was very active in public policy issues. Presently, he lives in South Carolina and works for a senator. He is an avid basketball fan and loves sports and politics.

Currently, Nu has no interest in locating his birth parents, although he notes that for some adoptees, conducting a birth parent search "really drives them and some are consumed by that." Some of his close friends are Vietnamese adoptees, and he occasionally speaks at adoption events and conferences.

PLEASE STATE YOUR NAME AND YOUR BIRTH DATE.

My name is Nu Wexler. My full name is Benjamin Nguyen Wexler, and my legal birthday is October 30, 1973. It's probably anywhere from six months to a year after that, but when I came to the country they had to pick a birthday. I think at the time my parents just wanted me to get into school earlier so they picked the day before Halloween.

HOW OLD WERE YOU WHEN YOU WERE ADOPTED?

I was probably one and a half, probably somewhere around there.

WHAT WAS IT LIKE GROWING UP NOT KNOWING YOUR EXACT BIRTHDAY?

It didn't bother me. It was just something that was kind of funny. It wasn't something I thought about a whole lot.

WHERE WERE YOU LIVING WHEN YOU WERE ADOPTED?

I was born in Vietnam, spent the first year, maybe a little over a year, in a French orphanage in Vietnam. We don't have much paperwork at all, so just judging by a couple of things, like when I came over here I had a coat, so my parents think that we were in the mountains because I would have needed a coat. But other than that, we really know very, very little.

DO YOU REMEMBER ANYTHING ABOUT VIETNAM OR WHERE YOU WERE LIVING?

No, not at all. I don't remember anything.

YOU MENTIONED THAT YOU ARE ASSUMING THAT YOU ARE "PART" VIETNAMESE.

Yeah, and that's basically because my ethnicity is kind of ambiguous. And their assumption at the time was that my father was an American serviceman and my mother was Vietnamese, but it's really not confirmed.

IS IT DIFFICULT FOR YOU NOT KNOWING THESE ASPECTS OF YOUR HERITAGE?

I'd say no. It's because most of my interest is just out of curiosity, and there might be something that I haven't discovered in twenty-seven years. When I turn thirty or forty I might be interested in finding out more about that. It's interesting because I have friends who are adopted, and it's something that really drives them, and some are consumed by that. I never really have been. I think it would be difficult to go and search for my parents anyway. I should say birth parents. I think that would be tough, and because of that, I've never really given it a whole lot of thought.

DO YOU HAVE ANY SIBLINGS?

I have a younger brother and a younger sister. Neither of them are adopted.

AND HOW OLD ARE THEY?

My brother is a year younger than me; he's twenty-six, and my sister is five years younger than me.

WHEN YOU WERE GROWING UP, DID YOU GET ALONG WITH THEM?

I did. We were a little different in certain ways. For one, my mother, my brother, and my sister all have blond hair and blue eyes, so they're different in that respect, but we did get along. I have different interests. I mean our family will debate nature versus nurture all the time, and there's a lot of the nature between them.

WOULD YOU CHARACTERIZE YOUR RELATIONSHIP WITH THEM AS ANY DIF-FERENT THAN OTHER FAMILIES WHERE CHILDREN AREN'T ADOPTED?

Different in that I have different interests. But it's not like I'm the black sheep of the family. I haven't done anything that's very different from them, if that makes sense.

GROWING UP, DID YOU PERCEIVE ANY DIFFERENCES IN THE WAY YOUR PAR-ENTS TREATED YOU VERSUS YOUR SIBLINGS?

Not really. I mean we would talk. My parents are very good about it be-cause they would go out of their way to say little things like, "You were cho-sen" and little things like that to make me feel more comfortable. But it was never a big issue. I didn't have any real resentment.

DID YOU TALK WITH YOUR BROTHER AND SISTER ABOUT YOUR ADOPTION GROWING UP?

It was something that we all talked about it a little bit, but we didn't nec-essarily sit down and have a discussion. When I talk to other adoptees, adoption looms much larger in their lives than it does mine. Sometimes I think about it, and I feel like I'm like dealing with it on a superficial level and I need more self-examination, but then it's just something that has never really been a huge issue.

DO YOU EVER THINK ABOUT WHETHER YOU HAVE BIRTH SIBLINGS?

Yeah, that's actually something, and again it's more out of curiosity. If someone were to say, "You know, you have a brother out there," or even a twin, I would be very interested in finding him. In some ways, it's almost re-ally out of curiosity. Because it's not like it would be any real shared experi-ences; it's not like it's someone I spent a couple of years with and then left.

My adopted father passed away when I was thirteen. He had colon cancer, and there is a history of colon cancer within his side of the family. It's interesting because my brother and sister think about that a lot, and they are very interested in it.

I'M SORRY ABOUT YOUR FATHER.

It affected part of my growing up and part of being adopted. My adoptive father was Jewish and because everything is genetic, it was the sort of thing that I never really accepted, like I was always just a little different in that respect. I never really could relate to that because so much of it is passed on through bloodlines. I just didn't feel like I was a part of it. I have a lot of respect for the culture, and I know a lot about the culture. But that was something that my brother and sister clearly had—a genetic connection—that I did not.

DO YOU KNOW WHAT INFLUENCED YOUR PARENTS' DECISION TO ADOPT?

I think my mom might have been already pregnant with my brother, so it's not like so many adoptions. We are basically eighteen months apart. At the time the babies in Vietnam were very high profile. It was at the end of the war, and it's not like she actually had to go out and find out more information about it.

WHAT ABOUT YOUR MOTHER'S RELIGION? DOES SHE IDENTIFY WITH ANY RELIGION?

Yes, she was raised Baptist.

THAT'S AN INTERESTING COMBINATION.

I know, very. Very. My aunts on my dad's side are practicing Jews, and my aunts on my mother's side are practicing Baptists. While we were growing up, I guess you can say we "split the difference." I was twelve when my dad died. I never took Hebrew lessons, and I never was going to have a bar mitzvah, but I knew about both cultures, and I guess I wasn't really old enough to pick one.

WHEN YOU THINK ABOUT MARRIAGE IN THE FUTURE, DO YOU THINK ABOUT MARRYING ANYONE WHO IS VIETNAMESE AMERICAN OR ANYONE FROM A SPECIFIC CULTURE?

You know it's something that growing up I never really had that as an option because I really didn't have any Asian friends, and it wasn't anything that I ever considered. I shouldn't say not considered—I didn't rule it out—it just wasn't there; it wasn't on the table.

WHAT DO YOU KNOW ABOUT YOUR VIETNAMESE BACKGROUND?

My mom thinks that I was on Operation Babylift that crashed. She thinks that I was on the plane because there were two planes. One of them crashed, and then they loaded everyone onto another. When I was little, I was terrified of planes, and they think that I probably was on one of them.

A couple of years ago I had met one of the guys who was a doctor on the plane. This was five years ago. I was reading the story in *Newsweek* about the crash and they interviewed him and it said that he was currently retired in Asheville, North Carolina, where I was. So I just went through the phone book, and I called him and introduced myself. We talked several times and he told me a lot about it. That has always interested me.

WAS HE AN AMERICAN DOCTOR?

He was an American doctor. He was in the Air Force at the time, and it was interesting because he had written a lot about it. I found out that he had in fact been in Vietnam, had adopted a little girl who died in the plane crash. He never told me that, but in reading it, it was that sort of connection. When you read something like that it is amazing.

Because of that I feel very fortunate.

IF YOU HAVE CHILDREN, HAVE YOU THOUGHT OF HOW YOU WANT TO INTE-GRATE YOUR BACKGROUND AND CULTURE WITH THEM?

Yes, I have. I wouldn't rule out adopting, but maybe given my experience, I definitely want to have a natural-born child with my genes. Maybe it's because I'm adopted. It is just one of these weird things that I can't explain, but at some point I definitely want to have—I shouldn't even say "my own kid"—but someone who is biologically related. I know there's a reason for it, but I don't quite understand it.

WOULD IT BE IMPORTANT TO YOU TO HAVE THEM BE FAMILIAR AND COM-FORTABLE WITH VIETNAMESE CULTURE?

I think it would be because I would think that they should probably know—because I don't know a whole lot. Then again, there are other parts about me. I would think that an interest in the other parts of my life would be more important than that.

SO YOU DON'T WANT YOUR ADOPTION TO DEFINE WHO YOU ARE IN THEIR EYES?

Exactly.

GOING BACK TO YOUR PARENTS, DID THEY EVER BELONG TO ANY SORT OF SUPPORT GROUP OR FAMILY ORGANIZATION FOR ADOPTIVE FAMILIES?

No, because I don't think there were any. When we went to the Vietnamese reunion, [my mom] loved talking to the other parents. I just thought it was hilarious because you had all this Vietnamese culture there and Vietnamese food. And you had all of these adoptees, maybe two hundred, and everyone had their parents who were, by and large, almost all white, and the parents were fascinated by the culture. The parents were dragging their kids, and the kids didn't have any interest in it. All of the children were more interested in socializing with each other.

NOT SURPRISING.

And all these white parents were really into the culture.

WHERE WERE YOU RAISED?

Until I was eleven, we were in Florida. While growing up, we had a summer home in North Carolina, so I grew up in Florida; and then when my dad was sick, we moved up to North Carolina to a summer home. It was in the mountains of western North Carolina, and I was there until I went off to college.

WHERE DID YOU GO TO COLLEGE?

I went to college at Furman University in Greeneville, South Carolina, for two years and then transferred to the University of South Carolina in Columbia, South Carolina.

WHAT DID YOU MAJOR IN?

My degree is in government and international studies, which in effect was a political science degree.

AND WHEN YOU FINISHED COLLEGE, WHAT KIND OF JOBS HAVE YOU HAD?

I went into politics right afterwards. I was always interested in campaigns and public policy issues. I worked on a campaign, I worked on another campaign, and then went to work for the South Carolina Trial Lawyers Association. And then I moved up here and worked on the Hill.

WHEN YOU MOVED FROM SOUTH CAROLINA TO THIS AREA, WHAT KIND OF SOCIAL OR POLITICAL CHANGES DID YOU NOTICE?

I really appreciate the diversity. I like that. It is kind of funny . . . my name, Benjamin Wexler, is very Jewish, and I go by Nu; but when I talk to people over the phone or someone hears Wexler, they'll flat out say, "You're not what I expected." It really is something that throws them.

WHEN YOU MEET NEW PEOPLE AND THEY ASK YOU ABOUT YOUR ADOPTION OR BACKGROUND, HOW COMFORTABLE DO YOU FEEL TALKING ABOUT IT?

People generally don't. Sometimes they'll ask about ethnicity. People just aren't direct about it. But people that do ask, and I'll talk about my adoption. I don't have a real hang up about that.

GOING BACK TO WHERE YOU GREW UP, WHAT WERE THE NEIGHBORHOODS LIKE, AND WHAT WERE THE CHILDREN IN THE NEIGHBORHOOD LIKE?

They were all white.

DID THE LACK OF DIVERSITY EVER BOTHER YOU? OR DID YOU THINK ABOUT THAT?

Maybe a little bit. I would want to raise my kids in an area that is more ethnically diverse. It is not something that was a need. I never went out and sought out certain parts of Asian culture when I was younger.

WERE MOST OF YOUR SCHOOL FRIENDS WHITE AMERICAN?

Almost all white. Very white.

WERE YOU EVER TEASED BY THEM?

A little bit. I don't think I was teased a whole lot. There were a lot of people who would make references to the Vietnam War. It is very much a part of my life; it is the reason—probably the reason I was born, and part of the reason why I am here now instead of there. So that was something I thought about.

DO YOU THINK THE KIDS IN YOUR SCHOOL OR YOUR NEIGHBORHOOD PERCEIVED YOU MORE AS VIETNAMESE OR AMERICAN?

Vietnamese, maybe. I should just say Asian. I think now things are changing, where people make a distinction between Chinese, Korean, Vietnamese, Cambodian, but to them I might as well have been Chinese. If you're Asian, you're Chinese. I was conscious of it, but I don't know how they perceived me. We all liked the same things and really the only difference between them and me was my skin.

DO YOU REMEMBER A TIME WHEN YOU FIRST STARTED TALKING ABOUT YOUR ADOPTION, OR WAS IT ALWAYS SPOKEN OF?

It was something that I always knew about. I remember certain times when I was little when my mom ran into someone. My brother, sister, and I were together, and she was introducing us. I was clearly adopted. I couldn't be "passed off" like people wouldn't notice. I remember her telling people, "This is Nu" or "He's adopted." And my name is different, so there was something a little different there. But I remember her telling people that, and I remember when I was six, when they were telling me the story of the Babylift plane crash, and that was powerful because it hits home. Other than that, I always knew I was adopted. I always knew it was there and accepted it.

WAS THIS SOMETHING THAT REALLY WAS TALKED ABOUT A LOT? DID YOU ASK A LOT OF QUESTIONS?

I asked some questions, but not a lot. Just generally basically, "What is there about me?" The other twist on the adoption is when I came over, a Catholic family in Miami adopted me. At the time I came over I was very sick. I had the big, distended stomach from malnourishment, and I was very sick. The back of my head is still flat because I spent so much time in this orphanage on my back. And so this family was Spanish Catholic, and I think they might have had me for a month or so. They thought I was going to die, and they brought me back, and my parents were the first people on the waiting list. Why a family like that would adopt a Vietnamese baby is something that I don't understand. It doesn't make sense to me. When they told me about that, I wanted to know how sick I was. There're so many things I don't know. When they picked the birth date—the way they do it is by the bones in your wrist, which are the best judge for infants of how developed the body is. So my dad's doctor at the time basically brought me in, x-rayed my wrist, and said, "Ok, we're going to pick this birthday and cheat on it a little bit." Little things like that interest me because I don't have any other stories.

DID YOUR FAMILY DO ANYTHING SPECIAL TO TRY TO INTEGRATE VIET-NAMESE CULTURE INTO YOUR FAMILY'S LIFE, LIKE FOOD OR HOLIDAYS?

Not really, no. In some ways I almost thought that an interest in American culture was a way of showing my loyalty. I wasn't really interested in going out and finding my natural mom. In hindsight, that might have been a way to say, "Ok, I'm accepting you as my mother, and one of the ways I am going to do that is not to pursue certain parts of the Asian culture."

DO YOU THINK YOUR PARENTS WOULD HAVE BEEN VERY SUPPORTIVE IF YOU HAD?

Oh, yes.

BUT THEY LET YOU CHOOSE YOUR LEVEL OF INTEREST AND THEN PURSUE IT WHICHEVER WAY YOU WANTED TO?

As for being born in Vietnam and growing up in the South, I would say that my connection with the South is probably about equal to my connection to Vietnam. It is just weird. That's as big a part of my identity as being in Vietnam.

WHAT ABOUT YOUR EXTENDED FAMILY? DID THEY PERCEIVE YOU AS THE "ADOPTED CHILD"?

I think they do, but if anything, gosh, it might be a net plus. It's not in a bad way. My mother's side of the family is very, very conservative. I remember when I was little, we used to debate interracial dating all the time. At one point my sister wanted to prove a point: "What if I start dating a black guy, how would you feel?" They said they wouldn't be happy with that. And I told them, "Now how about me? I've dated white women. How is that any different?" And they say, "Oh, no, that's different," but they couldn't justify it, and I knew they couldn't justify it. I think at one point my grandmother cited some passage from the Bible. I think there was a point where they're going through the lineage where somebody said the tribes shall not mix and that was her lame justification against interracial dating. They're like, "But you're different." My grandparents were very conservative and they had ideas about race, but they always wanted to make exceptions for me.

YOU SAID YOU'VE NEVER TRIED TO LOCATE YOUR BIRTH PARENTS. DO YOU THINK YOU MIGHT DO THAT IN THE FUTURE?

For the longest time I didn't do it because I didn't think it was possible. I don't think about it a whole lot. Going back to the country is another story. That is something that I intend to do eventually. The friends that I have who are Vietnamese, most of them know which orphanages they came from. If I went there, I would probably do enough of a research to try and find out.

WOULD YOU WANT ANY OF YOUR FAMILY MEMBERS TO COME WITH YOU?

Yeah. The last time we thought about doing it, my mom was going to. It is an experience that I probably would want to have with my mom. I think that she would want to do it, and we would probably do it together.

DO YOU THINK RACE OR CULTURE SHOULD BE A CONSIDERATION WHEN PLACING A CHILD WITH EITHER A FOSTER FAMILY OR AN ADOPTIVE FAMILY?

If parents are going to adopt a kid of a different race, they should be open-minded. I don't agree with the people who want to evangelize.

Do you have any suggestions or advice that you would give to parents who are considering adopting internationally?

I guess you have to be aware of the culture, you have to really consider where you are. I think it would have been easier growing up somewhere like here, rather than where I did. I don't know that it inflicted a whole lot of damage, but I think that overall you should be conscious of that. You have to be able to accept certain differences. You have to accept the nature part of the argument. You have to say, "Ok, I can't turn this kid into everything that I want. There are going to be certain differences, and I have to accept those."

11

RYAN KILLACKY

GENDER:	Male
AGE AT TIME OF INTERVIEW:	27
COUNTRY:	Vietnam
MARITAL STATUS:	Separated
OCCUPATION:	Correctional officer/student

Born in 1973, Ryan was adopted from Vietnam when he was one and raised in Illinois by Caucasian parents of Irish and Polish descent. One of five kids, he was the only adopted child in his family. As a kid, he was involved in sports and music and attended Catholic school. He recalled that his brother was his best friend while growing up, but felt that his parents were stricter with him than his siblings.

Ryan displayed little interest in discussing his adoption with his family while he was growing up. Describing himself as a "hell child" who was always in trouble, he attempted to run away from home several times from the time he was five to sixteen years old. His parents used "a lot of physical discipline," and after two brushes with the law, he spent six months in a youth home and was emancipated from his parents' custody at age seventeen.

Raised in a middle class, white suburban neighborhood, Ryan faced a lot of teasing in school. During his high school years, "interracial dating was not accepted," but he had a "hard time meeting Asian women." After graduating from high school, Ryan became interested in connecting with other Asians and Vietnamese.

Ryan began dating a Korean woman who was also transracially adopted. When they learned that she was pregnant, their families urged them to marry. His wife had been adopted when she was three years old and later returned to Korea, where she obtained information regarding her past. But adoption remained a "sensitive topic" with his wife, and they often had "conflicting views." After three years, Ryan and his wife divorced.

At the time of the interview, Ryan had completed two years of college at a private Christian school in St. Louis. While pursuing a bachelor's degree in criminal justice, he also works full time as a juvenile division correctional officer. Today, Ryan expresses interest in visiting Vietnam. Although he has no information on his birth parents, he has begun to speak openly about his adoption with his parents, who have been very supportive. Having emerged from an adolescence filled with anger at the world, hatred towards his birth parents, and problems with alcohol, Ryan asserted that today he feels better about life and his identity than ever before.

PLEASE TELL ME YOUR FULL NAME.

Ryan Peter Killacky.

HOW OLD WERE YOU WHEN YOU WERE ADOPTED?

I was a year old.

WHEN IS YOUR BIRTHDAY?

September 29, 1973.

AND AS FAR AS YOU KNOW, YOUR RACIAL BACKGROUND IS VIETNAMESE?

Correct.

WHERE WERE YOU LIVING BEFORE YOU WERE ADOPTED?

I was in an orphanage.

WHAT ARE YOUR ADOPTIVE PARENTS' RACIAL OR ETHNIC BACKGROUNDS?

Irish and Polish.

DO YOU HAVE ANY SIBLINGS?

Yes, I have an older brother and three younger sisters. They are all biological children.

WERE YOU ABLE TO TALK ABOUT YOUR ADOPTION WITH THEM?

No.

HAVE YOU EVER TALKED TO THEM ABOUT IT?

No, not really.

HAVE YOU EVER WANTED TO TALK TO THEM ABOUT IT?

In general, I never really wanted to talk about it, period.

DID YOU EVER PERCEIVE ANY DIFFERENCES IN THE WAY YOU WERE TREATED BY YOUR PARENTS?

I felt that, yes.

WHAT DID YOU FEEL?

The typical "black sheep" of the family. Kind of hard to pinpoint because I was very rebellious.

WHEN DO YOU THINK YOU STARTED ACTING OUT?

Well, I ran away from home the first time at the age of five.

HOW MANY TIMES DID YOU RUN AWAY?

From the age of five to about sixteen.

WHAT USUALLY HAPPENED?

Most of the time I was picked up by the local police.

AND BROUGHT BACK HOME?

Correct.

DO YOU THINK IT WAS BECAUSE OF YOUR ADOPTION OR ANYTHING RELATED TO WHAT YOU FELT ABOUT YOUR ADOPTION, OR YOUR RELATIONSHIP WITH YOUR SIBLINGS?

Well, actually it was a combination of things. A lot of it had to do with just that I always felt different. I felt that I was treated differently. They always seemed to be stricter with me, and for a long time I felt like I was always compared to my older brother.

HOW ELSE WERE YOU TREATED DIFFERENTLY?

Well, there was a lot of physical discipline.

WAS THERE ABUSE?

Honestly, I would say no. In today's standards, it would be yes. Personally, I don't think so. I mean I just remember growing up being hit a lot, and they were very strict.

WERE YOUR BROTHERS AND SISTERS HIT?

They were, but not to the same extent. It seems like I was always in trouble.

WHAT WERE YOU LIKE AS A KID? WHAT KINDS OF THINGS DID YOU DO FOR FUN?

I did typical things and was involved in sports, swimming, baseball, soccer. My parents allowed me to try different things—music, we all started piano, and we were required to play a musical instrument all throughout school.

DO YOU EVER WONDER IF YOU HAVE ANY SIBLINGS BORN TO YOUR BIRTH PARENTS?

Yes, all the time, all the time.

I'D LIKE TO TALK A LITTLE BIT MORE ABOUT YOUR PARENTS. CAN YOU TELL ME A LITTLE BIT ABOUT THEM AND THEIR SCHOOLING, WHAT KIND OF WORK THEY DO, AND THEIR GENERAL BACKGROUNDS?

My dad came from a small family, just him and his brother. They were basically raised in a seminary. My understanding was that his father was a police officer.

WHAT STATE WERE THEY RAISED IN?

Chicago, Illinois. My dad's education—he's got a doctorate degree and is an assistant professor at St. Louis University. He had twenty-three years with the FBI. My mom is actually getting her master's right now.

DO YOU KNOW WHAT INFLUENCED YOUR PARENTS' DECISION TO ADOPT?

My understanding was that after my brother was born, my mother had kind of complications with childbirth. I know she had a couple of miscarriages somewhere sporadic throughout the five of us.

DO YOUR PARENTS BELONG TO ANY RELIGIOUS ORGANIZATIONS?

They are Catholic.

DO YOU CONSIDER YOURSELF CATHOLIC?

Yes, but non-practicing.

CAN YOU TALK MORE ABOUT YOUR MARRIAGE AND THEN YOUR LATER SEPA-
RATION?

My son's mother is a Korean adoptee. The adoption thing was one of the
things that brought us together. We were together almost seven years; it
would be three years of marriage, and I have a four-year old son.

IS HE YOUR BIOLOGICAL SON?

Yes. Jordan.

WHAT IS HIS MOTHER'S BACKGROUND?

She was adopted at the age of three.

YOU TOLD ME BEFORE THAT SHE WENT BACK TO KOREA, AND SHE WAS ABLE
TO FIND SOME INFORMATION.

Yes. My understanding was she was able to locate the nanny that took
care of her when she was there. No information as far as her parents, but
she was born in Seoul, Korea.

WHAT IS HER ADOPTIVE FAMILY LIKE?

Their background is Norwegian, very conservative. They're Baptists, so
they're very religious.

WERE YOU ABLE TO TALK ABOUT YOUR ADOPTION WITH HER?

With my wife? Yes and no. It was a sensitive topic. Initially when we first
got in the courting period, we would talk about it, but it wouldn't be specific; but in the tail end it actually kind of divided us. We had conflicting
views. She had no real interest in associating with fellow Koreans, although
she would cook Korean. She would portray herself as being really into her
culture and the language, but at home within the confines of our house, she
wasn't. In general, she always worried about how she appeared to other
people.

HOW MUCH DO YOU TALK TO YOUR SON ABOUT YOUR CULTURE, YOUR VIET-
NAMESE HERITAGE, AND HIS MOTHER'S KOREAN HERITAGE?

Very limited because of his age, obviously. But he knows he's Korean-
Vietnamese. He knows his mom is Korean.

HAVE YOU THOUGHT MORE ABOUT WHEN HE GETS OLDER, HOW MUCH YOU WANT TO TALK TO HIM ABOUT YOUR EXPERIENCE AND HIS MOTHER'S EXPERIENCE, AND HOW MUCH YOU WANT TO SHARE WITH HIM VIETNAMESE CULTURE?

Very much. I'd be supportive as to what he wants. I will definitely encourage him, but I think that society will be a lot more racially mixed by the time he's old enough to really understand. But to answer your question, I'd be very supportive.

BEFORE YOU WERE MARRIED, WAS IT IMPORTANT TO YOU THAT THE PERSON YOU WERE WITH WAS ASIAN AMERICAN?

Yes. I would say that changed after high school. I mean all through high school, I dated American girls and a few Hispanics, but then afterwards I just preferred Asian.

DO YOU KNOW WHY YOU SHIFTED?

Well, during high school I always wanted to, but because they were more into education than actual dating, I had a hard time meeting Asian women. So I basically just dated American. I think it shifted because of me wanting to learn more and feel more connected.

WAS THERE A CERTAIN AGE WHEN THAT ALL SHIFTED?

It really kicked in probably when I was like eighteen or nineteen years old.

YOU SAID YOU DATED MOSTLY CAUCASIAN OR SPANISH GIRLS IN HIGH SCHOOL? WHAT WAS THAT LIKE?

It was different, definitely a race card. I definitely separated from a lot of girls because of the race issue more on their part than mine. Interracial dating was not accepted back in the days like it is now.

WERE PEOPLE PRETTY ACCEPTING OF YOU? THE PEOPLE WHOM YOU DATED? WERE THEY PRETTY ACCEPTING OF YOUR FAMILY SITUATION?

Yes. Basically, I fit in, but I was constantly explaining, especially when I would introduce my siblings.

IN TERMS OF YOUR EDUCATION, CAN YOU TALK ABOUT HOW MUCH SCHOOL YOU'VE HAD AND WHERE YOU'VE GONE TO SCHOOL?

I got my high school diploma, and I've got probably almost two years of college done. I am currently in school now for my bachelor's in criminal justice.

WHAT SCHOOL DO YOU ATTEND?

St. Louis University. It is a private Christian Brothers school. The only reason I'm really attending is because my father works there, so I'm getting hooked up there.

WHAT DID YOU DO WHEN YOU GRADUATED FROM HIGH SCHOOL?

I basically worked almost every kind of job possible. Right after high school, I had no work ethic; I'd quit a job the same day. All throughout high school, the majority of my younger years, I had planned on going into the military. So I'd never thought about college, and then lo and behold, five years later, I tried to get into the military, and I had medical reasons that disqualified me.

WHAT IS YOUR CURRENT JOB?

I am a full-time correctional officer, Department of Corrections, Juvenile Division, currently assigned the midnight shift, 10 P.M. to 6 A.M. Basically I deal with the incarcerated youth of today, ranging from truancy to pedophilia, rape, murder, you name it. The facility I work at is a medium maximum facility, which means we have everything—the worst of the worst.

WHAT SPARKED YOUR INTEREST IN CORRECTIONS OR CRIMINAL JUSTICE?

Mostly it is the influence of my father having been in the FBI. Most of his family was police. It's ironic—I am actually an auxiliary officer with the same police department and work with sergeants who used to pick me up when I ran away.

WHEN YOU FINISH YOUR DEGREE, WHAT KIND OF PROFESSION DO YOU SEE YOURSELF DOING?

Still in law enforcement.

CAN YOU TELL MORE ABOUT THE NEIGHBORHOOD WHERE YOU GREW UP?

Middle class, white suburban, pretty much.

WHAT WERE THE NEIGHBORHOOD KIDS LIKE?

Regular kids, middle class, white.

WERE YOU EVER TEASED BY THEM OR ALIENATED?

Not the neighborhood kids, but in school, yes.

CAN YOU TALK MORE ABOUT YOUR ELEMENTARY SCHOOL EXPERIENCE?

The typical teasing, you know, how you get all the different racial slurs and told to go back to your own country and all that other stuff.

AND I'M ASSUMING THAT THE SCHOOL WASN'T VERY DIVERSE?

Right. Believe it or not it was in a Catholic grade school where I got it the worst.

HOW DID YOU REACT WHEN CHILDREN WOULD TELL YOU TO GO BACK TO YOUR COUNTRY OR MADE SOME SORT OF RACIAL SLUR?

Very emotional. I mean just in growing up I internalized a lot of emotions, and then I'd get real angry.

WERE YOU EVER ABLE TO TALK TO YOUR PARENTS ABOUT THE THINGS YOU WERE EXPERIENCING? OR YOUR FEELINGS AND THOUGHTS ABOUT ADOPTION?

No, not really. I mean we would talk about it, and then especially when I was getting into more trouble. Counselors would say it was because of the fear of abandonment and all that stuff. Most recently I have started talking about it.

WITH YOUR PARENTS?

Yes.

AND HAVE THEY BEEN VERY SUPPORTIVE?

They have been. My mom says that I never wanted to talk about it or learn anything about it. I have a different opinion. I felt back then that they didn't have the information available.

AND YOU SAID YOUR PARENTS WOULD INTRODUCE ASIAN-LIKE ARTIFACTS INTO YOUR LIFE? WHAT KINDS OF THINGS?

Well, I mean, anything Asian. I collected panda bears growing up. In fact I still have my teddy bear collection, my son actually has it now. But just anything Asian. But like I said, it could have been something written in Chinese, eating Chinese food, going to Chinatown, or Koreatown for a parade.

WHEN YOU WERE YOUNGER, WERE YOU BOTHERED BY THE FACT THAT THESE THINGS WERE NOT SPECIFICALLY VIETNAMESE?

At the time, no, it didn't; but looking back, yes, it does.

WE'VE TALKED A LITTLE BIT ABOUT YOUR RELATIONSHIP WITH YOUR FAM-
ILY, DID YOU GO THROUGH ANY DRUG OR DRINKING PROBLEMS GROWING UP?

Drugs, no. Drinking, yes, actually, and this is surprisingly coming out in
the interview. I'm actually in AA, in Alcoholics Anonymous. Drinking, yes,
I definitely would say I went excessive.

WHEN DID YOU START GOING TO AA?

It's been a year, a year in April.

DO YOU REMEMBER WHEN YOU REALIZED THAT YOU REALLY NEEDED HELP?

It came out the night before my wedding. And then I would go six
months at a time not drinking by myself, and then for whatever reason, I
would go out and get obliterated.

HAS YOUR FAMILY BEEN PRETTY SUPPORTIVE IN THE PAST YEAR?

They have. I don't think they share the same thought of me being an actual alcoholic, only because I think society has portrayed it as a typical wino
living under the bridge image. They just think that I shouldn't drink.

IN YOUR OPINION, DO YOU THINK IT'S GENETIC OR DO YOU THINK IT'S A
PRODUCT OF YOUR ENVIRONMENT, OR BOTH?

I think it's kind of both. I mean my mom says that my biological mother
supposedly was an opium addict. . . . I don't use that as an excuse.

HAVE YOU EVER BEEN TO A PSYCHIATRIST OR PSYCHOLOGIST OR BEEN ON
ANY PSYCHOTROPIC MEDICATIONS?

I've been to both. I was on Lithium for an experimental period of maybe
six months prior to me trying to gain entry to the military. Because they
thought possibly I may have a chemical imbalance, but nothing ever came
of it. The majority of it, they said, was emotional problems due to the adoption issue.

WHAT DO YOU THINK?

That's what it is. Just recently, since I've started talking to a few others, a
lot of these emotions and feelings that I've carried inside have come out.

LOOKING BACK, IS THERE SOMETHING THAT YOU THINK YOUR PARENTS
COULD HAVE DONE DIFFERENTLY OR MAYBE SHOULD HAVE DONE DIFFER-
ENTLY?

I would say yes, because in the seventies and eighties there really wasn't
a whole lot information like there is now with computers and stuff. It was
still kind of a bitter topic.

HAVE YOU EVER TRIED TO LOCATE YOUR BIRTH PARENTS?

Not in actual physical contact. It was a dream that I wanted to do, but I was raised believing basically that my biological parents had died in the war, so I never really tried.

DO YOU THINK YOU WILL EVER SEARCH FOR THEM IN THE FUTURE?

Honestly, I don't think I can because of the fact that I don't know my original name. My Vietnamese name was given to me by the court, so I had no real identification.

HAVE YOU EVER BEEN BACK TO VIETNAM?

No.

DO YOU THINK YOU WOULD LIKE TO GO?

Yes. Actually my parents and I have recently talked about it. I've always said I was going to go back, but I never did.

DO YOU THINK YOU WILL EVER TAKE YOUR SON TO VIETNAM?

It would be one of those things that I would love to do, but because of the current situation, I don't know if that's practical either.

IN 1971, THE PRESIDENT OF THE NATIONAL ASSOCIATION OF BLACK SO-CIAL WORKERS CAME OUT WITH A STATEMENT AGAINST TRANSRACIAL ADOP-TION. WHAT ARE YOUR THOUGHTS ON THAT?

It's one of those debates that you know has no right or wrong answer—kind of like abortion. I think it's up to the individual person. I think it's narrow-minded, but is my opinion any better than theirs? No.

WHAT SUGGESTIONS OR ADVICE WOULD YOU GIVE THE PARENTS WHO ARE THINKING OF ADOPTING TRANSRACIALLY?

Again, just educate them. Support them one hundred percent. Raise them like they were one of your own.

NOW IF YOU WERE TO BE ADOPTED ALL OVER AGAIN INTO A HOME THAT WAS AS LOVING OR STABLE AS YOURS, WOULD YOU PREFER TO HAVE BEEN ADOPTED BY VIETNAMESE OR ASIAN PARENTS?

I would say yes.

WHY IS THAT?

Because then I would have been able to have been raised in a culture, a language, you know, just everything.

IS THAT SOMETHING THAT YOU FEEL IS REALLY MISSING FROM YOUR LIFE RIGHT NOW?

Yes. I don't know how you feel, but for me, it's tough having an Irish-Polish name.

ARE YOU GLAD THAT YOU WERE ADOPTED?

Oh, well, yeah. I mean, I could be dead if I wasn't adopted. I could be anywhere in jail, strung out on crack, you name it. Yeah, I am grateful. I have to really be thankful.

HAVE YOU EVER BEEN IN TROUBLE WITH THE LAW BESIDES RUNNING AWAY?

Yes. Basically the trouble I got into was usually when I ran away. The most severe thing I did was steal my father's FBI car in the process of running away. I was detained in a youth home for six months prior to being placed in a placement home for a year. I was emancipated at the age of seventeen from my parents' custody, which is still to this day kind of a sensitive topic, but it's because I felt so much anger and resentment that now it comes out. Fortunately that six-month period was enough to straighten me out. I dabbled with street gangs when I ran away, tried selling pot, and got caught. Fortunately that charge was expunged.

SO OVERALL YOU THINK THAT SIX-MONTH PERIOD WAS BENEFICIAL?

Oh, yes.

DO YOU THINK THAT IS PARTIALLY WHY YOU'RE STILL WORKING WITHIN CORRECTIONS, BECAUSE YOU CAN IDENTIFY TO SOME DEGREE WITH THE KIDS YOU'RE WORKING WITH?

When I took the job, I didn't think of that. I picked juvenile because I didn't want to be in adult because of my size. So to answer your question, no. I definitely relate to the untouchable mentality, but today's youth are also doing a lot worse than I ever did.

YOU SAID IT'S STILL A SENSITIVE TOPIC WITH YOUR FAMILY ABOUT THE CUSTODY ISSUE?

Well, yes. Just the whole experience. I think I've dwelled and focused on the negative things in my life for so long. To this day I wake up in tears. I have recurring nightmares, and the majority of it is being yelled at and being hit.

IT DOES SOUND LIKE YOUR PARENTS USED EXTREME PHYSICAL PUNISHMENT WHEN YOU WERE A CHILD.

Yeah, but you know the situation. It sometimes requires definite measures. My parents were at the point where they didn't know what else to do. I was a hell child.

DO YOU HAVE ANY REGRETS OR RESENTMENTS?

Yes, I have a lot of them. The emotional problems are because of the resentments and regrets. I mean there's a lot of things I regret doing.

HOW DO YOU DEAL WITH STRESS?

Now, I smoke a lot. I recently began listening to music. I'll drive around and listen to music.

WHEN YOU WERE A TEENAGER, YOU SAID YOU GOT IN TROUBLE WITH THE LAW, BUT DID YOU EVER ENGAGE IN SELF-DESTRUCTIVE BEHAVIORS?

Yes, in fact I have scars to this day that remind me. I cut myself. I burned myself with cigarettes, and I've got a pretty good scar on my forearm from one of those times. So yes.

WHEN DID YOU START DOING THE CUTTING?

I was sixteen, and that was the worst trouble that I was in.

WHAT MADE IT WORSE THAN OTHER PERIODS?

That's when I really started rebelling, you know, really running away. I started going out of state. I got as far as Minnesota one time.

HOW WOULD YOUR PARENTS REACT, OR HOW WOULD THEY DISCIPLINE YOU BESIDES CORPORAL PUNISHMENT.

Well, basically they did the tough love thing. They restricted any activities down to barely nothing. Limited my clothing because I would change clothes at school. There was a period where they took my house keys because they didn't want me in the house if they weren't home.

DID YOUR BROTHER OR SISTERS EVER GO THROUGH ANYTHING SIMILAR?

No, and I don't think they wanted to.

DO YOU THINK THAT CAUSED YOU TO BE MORE ALIENATED FROM YOUR FAMILY?

Yes.

DO YOU THINK THEY HAVE FORGIVEN YOU, OR DO YOU THINK THEY HAVE ANYTHING TO FORGIVE?

I would say yes, I think they did definitely forgive me. Now that we are older, we are close.

WOULD YOU CHARACTERIZE YOUR EMOTIONS MORE AS ANGRY OR AS SAD?

Both. I would turn sadness into anger.

AND WHO WERE YOU ANGRY AT?

Anybody and everyone. I've carried a chip on my shoulder for years. And just angry at the world.

WERE YOU ANGRY AT YOURSELF AS WELL?

Yes.

HOW DO YOU FEEL ABOUT YOUR BIRTH PARENTS?

You know I went through a phase of hating them, but a lot of it had to do with because I didn't know, you know what I mean.

A LOT OF UNANSWERED QUESTIONS?

Yeah. Had I been like born here and given up for adoption here, it's a little bit easier to track down information. I mean I always grew up saying, "I didn't choose to come here. Somebody else made that decision for me."

ESSENTIALLY, YOU WERE RIPPED APART FROM YOUR BIRTH COUNTRY, YOUR CULTURE, YOUR BIRTH FAMILY.

IF YOU COULD ASK YOUR BIRTH PARENTS ANYTHING, WHAT WOULD YOU ASK THEM?

What happened? I mean because I don't know the situation as to why they gave me up.

DO YOU LOVE YOUR ADOPTIVE PARENTS?

Yes.

SOME ADOPTEES HAVE ROUGH PERIODS DURING THEIR ADOLESCENCE, BUT NOT MORE SO THAN YOU WOULD CHARACTERIZE NORMALLY ROUGH TEEN YEARS. AND THEN SOME HAVE GONE THROUGH EVEN MORE EXTREME TEEN YEARS. WHAT WOULD YOU SAY DISTINGUISHES THEM FROM THE ADOPTEES WHO MAKE IT THROUGH THE TEENAGE YEARS WITHOUT TOO MUCH TURBULENCE?

I think one of the biggest things is the race issue, because we stand out.

DO YOU THINK YOU'LL EVER FEEL MORE COMFORTABLE IN ALL WHITE GATHERINGS OR SOCIAL SETTINGS?

No, I don't think so. I worry about all the racism and stuff like that. I'm just real cautious, that's all.

DO YOU FEEL MORE COMFORTABLE IN ALL ASIAN GATHERINGS?

Yes and no. I'm also alienated there because, I mean, I don't speak the language, which is the biggest thing. Not only that, but then when you get to talking to them, you tell them you're adopted, and it's just like, "Oh."

DO YOU THINK YOU WILL EVER DATE A VIETNAMESE WOMAN?

Yes, but I think it would be probably somebody that's adopted. I would definitely take my time, and there would have to be a lot of understanding and acceptance.

WHAT OTHER ASPECTS OF ADOPTION DO YOU THINK ARE IMPORTANT TO SHARE OR OTHER THINGS THAT I'VE FORGOTTEN TO ASK YOU, OR THAT I'VE MISSED IN TERMS OF YOUR STORY?

I think it's just important that we talk about it. Really, I am the way I am today because I never did talk about it.

WOULD YOU SAY YOU'RE FEELING BETTER ABOUT LIFE, ABOUT WHO YOU ARE TODAY, MORE SO THAN EVER?

Yes, but it's scary because I don't like all these emotions that come out. Literally since I've started this, I'm crying more now than I've ever cried in my life. I've just been really emotional.

I THINK IT'S A POSITIVE SIGN THAT YOU'RE UPSET AND EMOTIONAL RATHER THAN BEING REALLY UNATTACHED. I THINK IT IS A VERY HEALTHY SIGN. I'M HAPPY FOR YOU THAT YOU ARE ABLE TO FACE IT EVEN IF YOU ARE IN YOUR LATE TWENTIES. IT'S NEVER TOO LATE.

⑫

JUSTINE CASE*

GENDER:	Female
AGE AT TIME OF INTERVIEW:	28
RACE:	Vietnamese
MARITAL STATUS:	Single
OCCUPATION:	Executive assistant

Born in Saigon, Vietnam, Justine was adopted through Holt International when she was five months old. She came to the United States in 1975 as part of Operation Babylift and was adopted by a Caucasian couple. Justine's parents decided to adopt after her mother almost died in childbirth delivering her older brother. When told that they couldn't have any more children, her parents considered adopting from Japan. Because of the waiting list for Japanese babies, they decided to adopt from Vietnam.

Growing up, Justine moved frequently and recalled living in homogeneous neighborhoods. She was raised with her older brother, her parents' biological son, and characterized their relationship as filled with "normal sibling rivalry." Not able to recall any discussions about adoption issues with her family, Justine believed her family perceived her as being non-Asian, as

---

*Identifying information about this participant has been omitted or changed.

if "it just went out of their consciousness." When she was six, her parents divorced. Both of her parents subsequently remarried, although her mother divorced again when she was older. Being adopted made Justine feel special. It "provided some amusement," especially when she encountered people who, for example, remarked, "I can't believe she doesn't have an accent!" Throughout her childhood, Justine was constantly concerned about her father's struggle with alcoholism. Today, however, Justine and her father remain very close to each other.

Having always excelled in school, Justine graduated from a highly ranked liberal arts school where she obtained a political science degree and a minor in communications. She lives on the West Coast and characterizes herself as "really independent." When asked how she perceives herself, she identified herself as "an adopted Vietnamese and a Westerner," and as a "typical American girl from a typical American family."

Reflecting upon her future, Justine indicated that she would consider adopting from Vietnam, but also expressed her desire to have biological children and "having a family where you are blood related." Someday she hopes to travel to Vietnam, where she has many adoptee friends. She also expressed interest in locating her biological mother, who, she was told, had four children prior to Justine's birth. Currently, she characterizes herself as very spiritual and enjoys yoga.

How old are you Justine?

Twenty-eight.

Where were you born?

Saigon, Vietnam.

Do you know the name that you were born with?

Duing Thi Ngo Ny Chi. My middle name is Chi. They thought that was my first name because it reads backwards. Duing was my family name, and they thought Chi was my first name. Then I found out from a Vietnamese lady—when I showed her my name she was like, "Oh no, your name is Ny-chi." Ny and Chi were one name. I thought Ny was the middle name.

Were you adopted through an agency?

Yes. Holt International.

How old were you when you were adopted?

I was relinquished when I was three days old to the adoption agency. I didn't reach my parents until I was five months old. I was shipped out of Vietnam in April of 1975, when basically every American had fled.

Were you part of Operation Babylift?

Yes. I flew over in a plane with about two hundred other orphans in April of 1975, and we stopped in Guam or Hawaii. Then they landed in Seattle, and we all got shipped off to other places.

Where were your parents living when you were adopted?

East Peoria, Illinois.

Is that where you grew up?

We moved around a lot. My parents split up when I was six because my dad is an alcoholic. I lived in Illinois until I was nine, and then when I was nine, both of my parents married different people. My stepdad got transferred from Princeton, Illinois, to southern Minnesota. I lived in Minneapolis suburbs until I was done with high school.

And right now you are in California?

Los Angeles.

Are your adoptive parents both Caucasian?

Yes.

What about your step parents?

They are all Caucasian.

Do you have any brothers or sisters?

One brother. He is three years older and is my parents' biological child.

Growing up, what kind of relationship did you have with your brother?

It was good. We had the normal sibling rivalry. It sort of all mellowed out by the time he turned fifteen. Then it got real mellow, and we were able to work together to lie to our parents.

Did you ever talk about adoption issues with your brother?

I knew I was adopted since I was old enough to really comprehend. I don't think we ever really discussed adoption issues. They didn't even think of me as Asian. They really thought of me as just part of the family, and I wasn't treated any differently. It just went out of their consciousness. Like my brother still—when people bring it up to him, he's like, "I forgot about it totally, that she's a different race, and that she's not my real sister."

WHEN YOU WERE GROWING UP WITH HIM DID YOU PERCEIVE ANY DIFFER-ENCES IN THE WAY YOU WERE TREATED BY YOUR PARENTS OR FAMILY?

No. My grandma on my mom's side didn't know if she'd be able to accept me, but the moment she saw me, she knew she wouldn't have a problem. Before I arrived, I think there was some hesitation. My dad was stationed in Okinawa for a year, and my mom stayed with him over there. They just really fell in love with the "Oriental" race while they were over there. When they came back they talked about adopting a Japanese baby, but at the time that they wanted to adopt, there were none available—the waiting list was very long. They had my brother, and she almost died in childbirth. They told her to adopt because she couldn't have anymore kids.

CAN YOU TELL ME MORE ABOUT YOUR PARENTS?

They both come from blue-collar families in East Peoria, Illinois. They were high school sweethearts. She is the only one in her family of five kids who went to graduate school and did the college thing. She's a licensed psychologist. My dad studied computer programming, but he dropped out of it. He likes working with his hands—he's a mechanic, an auto body guy. Alcoholic. He recently moved to L.A. from Chicago. He lived in Chicago basically since I was nine or ten, and he was dying there. He had been married twice and divorced twice; my mom has been married three times and divorced twice. So he's really doing well out here. He had to get into an alcohol treatment program because he was killing himself with alcohol. I had no idea how bad it had gotten because I only saw him a few months a year since I was ten. It is always hard, but it seems almost every family is touched by some kind of addiction now—if it's not drugs or alcohol, it's shopping or gambling or something.

ARE YOU CLOSE TO YOUR FATHER TODAY?

Oh yeah. I see him every weekend. I've seen him more since he moved here in October than I probably have in my whole life since we stopped living with each other when I was five years old.

WHAT WAS IT LIKE WHEN YOUR PARENTS DIVORCED?

It was really hard for me. I was really shook up about it. I was maybe four or five when they were getting separated. But they fought all the time because my dad was an alcoholic.

Do you think your experience with divorce is different from other kids' because you were adopted?

It's hard to say. I've always been really independent.

What about the neighborhoods you grew up in, were they very homogeneous?

Oh, yes. It was like *oooh* when a black family moved in. So when I first visited New York, I felt this comfort level and level of anonymity.

And people aren't looking at you just because you are different.

Right. Every time I went out to eat with my family, I'd catch people looking at us out of the corner of their eye. People are just curious. Growing up being out of the norm, when you move someplace where you are the norm, you are going to miss it. Even the attention, in a way.

For a lot of us, being different has been such an integral and normal part of our life. As much as we may have felt uncomfortable, I think at some point we get so used to that it just becomes part of who we are.

At the same time I have this comfort knowing I am always going to be different. I used to waitress for six years through college. I talked to a lot of people, and they asked me about my life story. I told it a zillion times, over and over. It is always like, "Have you ever found your real parents? Have you ever searched for them? Have you ever wondered about them?" I always get the same questions. They are really intrigued by the whole concept of not having blood relatives or not knowing your roots. They are all very curious. It never really crossed my mind. And in other peoples' minds, it should have been my number one priority in life—to find my mother. They just couldn't fathom (a) giving up a member of their family for adoption and (b) not knowing your heritage or your language and customs. I'm like, "I didn't grow up with anything else, so I didn't wonder about those things."

Have you ever been back to Vietnam?

Hopefully next year I'll be able to go.

Have your parents ever expressed interest in going to Vietnam?

Oh, yes. They both want to go. My mom wants to go with me, but I decided that the first time I go, I want to go without my family. The second time I go, I'd like to go with my family and my boyfriend and take the Holt Motherland Tour. The tours are for very white Americanized Vietnamese adoptees and their white parents.

I DID THE HOLT MOTHERLAND TOUR IN KOREA AND IT WAS ALL ADOPTIVE FAMILIES.

Yeah, and they do bonding or whatever. Some of the other adoptees parents I've met—I'm so glad I didn't grow up with them! I've met some, and they are so icky. My mom is so cool compared with that! I lucked out because I wasn't abused mentally or physically. I've met some who have been, and they are messed up for life

WHAT'S YOUR BOYFRIEND'S ETHNICITY?

He's white. Irish/German mutt. So are my parents. They're very like mutts—German, English, French.

HOW LONG HAVE YOU BEEN DATING?

Four years in July.

DO YOU TALK ABOUT ADOPTION ISSUES WITH YOUR BOYFRIEND?

Not really. I think he knows that I want to go to Vietnam. He knows that I hang out with other adoptees sometimes. We have like a kind of little L.A. group of adoptees that gets together every now and then. We went to the Tet celebrations, the Chinese New Year's last month. He doesn't really go along on those. It is sort of a special unique kind of little thing. We don't really talk about it. He knows that deep down I'm like him. On the surface, I look different.

WHAT ARE YOU EXPERIENCES OR THOUGHTS ON INTERRACIAL DATING OR EVEN MARRIAGE?

I think hybrid children are really beautiful. Like most of the hybrid children I've ever seen have been totally gorgeous, so that is my whole take on that. As far as dating people of another race, I feel like it is more of a cultural thing that stands in the way than race. My boyfriend and I don't even look like we're a couple. He's tall and I'm short, so I think people think we are just friends. There's a perception that a lot of Asian women who aren't adopted are really status-seekers. They date for money and how nice a car you're driving. I'm not really shallow like that.

OVERALL, WHAT WOULD YOU SAY IS IMPORTANT TO YOU IN A PARTNER?

Sincerity, honesty and humor, and ambition.

DO YOU THINK YOU WILL HAVE CHILDREN?

Yeah.

DO YOU THINK YOU MIGHT ADOPT?

Yeah. Probably if I couldn't have kids of my own.

IF YOU HAVE KIDS, WILL YOU TRY TO DO ANYTHING TO CELEBRATE THEIR CULTURAL HERITAGE?

I would probably do more than my parents did. My parents didn't know a whole lot. They knew the chow mein noodles in the package and in the can. My mom did more of trying to expose me to cultural things after my mom and dad divorced, but she did it for all cultures. She took me to plays and art museums and different cuisines like Middle Eastern cuisine, Vietnamese cuisine, and Mexican. She tried to expose me to all these kind of things, and Vietnamese was just one of them. It took me a while to start liking the food.

DO YOU THINK YOU WOULD EVER ADOPT TRANSRACIALLY YOURSELF?

Like I said, if I couldn't have kids of my own. I think the whole joy of having biological kids is having a family where you are blood-related. Because I didn't grow up blood-related to anybody, I totally think that is important. I tried to explain that to a mother who said, "I don't understand why none of the adopted kids are adopting other kids."

TELL ME SOME MORE ABOUT YOUR EDUCATION.

I went to public school all the way from kindergarten to twelfth grade; and I always did really well in school. I got straight As all through elementary, and I was in advanced placement classes in senior high, which I am still thankful for. I got into a really prestigious private liberal arts school, and my parents didn't have any money to pay for me, but the state and the school gave me a shitload of financial aid, so I really lucked out. Through waitressing and bussing tables and working three jobs in the summer, I paid for college. And I graduated. I have a major in political science and a minor in communications and almost a minor in sociology.

WHEN YOU WERE GOING INTO ADOLESCENCE, DID YOU GO THROUGH ANY PROBLEMS WITH DRUGS OR DRINKING?

Not in adolescence, but in college I was smoking pot every day. But I wouldn't do anything until I was finished with my homework, and I was trying not to do it if I had to go to work. I graduated with a 3.64 GPA, and I didn't let it affect my studies. After I graduated from college—that's when I started having problems because celebrating my graduation from college went on for a year. The whole summer afterwards, I was celebrating and then it became the entire year. I realized that I had a problem and that's when I moved to New York from Minneapolis. When I was twenty-five, I really started trying to reverse all the damage that I'd done to myself, like becoming a vegetarian or eating really healthily. I exercise and I do yoga, and so I am really into cleansing the body, soul, and mind. Now that I'm twenty-eight, I have to think about having kids, so now I'm really into sobriety.

HAVE YOU EVER THOUGHT ABOUT SEEING ANYONE FOR MENTAL HEALTH TREATMENT?

Recently I thought maybe I should see a psychologist. I would probably talk about my dad being alcoholic, being adopted, about identity issues of growing up. My mom is a psychologist, and I always felt pretty mentally balanced and able to cope with the changes and stress in my environment. You can either deal with things in a selfish way or a constructive way. And I am trying to change my habits to be constructive instead of self-destructive.

WAS THERE ANY POINT WHEN ADOPTION BECAME A CENTRAL PART OF YOUR LIFE?

No. It was always on the back burner. It was in my history; it was in my past. You have to accept it and move on with life.

WERE YOU GIVEN ANY INFORMATION ABOUT YOUR BIOLOGICAL PARENTS?

I have a special history paper, which I guess my birth mother filled out with the adoption agency before relinquishing me. It basically says that she had four other children before me and her husband had fought for the South Vietnamese army and she ended up getting pregnant. Her husband came back wounded after the war. His whole family shamed her because he knew it was not his child and told her that she had to give it up for adoption, otherwise they would banish her from the family. So this is her reason for giving me up for adoption, although it could have been a totally made up story.

ARE YOU INTERESTED IN DOING A BIRTH PARENT SEARCH?

In April of 2000, I paid Holt a fee to try to find her, and I signed some papers that said if she ever went to Holt looking for me that I give permission for her to find me. I was in the first wave of Vietnamese adoptees who gave them money to look for her, and I found out that they had her name and that they wouldn't give it to me. I got really, really pissed off—this was in 2001. I think it was finally January last year where they were able to relinquish her name, and they gave me her name and the address where she was at when she gave me up. I'm really interested in seeing what my half-brothers and sisters—the four other kids before me—look like. And, of course, what she looks like in her old age because I might look like that in my old age. I know that is opening up a can of worms, opening up all these emotions about not having a birth mother that I know.

WOULD YOU BE INTERESTED IN MEETING YOUR BIRTH FATHER?

Yes, but I don't think she would know who he was. Maybe she does, maybe he was a neighbor who was like, "Hey, I'll feed your kids if you sleep with me," and maybe she knows who he is. I think I am full Vietnamese, so I'm thinking it was not a U.S. soldier. I think by the time I was conceived, most of the American soldiers had pulled out of Vietnam.

SEARCHING IS SO EMOTIONALLY DRAINING—EVEN JUST THE CURIOSITY OR WONDERING.

I WANTED TO READ YOU A QUOTE THAT THE PRESIDENT OF THE NATIONAL ASSOCIATION OF BLACK SOCIAL WORKERS SAID BACK IN 1971 AND GET YOUR RESPONSE IN LIGHT OF YOUR EXPERIENCE. HE SAID, "BLACK CHILDREN BE-LONG PHYSICALLY, PSYCHOLOGICALLY, AND CULTURALLY IN BLACK FAMILIES IN ORDER THAT THEY RECEIVE THE TOTAL SENSE OF THEMSELVES AND DEVELOP A SOUND PROJECTION OF THEIR FUTURE." THAT STATEMENT GENERATED A LOT OF CONTROVERSY AS YOU CAN IMAGINE.

It is sort of a racist statement. I think that back then people believed that it was wrong. I've met some black people adopted by white people, and I think they have issues. I think being raised in a family that provides chal-lenges makes you a stronger person.

DO YOU FEEL ACCEPTED BY THE VIETNAMESE OR THE ASIAN COMMUNITY?

It depends. I've met Vietnamese people my age who are really cool, and I've met other ones who are closed-minded.

HOW WOULD DEFINE YOUR RACIAL IDENTITY TODAY?

I would say I'm an adopted Vietnamese and a Westerner. I'm not a Cali-fornian, and I'm not a New Yorker, and I'm definitely a Midwestern girl deep down. On the surface I'm Vietnamese, and I have Vietnamese blood running through my veins. That's why I really enjoy yoga and spirituality and that kind of thing.

HOW MUCH OF ADOPTEES' HERITAGE SHOULD PARENTS INCORPORATE INTO THEIR LIVES?

You shouldn't force feed it. I think once the kids start searching on their own, just let them search. You can kind of point them to the library or the internet and say, "Hey, there are some folk stories on the internet about what mommies and daddies in Vietnam read their kids at bedtime in Vietnam. But there are also some on here from Sweden or Finland." Some parents I think today are searching for answers, like, "How many Vietnamese dishes should I prepare, and should we fly half way around the United States to go to a heritage camp?" As long as they do the best job they know how—that's all they can do. So, I can't say anything bad about transracial adoption except that if there are drawbacks, there are drawbacks to being a natural-born kid as well. There are difficulties and identity issues growing up as a natural kid—it happens to kids everywhere. It's just part of growing up.

WAS THERE ANYTHING SPECIFICALLY ENJOYABLE ABOUT GROWING UP IN A MULTICULTURAL FAMILY?

It made me feel special. Some kids have problems with feeling ordinary. It provided some amusement. I heard people in a hotel one time who said, "I can't believe she doesn't have an accent!" And I've had people who squint at my nametag from across the table, like "How do you pronounce your name?" I'm a typical American girl from a typical American family, you know, semi-dysfunctional.

ARE YOU GLAD YOU WERE ADOPTED?

I often wonder what my life would have been like and how I would have been different. Sometimes I dream about it. I used to dream about it when I was a little girl. I was like a Mafia princess, and they would come back for me.

WAS THERE EVER A TIME WHEN YOU THOUGHT YOU WOULD HAVE PREFERRED TO BE ADOPTED BY A VIETNAMESE FAMILY?

No, because it always seemed very patriarchal—that whole thing where you have to live with your family after you get married and bow down to your father and then your husband and then the brothers. What's up with that? I grew up with a single mother who did it all and was single for a long time. She was really independent, and that is really who I am.

DO YOU HAVE ANY SUGGESTIONS OR ADVICE THAT YOU WOULD GIVE TO PARENTS WHO ARE CONSIDERING ADOPTING TRANSRACIALLY?

I would say follow your heart. Don't do it because you want to have an Asian kid or a black kid. Try to develop their talents in general and their journey finding themselves. There's always going to be low self-esteem—that's part of growing up. And don't blame themselves even if the kids blame them for turning out bad. You have to let them go. Some parents try to cling on to their kids so much. There's a whole thing about how if you leave the cage door open and they come back. And it's true. Try to keep them caged up, and they'll fly away and never come back; but leave the cage door open, and they'll come back because they want to.

13

JENNIFER*

GENDER:	Female
AGE AT TIME OF INTERVIEW:	25
RACE:	Ethnically Chinese, adopted from Vietnam
MARITAL STATUS:	Single
OCCUPATION:	Teaching English to children overseas

Born in Guam to ethnically Chinese parents who were fleeing Vietnam during the time of her birth, Jennifer was twenty-five years old at the time of the interview. Adopted by Caucasian parents, whom she described as "ultra-conservative Christians," and raised with her younger adopted brother, she moved many times throughout her childhood. She grew up on military bases and attended at least twelve different schools while living throughout the country. She remembered that while living on the West Coast, Asian culture was the norm and "it was really cool to be Asian." But she also recalled living in the southeast, where she longed to be blond and blue-eyed, to blend in with her surroundings.

---

*Identifying information about this participant has been omitted or changed.

As a child, she described herself as fairly "happy-go-lucky." Growing up in an extremely religious family, her life revolved around school and church. During her high school years, she was very involved with school activities, but began questioning her religious upbringing. It was at that point when she began to branch out from her family and explore other religions and cultures. She recalled her adolescent rebellion as "intellectually" and religiously-based.

Her extended family was also ultra-conservative and "quite distinct in their attitudes towards race." Though they saw "everything and everyone in color," she was considered the exception to their worldview. They disliked the idea of her dating interracially, and were completely against her dating a non-Christian. She noted the contradiction that she experienced within her relatives, who viewed her as "one of their own—a white American southerner." At one point, she recalled being told by a family friend that she was a "lucky little girl because these white people saved her."

When Jennifer was nineteen years old, her adoptive mother passed away. Shortly after, she had a falling out with her adoptive father over his quick remarriage. She described that time as "horrific" because "in one moment I lost my mother and I lost my family at the same time. My father and I were estranged and barely talking to each other for the next five years."

During this time, she found her birth parents who had been living in the United States with her two biological siblings since the end of the Vietnam War. For a week, she visited her biological family and discovered that her brother and sister were "just as American as [she was]." After her estrangement from her father, she turned to her biological parents for support as she completed college and received her bachelor's degree in liberal arts. Later, she attended graduate school and received a master's degree.

Today, she still remains in close contact with her biological family and recently she has begun to reconnect with her adoptive father as well. She strongly identifies herself as being Asian American and has made close friends with other Vietnamese adoptees. She recently lived overseas, where she taught English to children.

PLEASE TELL ME YOUR FULL NAME.

Jennifer.

HOW OLD ARE YOU?

Twenty-five.

WHERE WERE YOU BORN?

Guam.

HOW WOULD YOU DESCRIBE YOUR RACIAL BACKGROUND?

I am ethnically Chinese. My birth parents were born in Vietnam and were Vietnamese refugees. They eventually landed in the refugee camp in Guam. I was premature, so I was born at the military hospital and adopted by a military family pretty much the day that I was born.

DO YOU HAVE ANY BROTHERS OR SISTERS?

I have an adopted brother who was adopted when we were stationed on the West Coast. He is in his teens.

AND WHAT IS HIS RACIAL BACKGROUND?

He is a mix. He is Hawaiian, Caucasian, probably a little bit Filipino, and a little bit of Asian mixture unique to Hawaii. I think he is also American Indian.

AND YOU DON'T HAVE ANY SIBLINGS THAT WERE BORN TO YOUR ADOPTIVE FAMILY?

No, my adopted mother couldn't have children.

WHAT IS YOUR RELATIONSHIP LIKE WITH YOUR BROTHER?

We didn't adopt my brother until I was twelve. It was a sort of typical relationship. I didn't really want a brother at this time. We were fine, and then I went off to college shortly thereafter, so I didn't really see him that much. And I haven't been home in eight years, so it's been a long time.

WERE YOU EVER BEEN ABLE TO TALK WITH HIM ABOUT YOUR ADOPTION OR HIS ADOPTION?

He never asks. And I don't think he is curious at this point. As a child I would always ask about my birth parents, about what my life was like, anything that my parents would know. But he's never shown any interest in that yet.

WOULD YOU FEEL COMFORTABLE TALKING TO HIM ABOUT ADOPTION ISSUES?

Definitely. I think he eventually should talk about it, but I just think right now he's at the stage where he wants to be like everyone else, like we all do. He just doesn't want to think about it.

CAN YOU JUST TELL ME SOMETHING ABOUT YOUR PARENTS? THEIR SCHOOL-ING, THEIR WORK?

My adoptive mother was a high school dropout. She was born in the South. My adoptive father was born on the West Coast, and he completed high school and joined the military. While he was stationed in the South, they got married.

DO YOU KNOW WHAT LED THEM TO THE DECISION TO ADOPT TRANSRA-CIALLY?

Well, because my mother couldn't have children; she just wanted a baby. They had actually been on adoption lists and had always fallen through, and so at the last moment they decided to put their name on the list for a Viet-namese War orphan. The government at that time was having a program where they were sponsoring adoptions for the refugees, so that is how their name came up.

DO YOU KNOW IF YOUR PARENTS RECEIVED SUPPORT FROM THEIR FRIENDS AND FAMILY WHEN THEY DECIDED TO ADOPT?

Yes, I think they did. Everyone knew my mother's situation and the fam-ily was all for it. They were very positive. And they were really excited that she actually got me.

WHAT ARE YOUR ADOPTIVE PARENTS' RACIAL BACKGROUNDS?

My adopted father is typical English. My adoptive mother's side is Span-ish/American Indian mix and very southern. They are from the fundamen-tal sect of Christianity. They belong to a very strict, literal Christian funda-mentalist group.

DID YOU PARENTS HAVE ANY FRIENDS WHO WERE VIETNAMESE?

No. I was pretty much the only Asian kid in a ten-mile radius.

HAVE YOUR PARENTS EVER TRAVELED TO VIETNAM?

No, they really haven't traveled outside the United States.

DO THEY KNOW ANYTHING ABOUT ASIAN CULTURE?

They didn't, and they never really strove to find out about too much of it. The only Asian culture we got was to eat in a Chinese restaurant. That was as much as they did. They really didn't care much about the Chinese cul-ture per se.

WHAT KIND OF FRIENDS DID THEY HAVE?

Mainly church people. Friends from church.

DID YOU FEEL ACCEPTED BY THE MEMBERS OF THE CHURCH?

I was always aware that I was different because everyone at church wanted to know my "story." They wanted to know how I was adopted, but they pretty much treated me like part of the family. There would be occasional things, like if they were talking about Chinese missionaries. I would be picked on. It was just normal stuff like that. It wasn't anything racist in the church.

DO YOU BELONG TO ANY RELIGIOUS ORGANIZATIONS TODAY?

No.

DID YOUR PARENTS' RELIGIOUS AFFILIATION AFFECT YOUR DECISION TO STUDY RELIGION?

I think so. Growing up in a fundamentalist family you are taught that all other religions are wrong. I was in the Christian bubble for so long that when I went to college, I began to meet other people. I just couldn't condemn them all to hell at this point, so I just became interested in other people's religion and what they believed. And my family was really excited. They thought I was going to become a missionary and that I was going to learn about everyone's religion so that I could convert everyone else. Now they are kind of worried about me, but at the time, they thought it was a great idea. They were just worried that I would "backslide" or change religions. But I think that is what spurred me. I was taught that everything else was wrong except for us, and when I got to college, I began to see that there was a whole world out there.

WHAT WAS THE CHURCH'S ATTITUDE TOWARDS OTHER CULTURES?

If they weren't Christian and they didn't accept Christ, it was pretty much "pray for these poor lost souls." When I used to get teased, it would mainly be because I was Asian and because of my race. It's kind of interesting because my mother's side is very religious, and they are very conservative— very southern, and quite distinct in their attitudes towards race. They see everything and everyone in color except for me—the exception. I'm the exception. They totally think that I am one of their own, and they keep forgetting. We just had a conversation the other day, and they are so against interracial dating. Well, "Who am I going to date?" But they don't see it.

DO YOU THINK THEY WILL EVER SEE THE CONTRADICTION?

In their beliefs they see me as one of their own, as a white American Southerner.

WHAT IS THAT LIKE FOR YOU?

Growing up, I would have loved it because I would be one of them and I was accepted, but now that I am beginning to understand what it is to be Asian and to accept being Asian, it kind of bothers me because I want them to see that there is a whole side to this being Asian ethnicity that should be accepted.

HAVE ANY OF THEM EXPRESSED AN INTEREST IN ASIAN CULTURE?

No, I mean maybe some of my cousins, but not my grandparents.

WOULD YOU LIKE THEM TO AT THIS POINT?

I think it would be nice just to see the world is bigger than where they live in the South.

COULD WE TALK MORE ABOUT YOUR CURRENT JOB?

Currently, I am an administrative assistant to a well-known professor. He travels and lectures around the world, and is quite famous.

HOW DID YOUR PARENTS FEEL ABOUT YOUR WORKING WITH HIM?

They thought at first that God had placed me there so that I could convert him, which is really funny because if anything, he converted me to a new world, to new ideas.

WHEN DID YOU DECIDE TO SEPARATE FROM YOUR PARENTS?

Once I actually started studying religion seriously in college. I pretty much had done what they told me until I got out of that environment because in that situation you are not taught to think independently. You are told what you should think, so it was very bad.

ARE YOU CURRENTLY MARRIED?

No.

WHAT'S IMPORTANT TO YOU IN A FUTURE PARTNER?

Well, I think someone who is definitely tolerant. Someone who has a more cosmopolitan view of life, someone who has traveled. I don't think I could marry a "good old country boy" anymore. Someone with a good education who likes to learn about other people and cultures.

IS IT IMPORTANT TO YOU TO MARRY SOMEONE WITH A SIMILAR RACIAL BACKGROUND?

No.

WHAT ARE YOUR EXPERIENCES OR THOUGHTS ON INTERRACIAL DATING OR MARRIAGE?

I am all for it. My family, of course, is against it. I think it is a good thing, so I definitely would not condemn it.

WOULD YOU LIKE TO DATE SOMEONE FROM VIETNAM OR A VIETNAMESE AMERICAN?

I think so, but it has been my experience that once they find out I'm adopted, they treat me a little bit differently. I am not Asian enough for them. It is harder to win their respect because they're always like, "Why don't you learn our language and customs?" so it's harder to be accepted into your own ethnicity.

WOULD YOU LIKE TO HAVE CHILDREN?

Definitely. And I think I would like to adopt children.

WOULD YOU LIKE TO ADOPT FROM AN ASIAN COUNTRY?

I think so. Even though I grew up obviously with an American white family, I think it is easier if the children are of the same nationality as you are. I am not against interracial adoption or transracial adoption. Knowing my experience, it would be a lot easier, a lot more acceptable, a lot less controversial had I been adopted by an Asian family.

WHEN YOU HAVE CHILDREN, DO YOU THINK IT WILL BE IMPORTANT FOR THEM TO BE EXPOSED TO VIETNAMESE CULTURE?

I think so, but I want to expose them to all different cultures and not just the Vietnamese.

WHAT KIND OF ACTIVITIES OR EVENTS WOULD YOU PARTICIPATE IN TO EXPOSE THEM TO OTHER CULTURES?

Well, celebrating different holidays, taking them to different communities, and getting involved in some of the ethnic holidays and celebrations going on. I think little things like Asian fairy tales will show them the world is a little bigger than what we live in.

WOULD YOU LIKE TO TAKE THEM OVER TO VIETNAM?

Possibly, but not until they are a little bit older. It would really depend on whom I marry. If I'm married to a Vietnamese, then I think it would be very important. If I'm not, then I'm not sure how important it would be for me because we are detached from the culture.

IF YOU DID MARRY A VIETNAMESE MAN, HOW WOULD YOUR PARENTS REACT?

I think they would be fine. I think it would be harder for me to marry a Vietnamese than for my parents to accept it.

CAN YOU TALK A LITTLE ABOUT YOUR SCHOOLING AND YOUR EDUCATION?

Well, I was a military brat. I changed schools thirteen times in twelve years. I went to a university in the Southeast for undergrad and got two degrees. I decided to get my graduate degree, and I will be leaving the country shortly to teach.

WHEN YOU WERE YOUNGER, WERE YOU EVER TEASED IN SCHOOL FOR BEING DIFFERENT?

All the time. It started as early as kindergarten. I was the only Asian in the school. I remember walking into restaurants with my family and the whole restaurant would stare. It was very tough for me, and I hated being in public sometimes. I really did. But on the West Coast it was the reverse. In the South, I didn't want to be Asian. I wanted to be blond; I wanted to be blue-eyed. I used to pray to be blond and blue-eyed. But you know when I lived on the West Coast, it was really cool to be Asian. That's what you wanted to be. You didn't want to be white, and so I didn't want any of my friends to come home with me. I wanted to live in this little world where I was accepted.

WAS THAT THE FIRST TIME IN YOUR LIFE WHERE YOU REALLY BEGAN TO APPRECIATE YOUR ASIAN HERITAGE?

Kind of. That's the first time I actually would say my middle name, which is a Chinese name meaning American Chinese. And I would never ever tell people my middle name. On the West Coast I would say that because I wanted to be accepted. Everyone else had Asian names and I wanted to have one too.

WAS THERE EVER A POINT WHERE YOU LIED ABOUT YOUR ADOPTION WHEN SOMEONE ASKED YOU?

I really couldn't because it was all in my name. It was obvious—the fact that I didn't know anything about Asian culture, and I didn't speak the language. I couldn't lie about it. Plus, my parents were so excited about having me in the first place that whenever a stranger came up to me, they would automatically tell them my story from the very beginning. They loved to tell the story, so I couldn't even hide it if I wanted to.

WAS THAT EMBARRASSING FOR YOU?

Yeah. I just got tired of always having to come up with an explanation. And the reaction that some people gave, like "Oh, you're such a lucky little girl that these white saviors helped you out."

CAN YOU TALK MORE ABOUT YOUR CHILDHOOD? WHAT IT WAS LIKE? WHAT WERE YOU LIKE AS A KID?

I was a pretty happy-go-lucky kid. All American. Mainly my home life evolved around school and church. We went to church three times a week. They were very strict. No skirts an inch above our knee, no makeup, and for a while no movies; it was a very strict upbringing. So that didn't help. I couldn't wear cool clothes, I couldn't wear make-up, I couldn't go to parties, and I wasn't allowed to go to any dances.

DID THEY GIVE IN AS YOU GOT OLDER?

Yeah, I think when I became a junior in high school they loosened up. They had to let me go to prom, and after that it was all down hill because I got my taste of freedom. It was so hard growing up in that restrictive type of atmosphere. I never turned to drugs or alcohol. I think my rebellion was more intellectually. Like when I started to question that whole Christian dogma, it was much more dangerous because it had a much more long-lasting effect. But that's the way that I rebelled against my upbringing.

HOW DID YOUR PARENTS REACT?

At first they would preach at me, and now I don't really talk to my family about religious differences or political thinking because it's just kind of pointless. They have their set views, and there's nothing I can do that will make them think otherwise.

DO YOU FEEL OTHERWISE FAIRLY CLOSE TO YOUR FAMILY? TO YOUR PARENTS?

Well, my adopted mother passed away in 1994, and shortly after that my adoptive father got remarried. There was a big falling out between he and me because he didn't tell me he was dating someone; he didn't tell me he was remarried. So when I found out, I was obviously very upset. At that point in his life, he wanted to get rid of anything and every one that reminded him of my dead mother and that life. So he got rid of the house; he got rid of everything that we owned, and he just needed to move on from my mother. It was horrible for me because in one moment I lost my mother, and I lost my family, and then my father pretty much decided not to talk to me for five years. We didn't really start talking until 2000 when, I think in the back of his mind, he thought the world was going to end and needed to get some closure.

SOME CLOSURE?

Yeah, some closure, to be forgiven. When my mother passed away, I was really upset and dealing with trying to be the mother figure to my brother and trying to be the support for my father. It was hard because I lost that life. It was a very hard lesson at nineteen to be cut off like that. And that's about a year before when I found my birth parents.

TELL ME ABOUT THAT. HOW DID IT HAPPEN?

I was eighteen when I found my birth parents. I don't know if that precipitated the cutoff between my father and me. It's really strange because adoptees spend their whole lives feeling rejected. When they start to search for their birth family, you would think that the adoptive parents would be closer to the adoptee because at that one point they're feeling the exact same thing that you're feeling—the fear of being rejected. It is too hard for the adoptive parents to think, "She's going to find her birth family. She's not going to want us." And for us—we spent our whole life thinking our birth family didn't want us.

HOW DID THE SEARCH START?

I started my last semester in high school. There was a project to discover your roots, and I talked to the teacher after class because I didn't want to talk about Oregon trail roots to my classmates. Most of them didn't know I was adopted, and I didn't want to have to deal with that whole issue. We decided I would do a journal of trying to find my birth family since they had been sponsored by a community on the West Coast. They had written my family when I was a year old.

DID YOUR PARENTS EVER SHARE IT WITH YOU?

No, they didn't. I only found it because I was snooping around one day and I found it in the hall closet. They had told me that if I wanted to find my birth parents when I was eighteen that they would help me and that they had stuff, but that was the first time I found it. I found an article from that town and from that article, I found out I had a brother, a sister, and a grandfather. Eventually I got in touch with the Director of Refugee Services in Washington during the Vietnam War, and he kind of remembered my parents. He didn't know what happened to them. So I basically I finished my high school report with that. I graduated and I didn't think too much of it.

That summer, I was working at a camp in Florida when I got a call from my friend's mother who was helping me out. What had happened was very strange. The director had actually found my family by accident. It happened to be that the director decided to go out to dinner with a friend, and they were going to go to a certain restaurant in the Seattle area, but instead of going to that particular restaurant, they said, "Let's go to another restaurant sixty miles out of the way" and they turned around. They got there and they're sitting at the table, and this man comes in through the door. He comes to them and asks for a quarter to use the phone outside. The director looked at this man and thought he looked really familiar and he said, "I know you." The man who had asked for a quarter was actually a Vietnamese refugee who the director had placed ten years ago. So the director says, "Oh, my gosh, do you happen to know a man by the name of _____." "Yeah, I was just talking to him last week." "Are you kidding, because his daughter is looking for him. Do you have his phone number?" He says "Yeah, I'll call you with it." It happened just like that. Just the random act of coincidence. So then I got this call from my friend's mother and she said, "You've found them! You need to call them—they're waiting to hear from you."

I had just turned eighteen, and I was just shocked. I never thought it was going to happen, not that quick. So later that evening, I called my birth parents from the laundromat. When they answered the phone, the first thing my birth father asked me was, "What is your middle name?" And I told him. He was crying, "Yeah, you're the girl. You're ours." When I was adopted at birth, my adoptive mother knew she wanted to name me Jennifer, but she didn't have a middle name picked out, so she asked the translator to ask my birth parents if they wanted to name my middle name. So they gave me this middle name, which I think is probably a made-up name, but they would know who I was. So once they heard my middle name, they knew I was actually their child. We made plans to go meet in August after my camp job got finished.

THAT'S INCREDIBLE!

I went there. I'm off this plane, off this little rural plane. They were the only Asians in the airport, so I knew. I was the only Asian who got off the plane. I loved it because the first thing you look for is if you look like them. I spent my entire life looking for someone. I didn't really see where I looked like my parents, but when I saw my brother, we looked so similar. It was such a surreal moment, and I remember just being in shock. My birth mother was crying, and that's the only time I've ever seen her cry. And I remember just feeling disembodied. It was like I was watching it happen. I wasn't part of it, and it was just very surreal. Now when other adoptees are about to find their family, I try to caution them and tell them things that I wish people would have told me.

WHAT DO YOU TELL THEM?

When I found my birth family and was staying with them, I realized how I didn't belong in that family anymore. I didn't have any of the same life experiences that they did; there's nothing that we could talk about except for this painful experience that was obviously very painful.

DID YOU TRAVEL TO WASHINGTON ALONE?

Yes, I traveled by myself. My adoptive parents didn't give any indication that they wanted to go, which is fine, because I think it was something I had to do on my own. And when I was eighteen, I was young and dumb and fearless. Now I would have a lot more trepidation going to be reunited.

DO YOU FEEL A SENSE OF SADNESS THAT YOUR ADOPTIVE PARENTS DIDN'T EXPRESS ANY INTEREST IN GOING?

No, because I knew it was hard for them, and I didn't know if I could mix the two up physically. I think I needed the time to adjust to this and then bring them into it. And, in fact, they never actually met. My adoptive parents never met my birth parents. My birth parents have met my extended adoptive family—my grandparents—during my college graduation.

DID YOU FEEL ANY SENSE OF RESENTMENT FROM YOUR PARENTS?

My father didn't say much. My adoptive mother was crying, but she was very happy for me because I had always said I was going to do this when I was a child. I know it hurts her because in the back of their mind they are afraid they are going to be rejected. You have this fine tightrope that you have to walk to try not to hurt anyone's feelings for a long time, trying to show that you appreciate both families. Your birth family doesn't want to be found and then be rejected, so it was very tough to handle.

WHAT WAS IT LIKE WHEN YOU MET THEM AT THE AIRPORT?

After the husband met me and my mother cried, it was really quiet. And I got to their house and the first thing I did was look at the pictures on the wall. I had sent them one or two pictures of me from high school, and they had taken that picture and they had blown it up into an 8 x 10 and put it next to their pictures of their other kids. That was a nice touch because it made me feel like they were accepting me as part of the family, but it was just so out of place because obviously it didn't belong there. I was thinking this would have been my life. I was looking at the pictures that would have been me, and it was just too surreal to me because you see where you're not there.

I tell adoptees this: "Be prepared for feeling very alone." I never felt so alone as when I was sitting in my biological sister's room looking at her pictures because that was her life, and I wasn't a part of it. So that was very hard. I think that was the only time I wept. I thought finding my family would make me feel more complete, but it made me feel more empty. I wasn't prepared for that. I wasn't prepared to not feel like I don't belong in this family either.

HOW OLD ARE YOUR BIOLOGICAL SIBLINGS?

My sister is a year older than I am, and my brother is two years older than I am. I met them, and we went to the West Coast and met a bunch of cousins and aunties and uncles. It was a crazy experience. I didn't realize how many of them had escaped from Vietnam and settled down on the West Coast. So that was pretty hard, and half of them didn't even know I existed. There was a lot of comparing me and my sister, which didn't endear me to her at all.

DID YOU LEARN WHY YOUR BIRTH PARENTS DECIDED TO PLACE YOU UP FOR ADOPTION?

Apparently they left Vietnam the day after Vietnam fell. They left and they got one of the last Navy boats out. My birth mother was about seven months pregnant at that time with me, and when they finally settled down in Guam, she fell getting off the boat, which precipitated labor pains. So she actually went into early labor. I was born a month premature. And at that point, they were in a refugee camp, and they had two small children and a grandfather to deal with, and they didn't know where they were going. So at that moment, they decided that it would be in my best interest to give me up for adoption. I guess they had decided when they were in the delivery room or maybe before she even went into labor. Two weeks after I was given up for adoption, they got places and sponsors. Had I been born on time, I would have never been adopted because they were settled. They were in a community, they were working, they knew what was happening to them, and they were able to take care of me from then. So it was a very strange luck of fate.

WHAT ARE YOUR BIOLOGICAL PARENTS' ETHNICITIES?

They are actually Chinese. They're Cantonese, both of them. They were born in Vietnam.

DID YOU STAY IN TOUCH WITH YOUR BIOLOGICAL FAMILY AFTER YOU LEFT?

Yeah. Actually, we still call twice a month. They pretty much accepted me back into the family as their own.

HAVE THEY EXPRESSED INTEREST IN MEETING YOUR FAMILY?

Not specifically, but they did meet my grandparents and my uncle during graduation at college. That was a good experience. It was a little bit funny because my adoptive family has this thick Southern accent, and my birth family has this thick Asian accent.

DO YOU FEEL THAT YOU'VE BECOME CLOSER TO THEM OVER THE YEARS? HAVE THE DYNAMICS OF YOUR RELATIONSHIP CHANGED IN ANY WAY?

Well, when my adoptive mother passed away in 1994, I kind of had to lean on my birth parents because I didn't know who else to turn to at that point. When my adoptive father decided to cut off all finances, I had to petition the school to change my financial aid over to my birth parents. So, it was a little bit embarrassing to me. But even now I don't call them mom and dad. It's very hard for me, especially since my adoptive mother passed away. For a long time I felt very disloyal thinking of my birth mother as my mother, because she didn't raise me.

DID YOU EVER GO THROUGH A PHASE WHERE YOU WERE ANGRY AT YOUR BIRTH PARENTS?

Yes, I did, especially when I started thinking about how they didn't give up my brother and my sister. I just actually resented them for a day or two because I wanted to believe in the story that they gave me up for a better life. What if it's just what I want to believe to make me feel better?

I THINK A LOT OF ADOPTEES ARE TOLD GROWING UP THAT YOUR BIRTH PARENTS GAVE YOU UP FOR A BETTER LIFE, BECAUSE THEY LOVED YOU, BECAUSE THEY WANTED YOU TO HAVE WHAT THEY COULDN'T HAVE, ETC. AND YOU GROW UP BELIEVING THAT AS THE ABSOLUTE TRUTH. DO YOU THINK THEY RESENT GIVING YOU UP FOR ADOPTION NOW?

I think they do, especially since looking back on it. If they had just waited two weeks, everything would have been fine. But they obviously didn't know how long they were going to be at the camp.

HAVE YOU BEEN ABLE TO RECONNECT WITH YOUR ADOPTED FATHER?

We're working on it. It takes a lot of time because trust has been broken and you realize you can't always rely on them. You realize that they're not perfect. At first I wondered if it was because I wasn't his own child, and I know that sounds stupid because obviously I was his child, but it seemed so easy for him to walk away, and at this point I was so tired of people just walking away from me.

HOW DID YOU ADJUST TO THE LOSS OF YOUR ADOPTIVE MOTHER?

First I went back to college, and I just threw myself into the college life.

DID HAVING YOUR BIRTH PARENTS AND YOUR BIRTH FAMILY IN YOUR LIFE HELP?

They were very, very good to me. They realized my loss. I remember writing a letter to my birth mother, and I said in that letter how it was very difficult for me to lose my adoptive mother, and how I was very thankful that I had lost one but found another, and how I was very lucky that I had two strong mothers in my life. For a long time, I didn't want to lean on her because I felt very disloyal.

WHAT ROLE DO THEY PLAY IN YOUR LIFE TODAY?

I guess they are kind of more like friends. They do provide me now and then with gifts and stuff like that for my birthday. They still consider me part of the family, very much so. I get invited to all the weddings and everything that is going on over there, but for some reason my birth siblings are not that close to me. And that's kind of awkward for me because I have a birth sister who is less than a year older than I, and she won't talk to me. And I don't know why.

WHEN DID YOU FIRST START TALKING ABOUT YOUR ADOPTION? DO YOU REMEMBER? DO YOU REMEMBER SOME OF THE QUESTIONS YOU ASKED YOUR PARENTS?

I never realized I was adopted, of course, when I was young. But the one question—I came up to my mother and I said, "Why are our noses different?" "That's because you are adopted sweetie." I was like three—I had no clue what that meant, but apparently it was a big deal for everyone else.

WAS THERE EVER A POINT WHERE YOU PRETTY MUCH REJECTED VIETNAMESE CULTURE?

I hated Asian culture. I would go to Chinese restaurants and order a hamburger. I hated Asian food. I hated being thought of as Asian. I hated

Asian art; I thought it looked horrible. I wanted to be an American because that's how I was raised and that's how I wanted to be thought of and that's what I wanted to be.

WHEN DID IT CHANGE? WAS IT IN COLLEGE?

Yes. It really was in college. I think my whole world shifted in college, a real 180 degree turn. And that's when I started to appreciate the beauty of the Asian culture and embraced it more as part of me.

WHAT CAUSED YOU TO CHANGE THAT PERSPECTIVE?

I think it finally took me accepting that I was Asian.

DID YOU EVER FEEL PRESSURE TO JOIN ANY SOCIAL GROUP OR ETHNIC GROUP?

I thought I would join some of the Asian clubs, but they weren't really nice to me.

IN 1971 THE PRESIDENT OF THE NATIONAL ASSOCIATION OF BLACK SOCIAL WORKERS SAID, "BLACK CHILDREN BELONG PHYSICALLY, PSYCHOLOGICALLY, AND CULTURALLY IN BLACK FAMILIES IN ORDER THAT THEY RECEIVE A TOTAL SENSE OF THEMSELVES AND DEVELOP A SOUND PROJECTION OF THEIR FUTURE." WHAT ARE YOUR THOUGHTS ON THAT STATEMENT?

I could definitely see where that comes from. I can definitely see where it would be easier to have been adopted by an Asian family, but I don't necessarily think that that's the only result. Overall, I think I had a great childhood.

HOW DO YOU DEFINE YOUR RACE?

I always say Asian American.

IN SELECTING ADOPTIVE HOMES FOR CHILDREN, WHAT DO YOU THINK IS IN THE BEST INTEREST OF A TRANSRACIAL OR BIRACIAL CHILD?

I know I put a lot of stock in being in an ethnic family, but I really do think it just comes with the family that raises you. If I have shown a semi-racist Southern family not to see color in me, then that's worth it. It is. That's really significant. And they love me just like one of their own, see me as one of their own. And so I can't say that I had a horrible experience, because I didn't. I was probably loved more than some of the children who are born into natural families.

HOW MUCH OF A TRANSRACIAL ADOPTEE'S HERITAGE SHOULD BE INCORPO-
RATED INTO THEIR LIVES BY THEIR ADOPTIVE FAMILIES?

If a family is interested in an adoptee's heritage, I think that would help.
It just says that they accept that part of your life.

WHAT DO YOU THINK WAS MOST DIFFICULT ABOUT GROWING UP IN A MUL-
TICULTURAL FAMILY?

That's difficult. I don't think it was difficult within the family. I think it
was difficult from outside the family. But most enjoyable was probably
knowing that I was wanted. My parents really wanted me as a child, and
they would say it all the time.

ARE YOU GLAD THAT YOU WERE ADOPTED?

I think so. Now looking back on it, definitely. I don't know what kind of
person I would have been had I stayed with my birth family, and I can't
imagine not having this life, so I can't imagine not being adopted.

DO YOU HAVE ANY SUGGESTIONS OR ADVICE THAT YOU WOULD GIVE TO PAR-
ENTS WHO ARE CONSIDERING ADOPTING TRANSRACIALLY?

I think when the adoptee wants to find their family, talk about it, and
don't just shut them off or get defensive, because I see a lot of problems
when that happens. And I think to be open to the fact that this child is going to deal with a lot of identity issues and that if they're angry, it's probably
something dealing with that. And there's going to be the normal situations
that natural kids don't go through. It's going to be a problem, and I think
parents really need to address this. I think it would have been helpful for
me. I think it would have been helpful also knowing that they didn't look
down at Asian culture.

MARIA*

GENDER:	Female
AGE AT TIME OF INTERVIEW:	41
RACE:	Born in Mexico of Arabic-Latino-Navajo descent
MARITAL STATUS:	Divorced
OCCUPATION:	Began a business that helps to reconnect Latino adoptees with birth parents

Maria, a forty-one-year-old woman of Arabic-Latino-Navajo descent, shared with us an emotional story filled with physical and sexual abuse, betrayal and sadness. Born in Mexico and placed for adoption in New Mexico, she was told that her biological mother did not want to place her for adoption, but was forced by the doctor to sign the adoption papers. Her family was very diverse, as her father was German-Mexican, her mother Irish-Cherokee, her brother Indian-Latino, and her sister German-Latino.

During the interview, she disclosed that her mother was a "very abusive parent both mentally and physically" and would burn, whip, and starve

*Identifying information about this participant has been omitted or changed.

Maria and her sister. She was forced by her mother to cut her hair above her ears and felt ugly throughout her childhood, but she recalls feeling "very close" with her father. She also disclosed that when she was twelve years old, her brother sexually abused her. At the age of seventeen, Maria ran away to Los Angeles and became a stripper to support herself. At one point, she also engaged in prostitution.

When Maria turned twenty-one, her adoptive father became very ill with a brain tumor but her mother prevented her from visiting him in the hospital. When he later died, she found out that his estate was worth over $10 million. However, Maria's mother wrote her out of his will, and she was ultimately disinherited from the family.

Maria later searched for and found her biological parents. She met her biological mother who upon discovering that Maria was married to a black man, told her she was not welcome into the family and wanted nothing to do with her or her daughter. Her biological father was more accepting, but his wife wanted him to cease all contact with Maria. Ultimately, he had to choose between his wife or Maria, and he chose his wife. So, Maria was once again rejected from her family.

Despite her difficult childhood and her turbulent conflicts with her biological and adoptive families, Maria has drawn upon her love for her daughter to find the strength to "go through the challenges in life." Dedicated to helping other adoptees discover "where they came from," she opened up an agency that helped Latino adoptees and birth families locate each other.

HOW OLD ARE YOU, MARIA, AND WHERE WERE YOU BORN?

Forty-one. I was born in New Mexico.

NOW YOU TOLD ME YESTERDAY, YOU THINK YOU MAY HAVE BEEN BORN SOMEWHERE ELSE?

Yes, a story was told that I was actually born in Mexico. The birth father, he didn't know anything about me. He didn't even know my mother was pregnant.

WHERE DID YOU LEARN THIS INFORMATION ABOUT YOUR BIRTH PARENTS?

I found them. I found them on my own. I think I was about twenty years old when I wanted to know my biological mother. My adopted mom and I never got along, so I just went searching by myself. I really didn't even know my mom's birth name or anything about her.

YOU SAID YOUR ADOPTIVE FATHER CAME TO THE HOSPITAL TO PICK YOU UP?

Yes, I guess he already knew about me in advance. The story was told that my birth mother really didn't want to give me up for adoption. A doctor forced her to sign the papers.

DO YOU HAVE ANY ADOPTED BROTHERS AND SISTERS?

Yes, I have one adopted brother and one adopted sister from different biological parents.

HOW OLD ARE YOUR BROTHER AND SISTER?

My brother is forty-four and my sister is forty-three.

AND WHERE WERE THEY ADOPTED FROM?

New Mexico.

DO YOU KNOW ANYTHING ABOUT THEIR BIOLOGICAL PARENTS?

My brother's biological parents, I'm told, were Indian and Latino. And my sister's biological mother was full-blooded Latino, and her birth father was German.

DO YOU HAVE ANY SIBLINGS WHO WERE BORN TO YOUR ADOPTIVE PARENTS?

No. We were the only children.

GROWING UP, WHAT KIND OF RELATIONSHIPS DID YOU HAVE WITH YOUR BROTHER AND SISTER?

My sister and I never really got along. I guess competition; I guess you could say that. I was the baby of the family. My brother and I, we always got along good. It was my brother and sister that never got along.

WERE YOU EVER ABLE TO TALK WITH THEM OPENLY ABOUT YOUR ADOPTION OR THEIR ADOPTION?

My brother? No. My sister, because I am trying to help her locate her biological mother.

WHEN DID SHE START TALKING ABOUT DOING A SEARCH?

When I opened my business helping other adoptees and helping birth parents find their lost children.

No. We've known since we were real little that we were adopted. But to be honest, I never really thought that much of it until I got older, I think maybe nineteen or twenty.

CAN YOU TELL ME A LITTLE BIT ABOUT YOUR ADOPTIVE PARENTS, THEIR EDUCATION, THEIR CAREERS?

My father was in the army and had an honorable discharge. My adopted mother is a mixture of Irish and Cherokee Indian. She was originally from Oklahoma, born and raised there, but she was brought up in Arkansas. But I don't know the story on her. I know she was married before she met my father. My mom and father met when my father walked into a shoe store where she was working.

She and I never really got along. She was a very abusive parent both mentally and physically all of her life, and we never really got along.

DO YOU WANT TO TALK A BIT MORE ABOUT YOUR EXPERIENCE WITH YOUR ADOPTIVE MOTHER?

She wasn't a very attentive mother. She was very prejudiced. My father wasn't, because he was from New York. I can remember since I was a little girl that me and my sister used to get put in hot water to bathe. She used to whip us with belt buckles. I can remember her setting my sister's fingernail on fire when she got caught smoking cigarettes. I can remember the times that we would go hungry. She would send us to bed hungry, and we wouldn't have anything to eat up to our high school years. We were always made to have our hair cut short above our ears to look like a boy. Mentally, all our lives, we had insecurities. I always felt ugly as a child. I never really felt accepted. I felt out of place. We could never talk to our mother about anything. You know a normal child—when they come home from school they should be able to talk to their mom, but we were never able to. She was never loving towards me or my sister, but she always favored our brother for some reason.

WAS SHE EVER ABUSIVE TO YOUR BROTHER?

As far as physically, no. We were brought up having everything that we ever wanted. We never went without nothing. My father owned his own successful business. He was a loving father, very attentive towards us. We were very close with him. For some reason our mom just didn't care for me and my sister. She was very abusive towards us.

DID YOUR FATHER KNOW ABOUT THE ABUSE THAT WAS GOING ON?

He knew of the yelling. As far as the physical abuse, no, he didn't. And if he did know, he never really stood up for us. There were so many secrets that went on in the household. I ran away from home three times.

WHEN WAS THE FIRST TIME YOU RAN AWAY?

The first time when I was sixteen.

DID SHE EVER SEXUALLY ABUSE YOU OR YOUR SISTER?

No, she didn't do that.

SO IT WAS ALL PHYSICAL AND EMOTIONAL ABUSE?

Right. I can think of a time that she held my head under water in the bathtub when I was little. I think I felt more mentally abused when we were always told we were ugly; we were never told we were loved, never accepted by her. We used to wish that she would die. My adoptive father died at an early age. He was only fifty-two. He had a major brain tumor, and he died in 1981. We knew he was always wealthy; we just didn't know how much. I didn't find out until my adoptive mother passed away in 1997 that he had an estate worth over $10 million, but I was disinherited. We were cheated, me and my sister. We were cheated out of everything that my father wanted to leave with us.

BUT NOT YOUR BROTHER?

No, he got everything.

WHAT HAPPENED?

Well, supposedly, three months before my father died in 1981, he had a new will and a new trust. He had a fifty-one-page trust. He had it changed, but I found out that it wasn't him who changed it. It was my adoptive mother who changed it. She became his power of attorney, so she had authority to change the will and the trust, and she disinherited me and my sister.

My father had it where if he was to pass away, all the children would get one-third equally, but she disinherited me and my sister. But I didn't know about the will until 1997.

Also, in the state of New Mexico, everyone—even if they are only left a dollar—is entitled to copies of all wills and trust agreements. Well, I was never sent one. My brother and sister were still living in the state of New Mexico. They were sent a waiver of confidentiality to sign over so she could become the successive trustee. And they signed it. But I was never mailed one. They didn't include me in that.

SO YOU NEVER SIGNED ANY LEGAL DOCUMENT?

No, I would never give up, never relinquish my inheritance rights. But they never sent me one, and I was never mailed one, and the court couldn't find my signature on record. Supposedly my mom forged my signature.

WHAT HAPPENED WHEN SHE PASSED AWAY?

I wasn't even there. Supposedly she died of congestive heart failure. I think it was maybe four days after she died, I talked to my brother. He had been trying to get a hold of me to tell me that Mom had passed away and that he needed my social security number. There was a trust will and I finally asked him for copies of it. I got my own lawyer, and when I did that, I guess that upset my brother. So long story short, we didn't get anything.

SO YOUR BROTHER DIDN'T GET ANYTHING EITHER?

Oh, no, he got everything. He got everything from the estate. My mother had over, I think, $300,000 worth of jewels. He got that. He got everything.

SO SHE LEFT EVERYTHING TO YOUR BROTHER?

Yes, everything. We were disinherited.

HAS YOUR BROTHER INDICATED THAT HE IS WILLING TO SHARE ANYTHING?

No, he did not want anything to do with me or my sister.

SO HE IS ANGRY AT BOTH OF YOU?

Yes, very much. I left home when I was only seventeen, and he thought I wanted nothing to do with the family, which wasn't the case. I wanted to get away from my adoptive mom.

HOW WAS YOUR ADOPTIVE MOTHER RAISED? DO YOU KNOW ANYTHING ABOUT HER FAMILY? WAS SHE ABUSED WHEN SHE WAS GROWING UP?

No. Her mother had to raise two daughters, and they grew up very, very poor. But they were never abused. And my aunt is totally different from what my mom was, totally different personality, a wonderful auntie.

DO YOU THINK SHE WAS ABUSIVE BECAUSE YOU AND YOUR SISTER WERE FEMALE OR BECAUSE YOU WERE ADOPTED?

The story was told that she really never wanted us. It was my adoptive father that wanted children. She really never wanted the girls.

SO SHE JUST WANTED YOUR BROTHER?

Yes. She felt insecure with me and my sister. She always felt jealous.

DO YOU THINK SHE FELT THREATENED OR COMPETITIVE IN SOME WAY?

I believe she did because we were always close with our dad. We were
not allowed to hug our father in front of her. She would make sexual accu-
sations about what we were doing . . . hugging our father. Very sick minded.

WHAT KIND OF MARRIAGE OR RELATIONSHIP DID YOUR PARENTS HAVE?

To be honest, it was a very good one. They would never argue in front of
the children. Now I know that my mother nagged my father constantly. She
was spoiled.

WAS THERE ANY ABUSE BETWEEN YOUR PARENTS?

As far as my father hitting her? No, no.

WAS SHE EVER EMOTIONALLY ABUSIVE TO YOUR FATHER?

Oh, yes, all the time. Mentally, yes. Constantly. She always just would nag
at him about the littlest things. She wasn't physically, but mentally, yes, very
much.

WHAT KINDS OF THINGS WOULD SHE SAY OR DO?

She would threaten to leave him. She would tell him he was no good.
"You think you're better than everyone because you made a successful business. I'm not getting enough time with you." My mother was catered to. My
dad would buy her furs, jewelry. She had everything a woman could ask for.
I remember she used to go shopping every day just to buy clothes just to
hang them in different closets and say, "I have all these clothes." She was
spoiled. She had everything, and it never was enough for her.

DO YOU KNOW WHAT HER FIRST MARRIAGE WAS LIKE?

Yes. Supposedly she was very domineering over her husband. I was told
that he was abusive towards her. Whether there is any truth to that I have
no way of knowing that. I know that she tried to get pregnant but she
couldn't have any children.

AND THAT'S WHY SHE DECIDED TO ADOPT YOUR BROTHER?

Yes. I can remember times when she used to drag us by our hair—me
and my sister—and make us go to the beauty salon, and make us get our
hair cut shorter. We would beg and cry, and say "Mama please don't; please

don't." She would knock us around and make us. And one time my father said, "Their hair is getting longer; they look beautiful. Let their hair grow long." And she just went off when he went to work. She just went off on me and my sister.

WAS THERE A TIME WHEN ANYONE OUTSIDE OF YOUR FAMILY STEPPED IN? DID ANYONE OUTSIDE OF THE FAMILY KNOW ABOUT THE ABUSE?

I think people knew about some of her ways, but no one really knew about the abuse going on in the house. My sister did go and tell the school teacher.

WHAT HAPPENED?

I don't know. I really don't know.

SO NOTHING HAPPENED? DID SHE THREATEN YOU?

Oh, yes, she used to threaten me and my sister a lot. I don't know if she would ever follow up on it. I think she just wanted to intimidate us. She would tell us if we told our father, she'd get rid of us, or she said "I'll kill you." But I don't think she ever would literally do that. I think she just did it to scare us.

WAS SHE ABUSIVE FOR AS LONG AS YOU COULD REMEMBER?

Yes, even after we left home. She never wanted nothing to do with me. And this is the gospel truth of a story: before my father passed away, the last time he ended up at the hospital, and I called home and I asked my mom if I could talk to my dad, and she specifically told me he's in the hospital and he'll be home in about three days. And I told her I'd like to come home and help take care of dad, because he had cancer. She said, "Oh that's not necessary." And then I said I'd like to come visit him at the hospital, and her line to me was, "It's only for immediate family." Well, I didn't know he was on his deathbed then. About four days later my brother called and told me my dad had passed away. I didn't have the money, and I wanted to come to my dad's funeral, but no one wanted to pay my way, so I didn't get to go to his funeral. My mother bad mouthed me and told everyone I didn't care about my father, and everyone thought I didn't care about my dad because I wasn't at the funeral. But that wasn't the case. So that has really affected me all my life—feeling guilty.

SO YOUR MOTHER DELIBERATELY PREVENTED YOU FROM SEEING YOUR FATHER DURING THAT TIME?

Yes. She lied to me.

SO SHE ULTIMATELY TRIED TO CONTROL EVERYTHING?

She always did. I can remember when my daughter was born—she's fifteen now. My mom's first expression she would say over the phone was "What color is she?" Her father is black. He is very well educated, nice. If it weren't for him, I don't know where I'd be in life. Well, she didn't want nothing to do with her granddaughter. She never accepted her. My brother has other children, and she has always bought gifts for Christmas for them, and cards, but she has never acknowledged my daughter, never, not even a card for her.

And the trust fund that was set up to be left to the children—they made it where nothing was left to my daughter. I feel disinherited now, then, and forever.

CAN YOU TALK A LITTLE BIT ABOUT WHAT IT WAS LIKE GROWING UP IN A MULTICULTURAL FAMILY?

My brother and sister were always told their culture. We lived in New Mexico where it is predominantly Latinos anyway. For some reason I always felt that I was Hispanic, even though I was never told growing up by my mom. I was never told. I always thought that I was.

WHAT WERE YOU TOLD ABOUT YOUR HERITAGE?

I was never told anything.

DO YOU KNOW ANYTHING AT ALL ABOUT YOUR HERITAGE FOR SURE?

Oh, yes, because I met my biological mother. But it's funny, growing up, all my friends were Hispanic and I always felt at home with Latino background and culture.

DID YOU HAVE ANY RELIGIOUS UPBRINGING?

We were sent sometimes to church, not with our parents, because they never went. I can tell you that before my dad passed away, he turned really religious, and he really turned his life around.

HE SOUNDS LIKE A WONDERFUL MAN.

He was. I wish I had the guts enough to have stood up to our adoptive mom years ago. I was always scared.

AND CHILDREN SHOULDN'T HAVE TO GO THROUGH THAT. THEY SHOULDN'T FEEL LIKE THEY HAVE TO STAND UP TO THEIR PARENTS.

I think that's why now I help adoptees find their birth parents, or vice versa. I don't want anyone to go through what I did. I believe everyone needs to know their identity. That's why I opened this Latino Search Services. I did it for the Latino community because that's my community, and I feel that they need help out there.

WHO WERE YOUR PARENTS' FRIENDS?

They had a lot of friends. Oh, gosh, my father was very well known in the state of New Mexico, I think for his integrity. When we were younger, he had a lot of friends. I think he started getting really successful when I was about twelve years old. My dad started from scratch I was told. He came from New York to New Mexico with only $500 in his pocket. And he started a very successful business from scratch by himself.

DID YOUR PARENTS HAVE A LOT OF FRIENDS OR VISITORS?

I think when we were younger, my mother used to have a lot of house parties to show off. I remember a lot of people used to come to the house.

DID YOUR MOTHER ACT DIFFERENTLY WHEN YOU WERE AROUND OTHER PEOPLE OR OUT IN PUBLIC?

Oh, yes. She would act all *lovey*.

DOES YOUR DAUGHTER TALK WITH YOU ABOUT YOUR ADOPTION AND YOUR FAMILY?

Oh, all the time. We are very close.

WAS IT IMPORTANT FOR YOU TO HAVE A BIOLOGICAL CHILD?

Not really, it just happened. I used to pray that I'd have a little girl, then I had one, and what I prayed for I got . . . an angel.

WHAT KINDS OF QUESTIONS HAS SHE ASKED ABOUT YOUR ADOPTION?

She's very upset that her grandmother, my mom, would have nothing to do with her, disowned her. She's very upset with what the woman did to me as a child. And she said she wishes my mother was alive, so she could tell her how she really felt.

HOW IMPORTANT IS IT TO YOU THAT SHE IS EXPOSED TO YOUR BIRTH CULTURE?

I feel it is important that she accepts all her cultures. Because she is biracial, I tell her everything that I know of my culture, and she has been to New Mexico.

Is FLINT PRETTY DIVERSE OR IS IT HOMOGENOUS?

Flint is predominantly—I'd say half black, half white. There's really not any Latinos here, I'd say maybe two percent here in Flint.

DO YOU ENCOURAGE HER TO HAVE A DIVERSE ARRAY OF FRIENDS?

Oh, yes. My adoptive mother was very racist, prejudiced. She used to call me the most awful names because I had black friends growing up. I don't want my daughter like that.

WHAT ARE YOUR THOUGHTS ON INTERRACIAL DATING OR INTERRACIAL MARRIAGES?

I don't have any problem with it. It doesn't bother me. To be honest, if a child is adopted, I feel that they should be adopted in their own culture. It's not because of the race issue, it is because they are not really taught about their culture and they should be. I really think that the Hispanics should adopt their own, whites too. Or if they should adopt, I feel that they should give knowledge to that child because so much of that child is missing.

WHAT WAS YOUR EXPERIENCE BEING IN AN INTERRACIAL MARRIAGE? OR ANY OTHER EXPERIENCES?

Dating a black man, I was always an outcast. The black sheep of the family. They were ashamed of me.

BOTH OF YOUR ADOPTIVE PARENTS?

I can't say for my father, but I assume yes. I know my adopted mom was very ashamed of me. She thought I was low class because I dated a black man.

WHAT ABOUT YOUR BROTHER AND SISTER?

He's very prejudiced. My sister, no. Didn't bother her.

BUT IT BOTHERED YOUR BROTHER?

Oh, yes, because he was raised like my mom. I thank God to this day that I am not like that, because she was so prejudiced growing up, the way she was raised, and then the way I was, I couldn't be like that growing up.

WERE YOU EVER MARRIED TO YOUR DAUGHTER'S FATHER?

Yes. I lived with him for a long time, but we didn't get married until 1992.

HOW LONG WERE YOU MARRIED?

Four years.

AND YOU SAID YOU ARE STILL LIVING TOGETHER?

Yes.

SO I ASSUME YOU ARE STILL CLOSE?

Yes, I love him very much.

WHAT'S IMPORTANT TO YOU IN A PARTNER?

Someone who is very understanding, sympathetic, someone who has a sense of humor, someone who is loving.

SO PRIMARILY YOU'VE BEEN WITH AFRICAN AMERICAN MEN, THEN?

Yes, to be honest I've never felt comfortable around Caucasian men. I never have because I was raped when I was very young, when I was seventeen; so I've never felt comfortable around a Caucasian man. I have Caucasian female friends, but never male friends. I would never date a Caucasian male. I was seventeen. I had run away from home. This was when I went with my girlfriend. We went to Las Vegas to do some sightseeing, and she went to go park the car, and this man grabbed me and took me in a car, and took me to some place. To be honest, I blocked most of it out.

HAVE YOU BEEN WITH AN ABUSIVE PARTNER?

I can say my ex, mentally abusive. Physically, no.

WAS IT SOMEWHAT SIMILAR TO THE WAY YOUR MOTHER TREATED YOU?

Sometimes, yes.

IS HE STILL SOMEWHAT ABUSIVE?

Somewhat. My problem is that I am a very sensitive person, and sometimes I take things too seriously, and I think a lot has to do with my childhood. I think because of what happened to me growing up, I have forgiven my adoptive mother for them, but I can't forgive what has been done, and it affects my well-being to this day.

GOING BACK TO YOUR EDUCATION, HOW MANY YEARS OF SCHOOLING HAVE YOU HAD?

I dropped out of high school when I ran away from home. I was seventeen. I went to L.A. From there, I went to Michigan. I started dancing; I became a stripper so I could pay my way through modeling school, because I wanted to model. So I danced for three years. I felt so special. I felt wanted. I felt beautiful, something I never felt growing up. It made my self esteem go up; it helped me pay my way through modeling school. It was crazy, but it never hurt anybody. You know what is strange? Most people who leave home turn to alcohol, drugs, cigarettes, and I never did any of them.

SO YOU STAYED AWAY FROM DRUGS AND ALCOHOL?

That's why I don't believe people who say if you are around that environment, you'll do it. It's not true. I didn't do it.

HOW OLD WERE YOU WHEN YOU STARTED STRIPPING?

I'd say, about nineteen and a half.

DID YOUR FAMILY KNOW WHERE YOU WERE OR WHAT YOU WERE DOING?

They knew I was in Michigan. They didn't know what I was doing. Not until my big sister found out. I had to. I never asked for anything when I ran away from home. I never had help; I was never given any money. I've never had anyone buy me anything. I've always had to take care of myself, and to this day I have a guilty conscience about what I did in my past, but I had to survive. I was homeless for a while.

WHEN DID YOUR LIFE START CHANGING?

When I ran away from home . . . I'll never forget, my adoptive mom was on the phone with the psychiatrist and said she was bringing me back in. I didn't want to see that man because he was making sexual moves on me. I remember breaking out my screen window on my bedroom, and I jumped out the window, and I ran and I ran and I never looked back.

AND YOU WERE ABLE TO PUT YOURSELF THROUGH MODELING SCHOOL?

I had to. I didn't have any help. I went through two different modeling schools and paid my way through it with dancing. I would work nights from eight at night to two in the morning.

WHAT WAS THAT LIKE FOR YOU?

To be honest, it didn't bother me at first, because I was on stage and no one could touch me or bother me. I felt like I was on top of the world. I would get standing ovations, or I would come to work and they would be hollering for me, and I felt so proud. It sounds crazy now, but that's how I felt. I had lots of attention. I felt the world was mine. I was at the center of attention; I had my own dance routine, my own music. I felt comfortable. I made good money, I saved it, and I wanted to start modeling.

WHEN WAS THE FIRST TIME YOU GREW YOUR HAIR OUT?

When I ran away from home.

DID YOU STAY IN TOUCH WITH YOUR FATHER OR YOUR SISTER?

It wasn't until a year later that they heard from me. Somehow I got involved with a big-time pimp. It is embarrassing to say, but it is true. I'm going to start crying. I couldn't go back home, and I didn't have any means or money, so somehow I just fell into prostitution. That's all I can remember. I was picked up by the police one day for prostitution. And they put me in jail, and they asked me for my social security number. I gave them a wrong one and they knew that, they knew I wasn't the age I told them. I remember about three in the morning, I had a correction officer come in and wake me up. She said, "Someone is here to see you," and I said "Who?" and she said, "You just got bailed out." And I said, "Who's paying my bail?" And the next thing I know, they told me to go outside.

I walked outside and I saw this really nice Cadillac, and I saw two women in the car. One woman got out and she said, "You don't know me, but I know you." And I said, "How do you know me?" She said, "Let's just say a guardian angel just sent me to get you." I asked her if she was a model, and she laughed at me. She was so beautiful, and she had the beautiful car. So I'm young and stupid and I was seventeen, and we went to Hollywood, and we went to a really nice restaurant. I remember sitting at a booth and two women were talking to me, asking me what was my situation and what I'm doing and I told them. They said, "Well, we're having someone meet us here for a date breakfast."

So the next scene I remember is looking out a window (now this is Hollywood), and I see a man pull up in a Rolls Royce—a fancy car. And I said, "Is this man a movie star? Look, there's a movie star pulling up!" They laughed at me and said, "That's our breakfast date." I remember the gentleman walking in; he was tall, nice looking, black man in a nice suit. He had on gold jewelry, and I remember him walking in. He sat down at the table, and a long story short, he was a very rich and powerful man and especially in Los Angeles. I rode with him in his car, and he said we're meeting some people that he wanted me to meet, so I followed him. I remember sitting in the car, and I felt like I was a movie star. You want to know why I felt like I was a movie star? Because this man was talking to me, and I felt like I was somebody.

So the next scene I remember, we were in Ventura, and we went to his home. His home was beautiful. I felt like, "Oh my goodness." It was beautiful. I didn't know he was a pimp. All I know is that he had about eighteen women there . . . they didn't live there, they were just there. They were dressed so nice, and they had gold jewelry, nice dresses; they were so beautiful. They were women that you see on magazines. And then, from there he told me that I'm going to be taken care of and I don't have to worry about anything, and he asked me if I'd like to go with one of these women, and they were going to put me up at the apartment, and I said "sure," gullible. They asked me if I was a virgin, and I told them yes except for the fact that I was raped. And they asked me if I wanted to offer my services to men, and I said no. And they said, "Well, how would you feel if you just entertain them while we do all the work, and you just let them in and talk with them and feed them drinks." So that's what I did when I was in L.A. You're the only one that knows this.

THANK YOU SO MUCH FOR SHARING.

It's embarrassing. I've done some crazy things. And even today, I'm not sorry that I went to L.A. I think for the lifestyle I'm sorry, but I didn't have a choice. I didn't have a family to go to, and I didn't know what to do.

AND IT SOUNDS LIKE IN SOME WAYS IT WAS BETTER THAN PUTTING UP WITH YOUR MOTHER'S ABUSE.

I wasn't abused in any way when I was in L.A. I had my own place. I was living like the rich. We had our own housekeeper come in; we had our maid service. We had our own beautician come in. We had limousine service.

AGAIN, THANK YOU FOR SHARING. IF YOU DON'T MIND, I WOULD LIKE TO GO BACK TO YOUR CHILDHOOD. WHAT WAS IT LIKE GROWING UP NOT KNOWING YOUR EXACT HERITAGE? I KNOW YOU FOUND THIS INFORMATION OUT LATER IN YOUR LIFE, BUT WHAT WAS IT LIKE GROWING UP?

It kind of bothered me because everyone would always ask me, "What is your culture? What is your nationality? What is your race?" but I never knew.

DID YOU HAVE ANY UNUSUAL BEHAVIORAL PROBLEMS GROWING UP?

Insecurities. I used to have nightmares all the time.

DO YOU REMEMBER WHEN THEY STARTED?

Ever since I can remember . . . five or six. I remember always being scared. I had a lot of anxiety, but back then I didn't know what anxiety was.

MOVING INTO YOUR LATER CHILDHOOD, DID YOU GO THROUGH A PARTICULARLY MEMORABLE ROUGH PERIOD IN YOUR ADOLESCENCE?

It was hard in school for me, being made fun of because our mother cut our hair short. We weren't allowed to dress ourselves. She would lay our clothes out for us every day, even when we were sixteen or seventeen. She would tell us what we could wear.

WHAT KIND OF CLOTHES WERE THEY?

Boys. Sometimes they were girl's clothes. But what was strange, she would buy us really cute outfits, but we could never wear them. They were just hanging up in the closet. So I think it was painful in school.

DID YOU EVER RECEIVE ANY MENTAL HEALTH TREATMENT OR WERE YOU EVER TAKING ANY PSYCHOTROPIC MEDICATIONS?

No, I never was. I never did. I remember having to go to a psychiatrist, I think, in my tenth or eleventh grade.

THAT WAS RIGHT BEFORE YOU RAN AWAY?

Right.

DO YOU REMEMBER WHY YOUR MOTHER TOOK YOU TO SEE ONE?

Yes, because I was taking things from the house and getting rid of them. Just to be mean, I would take my mom's jewelry and throw it away; and she would ask about it, and I would deny it.

WAS THERE A TIME WHEN YOUR ADOPTION BECAME MORE OF A FOCAL POINT OF YOUR EVERYDAY IDENTITY OR WHEN YOU BEGAN TO THINK MORE ABOUT YOUR ADOPTION?

To be honest, I think I didn't really start until about four months before I met my daughter's father. I just really wanted to know my identity. I really wanted to know where I'd come from, wanted to know who my mom was. I never had an attitude, and I never was upset because she gave me up for adoption.

WHEN DID YOU START SEARCHING FOR YOUR BIRTH PARENTS?

I started searching when I was in Michigan. I think that was in 1983, and I found her within two weeks. I didn't know her name, her culture, or anything. I didn't even know where she was from. I think God works in mysterious ways. I met her about six months later. It was 1984 that I met my biological father.

WHERE DID YOU MEET YOUR BIOLOGICAL MOTHER?

She was living out West. I remember flying out there; she picked me up at the airport. She had a rose for me. And when she saw me, she started crying and asking me to forgive her and all that. And I told her there's nothing to forgive. And she took me to her apartment, and that's where I met my other brothers and sisters.

Do you get along with them?

I don't see them anymore. Everything was going ok until the time when Shasta was born. That's when me and my biological mom had a fall out because she told me that my husband wouldn't be allowed in her home. She said if he would come to her door, she would slam the door in his face.

Because he is African American?

Yes. And then her racial attitude started coming out, and that really upset me. And it was reminding me of my adoptive mom again, and that blew me off. I got mad.

Are you connected with her at all today?

No, she doesn't want anything to do with me. But that's ok.

Is that disappointing?

Now, no. Then, yes. I felt like I've had her all this time without me, so no big deal.

Did it feel like you'd lost her twice?

Now, no. Then, yes, it did. I think the last time I saw her was in 1991.

And you don't stay in touch with any of your siblings either?

No. My brother died, the one I was real close with. They didn't even tell me about the funeral or anything.

What year did you make contact with your biological father?

I was pregnant. It was in 1985. He started crying. He was glad to find me. And he paid my way through modeling, and he was sending me money during modeling school. We got real close and we sent pictures, and then he said he wanted to meet me. I stayed three weeks, and we got really, really close, and everything was going ok until his wife found out that I came down. She swore up and down that he had an affair on her, which he didn't. She really blew up, and she told him it was either me or her. I was disinherited again.

Did you totally break your connection with him?

I have tried through the years, but he told me "Please don't write. It just causes problems at home."

When is the last time you had contact with him?

1986.

DID YOUR ADOPTIVE PARENTS KNOW THAT YOU HAD FOUND YOUR BIRTH PARENTS?

Well, my father was dead then. He died in 1981. My adoptive mom knew.

WHAT WAS HER REACTION?

Oh, she was mad, upset. She said, "How could you want anything to do with that bitch?" and all these names. "She gave you up; she didn't want you!" She was upset, said I hurt her. But I didn't do it to hurt her, I did it because I needed to know. I have medical reasons, my daughter.

YOUR BIRTH MOTHER'S HERITAGE IS LATINO?

Her father was Latino. Her mother is Latino and Navajo Indian.

YOUR ADOPTIVE MOTHER'S HERITAGE IS?

My adoptive mother was Irish and Cherokee.

AND YOUR BIRTH FATHER?

He was Arabic. He was from Greece. He said he left there for political reasons and went to New Mexico.

CAN YOU TELL ME ABOUT THE BUSINESS THAT YOU OPENED?

Yes. I have been doing this for two years. I started because of me being an adoptee, and I just feel that adoptees need to know where they come from. There are so many out there who are hurting. Their adoptive parents are denying them their birthright. They need to know, and I feel obligated to help them.

I THINK IT IS WONDERFUL WORK. HAVE YOU BEEN ABLE TO REUNITE MANY ADOPTEES?

A lot of them. I have had a lot of birth parents that I've helped now find their children. Some I haven't. Some get very angry, and ask why I can help others. I do the best I can. I never promise I can locate.

ARE THERE ANY TABOOS WITHIN THE LATINO CULTURE ABOUT ADOPTION?

They are left in the dark; they don't know where to turn. That's why a lot of them come to my site.

DO YOU THINK THERE IS ANYTHING SPECIFICALLY WITHIN THE LATINO CULTURE THAT MAKES IT DIFFICULT TO REUNITE FAMILIES?

I think it is because of their language. Because a lot of them don't know English well, and they don't know how to read. They don't have the finances to hire a lawyer or a private investigator or court agencies to help them find their children or their parents.

WHAT KINDS OF STEREOTYPES ARE STILL PREVALENT REGARDING LATINO OR HISPANIC?

I think the stereotype of Latinos are for being stupid. We don't speak English right; we have no business being here in the United States. The only people who say that are ignorant, not educated.

ARE THERE CULTURAL CLASS CLASHES BETWEEN LATINO-AMERICANS AND LATINO IMMIGRANTS?

Yes. If you're Latino American, you're not Mexican enough. If you're Mexican American you're not American Latino enough.

IN 1971, THE PRESIDENT OF THE NATIONAL ASSOCIATION OF BLACK SO-CIAL WORKERS MADE A STATEMENT: "BLACK CHILDREN BELONG PHYSICALLY, PSYCHOLOGICALLY, AND CULTURALLY IN BLACK FAMILIES IN ORDER THAT THEY RECEIVE THE TOTAL SENSE OF THEMSELVES AND DEVELOP A SOUND PROJEC-TION OF THEIR FUTURE." WHAT ARE YOUR THOUGHTS ABOUT THIS STATEMENT IN LIGHT OF YOUR OWN ADOPTION EXPERIENCE?

Honestly, I feel that only a minority couple should adopt a black child, and the reason why I say that is because I have seen other races of children being adopted by the Caucasian family, and they are not accepted by some of their friends; they are not accepted in school. They are treated differ-ently, and they are not really taught what they should be. I feel that all cul-tures should be taught their history, and I don't feel that the Caucasian race can really educate a black child on knowing their identity.

WITHIN YOUR OWN FAMILY, DO YOU FEEL YOU HAD SOME CONNECTION TO YOUR ADOPTIVE MOTHER AND SIBLINGS BECAUSE YOU SHARED SOME COMMON HERITAGE?

I never thought about that. I can tell you that I feel I would have been better off if I was raised by my biological parents. The reason for it is be-cause of my abuse, of course, number one, but I think of cultural reasons too.

WHAT KINDS OF IDENTITY PROBLEMS HAVE YOU EXPERIENCED AND WHAT ARE SOME OF THE WAYS THAT YOU'VE DEALT WITH THEM?

I think growing up people wondered what race I was. Some would think I was white, but some would think I was Latino. But then I would have a last name that's German, and then I would have to tell them I was adopted.

How do you define your racial identity today? And what are some of things that have contributed to shaping you to who you are both in your racial identity and in your personality?

I think maybe being brought up around Hispanics all my life and knowing my culture, now really knowing it. Even though I have mixed cultures in me, I say Latino, I think, because everyone says I look more Latino and Indian than anything.

Do you feel generally accepted by cultures other than Latino or Hispanic communities?

I feel I am more accepted in the minority culture in general.

Do you generally feel that you have been accepted by various sections of the white community?

I have been accepted, I think, because of what I do—my business. But if I were to meet them in person, I don't think I am much accepted because of race.

How much of a transracial or biracial adoptee's heritage do you think should be brought into their life by their adoptive parents, especially if their adoptive parents are from a different culture?

I think all children should learn all cultures, if possible. But mainly I feel it is very important that you know your own culture.

If you had been older when you were adopted, do you think it would have been better for you to have been adopted into a Latino family?

Definitely. Yes, I really do.

Are you glad that you were adopted?

No. Honestly, no because of my mom.

Do you have any suggestions or advice that you would give to parents who are now considering adopting transracially?

Yes. I think they should go to counseling to make sure that this is really what they want to do. I think they should consider before they adopt a child from a minority culture whether they can really set forth and bring the knowledge to a child who is going to want to know their heritage when they get older. I think that is very important that their identity be told. Most important, I think a social worker should come into the home once a month until the child gets to be at least the age of twelve because there are so many children who are being abused by adoptive parents. I think the state needs to check on the children, because a lot of the children aren't strong. They are committing suicide, and it is affecting them mentally into their adulthood. Those are the most important things: that adoptive parents get counseling and think twice before they adopt a child, and have a social worker to come out. Most importantly, you need to give that child love and reassurance knowing that they love them.

DO YOU THINK IT IS POSSIBLE FOR CHILDREN WHO ARE ADOPTED OUTSIDE OF THEIR MINORITY RACE TO REALLY COME TO A SOUND CONCLUSION AS TO WHO THEY ARE AND WHAT THEIR IDENTITIES ARE?

I am sure that some have. I am sure there were some that weren't taught by their adoptive parents, but when they got older, they went out and sought their own identity, just like I did. So it can be done. I mean I did. I think it is really according to the individual.

WHAT HAS HAPPENED TO ALLOW YOU TO BECOME COMFORTABLE WITH WHO YOU ARE AND TO MOVE FORWARD?

My daughter. My daughter. My daughter has given me the strength to know that I can do anything that I set my mind to, and I will go through the challenges in life, but she is my strong point. And my three little tiny dogs . . . and they are adopted, too, from animal shelters.

15

POLLY BETTENCOURT

GENDER:	Female
AGE AT TIME OF INTERVIEW:	35
RACE:	Filipino
MARITAL STATUS:	Married
OCCUPATION:	Full-time mom

Born in New York City to a biological mother of English descent and a biological father of Filipino and Spanish origin, Polly was adopted at the age of four and a half months by Caucasian parents. Raised with her non-adopted older brother and sister in a predominately white middle-class suburb of New York, her "best friends at one time were Korean and Chinese."

As a child, Polly grew up with the label "the adopted one," but she viewed the label as a "normal thing in [her] family" that helped her to feel part of her family. She was never exposed to Filipino culture due to the lack of resources, books, and community, and "didn't even know what a Filipino looked like." She was given "books about Chinese kids" and "Korean kids' books" because they were the "closest thing they could find" about Asian culture.

Because her mother was also adopted, Polly felt a special connection with her—a "different kind of understanding" of each other. Her mother was very open to talking about adoption, and she has been able to talk about adoption issues with her siblings even to the present day. She described her experience growing up in a multicultural family as a way to "see beyond" her physical features.

After the birth of Polly's first son, she located her birth mother, although it took her "a long time to have the courage" to do so. She also learned that she had a maternal half sibling who was also placed for adoption and has since begun to search for him. She has maintained contact with her biological mother and learned that her biological grandmother lives within driving distance. Polly tried to find her biological father, but she has not been able to locate him. However, she did learn about his heritage and discovered that she has four paternal half siblings.

At the time of interview, Polly was thirty-five and had two young children. Her children's father was also adopted and was able to identify with many of the issues that Polly faced. Her current husband has helped to raise her children, although initially he felt somewhat disconnected to them because they are not his biological children. Recently, he has spent more time with her children and feels much more connected to them now. Her husband and children "have been friends for four years now and . . . [his] consistency and willingness to be there for them have shown the kids that he is trustworthy." Despite her Filipino heritage, she identifies herself today as being "white," as it reflects her culture and upbringing, and describes herself as "totally ignorant" of Filipino culture. As she continues to search for her biological brother and father, her husband has been incredibly supportive and understanding.

―――――∽∞∾―――――

WHAT IS YOUR NAME?

Polly Bettencourt.

HOW OLD ARE YOU?

Thirty-five.

WHERE WERE YOU BORN?

I was born in New York City.

WHAT IS YOUR RACIAL BACKGROUND?

When I was a kid, they always told me I was half English/French and Welsh on my mother's side (it turns out it's mainly English), and on my father's side it was Filipino and Spanish, which basically means it was Filipino because all Filipinos are part Spanish.

AND YOU SAID YOU GREW UP IN A WHITE FAMILY AND WITH LITTLE EXPO-SURE TO THE FILIPINO CULTURE?

Yes. I grew up in the suburbs of New York. I didn't even know what a Filipino looked like.

HOW OLD WERE YOU WHEN YOU WERE ADOPTED?

I was actually in foster care for four months because I was labeled handicapped because I had hip dysplacia. So they had me in a cast for four months.

ARE YOUR ADOPTIVE PARENTS FROM NEW YORK?

My mother is originally from Minnesota, and my father is from New York.

DID BOTH OF YOUR PARENTS RAISE YOU?

Yes, though my father died when I was eleven. His mother lived across the street.

FROM AGE ELEVEN ON, WAS IT YOUR GRANDMOTHER AND YOUR MOTHER WHO RAISED YOU?

Yes.

DO YOU HAVE ANY SIBLINGS?

An older brother and an older sister. My brother is four years older, and my sister is six years older.

WERE THEY ADOPTED AS WELL?

No.

DID YOU GUYS TALK ABOUT ADOPTION AT ALL?

Yeah. Growing up it was really open. My mother told us before I remember because it was so obvious that it was hard to hide. My brother and sister are both blond. My sister has kind of hazel eyes; my brother has blue eyes. And they sunburn really easily. I have a darker complexion and darker skin, and as a kid I looked really Asian. I don't look like that anymore.

ARE YOU CLOSE TO YOUR BROTHER AND SISTER TODAY?

Yes.

AND DO YOU STILL TALK ABOUT ADOPTION ISSUES WITH THEM?

Yes, I do.

WHEN YOU WERE GROWING UP, DID YOU PERCEIVE ANY DIFFERENCES IN
THE WAY THAT YOU WERE TREATED BY YOUR PARENTS?

No. Maybe if anything, I was given slightly more understanding than they
were. If anything, I was a little bit more spoiled.

IN SOME FAMILIES IT IS A TABOO—YOU JUST DON'T TALK ABOUT IT. EVEN
THOUGH IT'S EVIDENT.

Actually, I have two kids, and their father is also adopted.

WHAT IS YOUR HUSBAND'S RACE?

He's white. He's from England.

CAN YOU TELL ME A LITTLE BIT ABOUT WHAT IT WAS LIKE GROWING UP IN
A MULTICULTURAL HOUSEHOLD?

Where I lived was in a white suburb, Westchester, and there were like
three black kids in my high school—it was that white—and a couple of
Asian kids. When I was a teenager, my mom said she'd turn around and look
in the back seat and couldn't tell which one was hers because my best
friends were Korean and Chinese. But other than that, everybody around
me was white, so I was raised white, middle class. The basic suburban living.

DO YOU KNOW OR DO YOU WONDER IF YOU HAVE SIBLINGS WHO WERE BORN
TO YOUR BIRTH PARENTS?

After I had my first son in 1993, I found my birth mother. She had another child before me, and that child was given up for adoption also. So I
have a half sibling.

HAVE YOU MADE CONTACT WITH HIM?

I just recently tried to find him. He was born in Ohio, so I sent a letter
to someone, and they found that on the day that I think he was born, there
was only one boy given up for adoption. So I wrote a letter to that person,
and he hasn't responded.

MAYBE HE'S STILL ABSORBING THE LETTER. WOULD YOU LIKE TO MEET
HIM?

I would.

HAVE YOU MAINTAINED CONTACT WITH YOUR BIRTH MOTHER?

Yes. Sometimes we'll go a few years without talking, but yes, we have
maintained contact, and my grandmother only lives a couple of hours away.

Your biological grandmother?

Yeah.

Do you know anything about your biological father?

I tried to find him and all I got was an address in L.A. He had financial problems and four kids, and the first one was born two years after me. I guess I have half siblings out there.

What was it like when you found your birth mother?

I was really slow about this stuff. When I turned twenty-one, I wrote to New York State. It was 1988, and all I could get was non-identifying information. There was one piece of paper, and it told me almost what I just told you—their races, height, ages, and some interests. So I don't know—it took me a long time to have the courage to find my birth mother. After having my first son, he was kind of blond with blue eyes, I was like "Oh my God, now I have to find her."

Do you see any resemblance?

Yes, I do look similar to her. And then she told me how she met my father. He worked in a hospital in Connecticut, and I called that hospital in Connecticut, and they sent me his picture from his file, from when he was twenty. My son looks just like him. My second son looks just like me. As a kid I looked more Asian, and now I look just white except that I'm darker and my cheekbones, my nose, my eyes are a little bit more like my mother's.

Have your sons met your birth mother?

Yes. I tried to explain it to them a little. I don't call her my mother, because she's not the person who went through everything. I call her my birth mother and my biological mother, and I call my mother my "mom." She's "Gran" to them now.

Can you tell me more about your parents, their schooling, what kind of work they did?

My mother was raised in Minnesota. Her family was wealthy, so she went to boarding school and she went to Sarah Lawrence College. She met my dad when she worked with his mother. They were both teachers, and she met my dad when he came back from the Army. He was an engineer and he went to NYU. His parents were divorced in 1941, and his grandparents were divorced. They were rebels. I've been working on this genealogy stuff, and it's pretty interesting

DO YOU FEEL LIKE IT'S YOUR HISTORY AS WELL?

The resolution I just came to was that I grew up close to my grand-mother, and she always told me stories of her childhood and her family, so when I read the genealogy, it resonates for me because it reminds me of the stories she told me. I don't really have much interest in looking up my own genealogy except for this really weird coincidence. My biological grand-mother—she was born in Connecticut and her maiden name was Wicker. My adopted grandmother's given name when she was born was Frances Wicker Dennis. It freaked me out. And so far the only connection I can find is in England in the 1600s. That kind of makes me feel more connected to my family.

What I learned when I met my birth mother was how much I am like the family I grew up with. There are certain things that resonate for me with my birth mother and my grandmother. When I found my grandmother, I felt really connected to her, like we were similar and related, and we had a similar sense of humor. But I can see that the things I do, and from my re-actions, that a lot of things are more similar to my adoptive parents.

WAS YOUR BIOLOGICAL MOTHER BORN IN THE UNITED STATES?

Yes. She's really white. My father is Filipino. He was born in the Philip-pines.

HOW DID YOUR ADOPTIVE FATHER PASS AWAY?

He had pancreatic cancer. It happened really fast.

WHAT WAS IT LIKE TO LOSE A PARENT?

It was really traumatic. I was eleven, my brother was fifteen, and my sis-ter was almost seventeen. Our family spent the next ten years not talking to each other. It took us until our twenties to deal with it.

WHAT WAS IT THAT KEPT YOU FROM TALKING? WAS IT JUST TOO MUCH GRIEF?

Yeah. Too much sadness. My mom wasn't around. It was a strange mix of things. My mom went back to school to get her master's in psychology.

WHAT INFLUENCED YOUR PARENTS' DECISION TO ADOPT AFTER THEY HAD TWO BIRTH CHILDREN?

When my mom wanted to adopt, she put down that she wanted a non-white child with a handicap, so there was some philanthropist in her.

Did your parents receive a lot of support from friends or family when they made this choice?

The one thing she always told me was that her mother was really upset that I wasn't white, but then when she met me, I wanted a hug and she fell in love with me. But then she died when I was a baby, I think in 1969.

What about your dad's mother?

I grew up around her, so I saw her every week. She was always really loving and treated me as well as everybody else. She always called me "the adopted one." That was part of my label, I guess. I think that was just a normal thing in my family because I was so different looking. It was the only way I could say that I'm really part of this family.

Did your parents know any Filipinos before they adopted you?

No, I don't think so. I never asked, but they never introduced me to anyone Filipino. When I was a kid, they always used to give me books about Chinese kids because that was the closest thing they could find. I had all these stupid Chinese kids' books and Korean kids' books.

Do you have any connections to Filipino culture?

No, because I still am totally ignorant of it. I went to the Filipino Consulate once, and looked around and said, "God, I don't look like any of these people! I don't get it!"

Do you and your husband talk about adoption issues?

Yeah, because I tell him whatever I'm thinking about. I've been doing all this genealogy stuff lately, so I've been thinking about it a lot. And finding my brother or half brother—and that makes me talk about it a lot.

Is he pretty supportive?

Yes. He'll say some funny things once in a while. Like at first he would refer to my birth mother as my mom, and I had to correct him. He'll say something about how I'm not really related to my family, and that makes me really mad. And I think, "You don't understand."

What was it like when you had your first child? He's the first person you've ever seen who shared your genes.

It was kind of shocking because he didn't look like me. I thought that he would just look like me with the darker hair.

HE LOOKS LIKE HIS FATHER?

He looks totally like his father.

WOULD YOU LIKE FOR YOUR SONS TO LEARN ABOUT FILIPINO CULTURE AT ALL?

I read one book that was good, and that is all I know about Filipino culture. Someday I'd like to take them there.

DID YOU EVER THINK ABOUT GOING OVER TO THE PHILIPPINES?

This goes back to my parents' ignorance. My mom—once I told her that I thought about going there—and she said, "Oh, my God, you'll get killed. You can't go there looking for people. They'll kill you over there."

DO YOU HAVE ANY ASIAN OR FILIPINO FRIENDS?

None. They are all white. The city is mainly white. I was just reading in today's paper that we are not very diverse. That figures. A lot of Latinos. I've met a few Filipinos.

DO YOU FEEL DISASSOCIATED FROM THEM?

Yeah. They've been generally older. Most of my friends are white. My husband is really white; my kids are really white.

WERE YOU EVER TEASED IN SCHOOL FOR BEING DIFFERENT?

I remember in elementary school, they would always ask me if I was Chinese. "You're Chinese, aren't you?" That was the extent of it. It wasn't really teasing, but I didn't like it either.

DID PEOPLE ASK YOU WHY YOU DIDN'T LOOK LIKE YOUR PARENTS OR YOUR SIBLINGS?

I think they must have. That's why I like my label "the adopted kid." When I first met my kids' dad, I didn't know he was adopted or anything. We were just chatting and I was like, "My brother and sister were born, and I was adopted." He was the one that actually made me realize that I had said that as part of my identity. The look on his face was what made me realize that he was kind of shocked that I would say that. I was like, "What?" and he said, "Why are you telling me that?" I said, "I don't know. I tell everybody that."

WAS IT A PREEMPTIVE STATEMENT BEFORE ANYONE COULD SAY ANYTHING?

That's it. It was the way I was just brought up to introduce myself, to say, "I'm the adopted one."

DO YOU REMEMBER SOME OF THE QUESTIONS YOU ASKED WHEN YOU WERE A KID AND TALKING ABOUT ADOPTION?

My mom was really cool because she remembered my first name. She remembered my last name wrong, but she remembered my first name. And my sister says I went through a phase wanting to be called Heather. Like I wanted to identify with that part of me. But now, I'm like "that's way too white." Not like Polly isn't, but that doesn't suit me as well.

WAS THERE A POINT IN YOUR LIFE WHEN ADOPTION BECAME A CENTRAL PART OF YOUR LIFE, LIKE WHEN YOU FOUND YOUR BIRTH MOTHER, OR WHEN YOU DECIDED TO SEARCH?

I think around eight. The whole time when I wanted to be called Heather. My mom told me my sister felt left out at one point for not being adopted.

AT WHAT POINT DID YOU DECIDE TO START LOOKING FOR YOUR BIRTH MOTHER?

I was interested as a teenager, but then they always stopped you. They always said, "We can't tell you anything until you are eighteen," and by the time I was eighteen, you had to be twenty-one.

AND YOUR MOM—WAS SHE SUPPORTIVE?

Yes.

HAS YOUR MOM MET YOUR BIRTH MOM?

No. She's supportive, and yet she told me that it is hard for her to be supportive. But she is, which is really impressive.

THAT REALLY TAKES A LOT OF STRENGTH.

Yeah. She told me that when I first found my birth mother, her first feeling was the same feeling she had when I was a baby—that somebody would come and take me away. I didn't know that.

I THINK THAT IS THE BIGGEST FEAR. WHEN PEOPLE LOOK FOR THEIR BIOLOGICAL FAMILIES, THEIR PARENTS FEEL LIKE THEY ARE GOING TO LOSE THEIR KIDS, EVEN THOUGH THAT IS RARELY THE CASE. WHAT WAS IT LIKE THE FIRST TIME YOU SAW YOUR BIRTH MOTHER?

It was overwhelming. My first thought was I didn't look as much like her as I wanted to. I realized she is as white as my family. I always felt that I wasn't white enough, but she was as white as they are, so that made me feel more accepting.

BACK IN 1971, THE PRESIDENT OF THE NATIONAL ASSOCIATION OF BLACK
SOCIAL WORKERS CAME OUT WITH A STATEMENT, AND I WANT TO GET YOUR
THOUGHT ON THIS QUOTE. HE SAID, "BLACK CHILDREN BELONG PHYSICALLY,
PSYCHOLOGICALLY, AND CULTURALLY IN BLACK FAMILIES IN ORDER THAT THEY
RECEIVE THE TOTAL SENSE OF THEMSELVES AND DEVELOP A SOUND PROJEC-
TION OF THEIR FUTURE."

Part of me agrees with that because I would have liked to have known a
little bit more about my culture. That might have made me feel more complete as a kid. But I can't be sure because adoption—especially the way it
was done then, the secrecy—is what makes you not feel complete. It's not
about the other stuff. I think there are a lot of black babies that are put up
for adoption who are not all black, they're biracial, but considered black and
that is unfair.

PEOPLE ONLY SEE WHAT'S DIFFERENT. TODAY, HOW DO YOU DEFINE YOUR
RACIAL IDENTITY OR HOW DO YOU IDENTIFY YOURSELF?

Oh, I'm white. That's the biggest question I've had. I asked the college
counselor that one because on college applications they want you to put
down your race. I ask them if they want to know your culture to make assumptions about how you were raised, or do they just want to know your
blood? Because if they want to know my culture, that's not Filipino. Mom
has always told me always mark Filipino. "You'll get more; you'll get into
college faster because you're a minority." But I'm not a minority.

DO YOU THINK THERE IS MORE PRESSURE PLACED UPON TRANSRACIAL
ADOPTEES BY SOCIETY AND BY THEIR FAMILIES TO COME TO A CONCLUSION AS
TO WHO THEY ARE EARLIER THAN OTHER KIDS JUST BECAUSE THEY LOOK DIF-
FERENT OR THEY'RE THE "ADOPTED ONE"?

Yes, I think there's pressure. I think there is definitely pressure on a kid
to deal with that.

SO WHAT DO YOU THINK ARE THE MOST IMPORTANT FACTORS WHEN CHOOS-
ING AN ADOPTIVE FAMILY FOR A CHILD?

I think the best thing would be to look at their interests and backgrounds
more so than genetics.

DO YOU THINK IT IS IN THE BEST INTERESTS OF CHILDREN TO BE PLACED
INTO A HOME REGARDLESS OF RACE OR CULTURE?

I think that is far better than being a foster child, yes.

What was the most enjoyable part of growing up in a multicultural family?

I think it's really good that we learned to see beyond what we look like. I think that we're a little deeper for it. Even when I think my brother is really shallow, I know that he looks at people for who they are, not for what they look like.

What is essential for parents to do who are raising children with different backgrounds?

Treating them as individuals and listening to their needs. I think the best thing for me was whenever I was curious about something, my mom tried her best, and she tried to remember that information for me. She never denied that I was adopted or denied that I was a different race.

Do you think it is possible for transracial adoptees or biracial children to come to a sound conclusion as to who they really are and where they come from?

Yes, I think that is possible. I think the resolution of why you were given up for adoption—that is the hard part.

And that's the first question that little kids usually have: "Why? What did I do?"

Are there any other aspects of adoption you would like to share or any other experiences that you feel are important?

It has made it harder for me to see why people separate themselves so much.

16

MICHELE MATTHIS

GENDER:	Female
AGE AT TIME OF INTERVIEW:	36
RACE:	Born in the U.S. of Hispanic-Indian descent
MARITAL STATUS:	Married
OCCUPATION:	Civil servant

Michele's story is quite unlike the others who were interviewed in this book. Born in Kansas in 1964, Michele was raised by her biological mother who is of Hispanic and Native American descent. Her biological father, whom she remembers meeting only once when she was nine years old, is Hispanic. Her mother divorced him shortly after the birth of Michele's younger sister. When Michele was nine years old, her mother married an African American man who later adopted both Michele and her sister, thus solidifying his relationship to them as a father figure. Later, her youngest sister was born to her mother and adoptive father.

Identifying herself as a "military brat," Michele and her family moved quite frequently. Growing up, she experienced a normal level of sibling rivalry with her sisters, but she never felt that her father treated her differently from her youngest sister (his biological daughter). Prior to her adoption, Michele asked many questions regarding her biological father. When her adoptive father initiated the legal proceedings to adopt her, she stopped asking questions.

Her parents had many friends from various cultures, although she describes times during her teenage years when she was subject to various racial slurs. Despite the comfort she felt within her own home, she was shocked at prejudices directed towards African Americans and Hispanics. At one point, she lived on a military base in Texas where she was exposed to racial slurs when attending schools outside the base. While living in Texas, she described the hostile attitudes directed towards her when dating interracially—especially when people learned that her adoptive father was African American. However, having been raised in that culture, Michele considered herself very much a part of the African American community.

During her adulthood, Michele's parents divorced and both remarried. She describes her relationship with her stepfamilies as comfortable, and she still remains connected with both of her parents. In 1994, Michele married an African American man, and they later had two children, ages five and two at the time of the interview. Since graduating from high school, she has worked for the government and continues to do so today. Overall, she describes her adoption experience as a "wake-up call" but very positive. One of the most enjoyable aspects of her adoption, she maintains, was being exposed to her father's family and learning about their culture. Today, Michele expresses no interest in contacting her biological father or searching for her biological siblings. She remains close to her sisters and her parents' new families. She is very protective of her children, and while she wants them to know where they are from, she hopes to shield them from the racism that is still very much alive.

MICHELE, WHERE WERE YOU BORN?

In Kansas.

WHAT IS YOUR RACIAL BACKGROUND?

Hispanic, Indian.

HOW OLD WERE YOU WHEN YOU WERE ADOPTED?

I was a junior in high school, so I was probably fifteen.

HOW OLD WERE YOU WHEN THE ADOPTION PROCEEDINGS BEGAN?

My dad started the process when I was a freshman in high school, and it became final when I was a junior in high school. We were in Germany when we got the papers. He had been married to my mom for years, and then he said he wanted to adopt us.

WHO WERE YOU RAISED BY? WERE BOTH OF YOUR PARENTS ADOPTIVE PARENTS?

No, just my father. My mom was a single mom raising my middle sister and me, and she met my father when I was probably about eight or nine.

WHERE WERE YOU LIVING?

Well, I'm a military brat. I was all over the place. When he started the adoption process, we were at Ft. Hood, Texas. When it finally came through, we were in Stuttgart, Germany.

DO YOU REMEMBER ANYTHING ABOUT YOUR BIOLOGICAL FATHER?

Not really. I know my mom said he was probably Air Force or Navy. I know he was in the same town; they all grew up there and were raised there. I know his name.

WAS HE MARRIED TO YOUR MOTHER?

Yes. They married after I was born, and so my middle sister has my real father's name. I have my mother's maiden name when I was born.

DO YOU HAVE ANY OTHER BROTHERS OR SISTERS?

Yes. I have a middle sister who is also by my real father and then my younger sister who is by my father now. I'm the oldest. My sister Karen is the middle, and Jo is the youngest. And Jo is from this marriage.

AND SO DID YOUR ADOPTIVE FATHER LEGALLY ADOPT YOUR MIDDLE SISTER TOO?

He adopted both of us.

WHAT WAS YOUR RELATIONSHIP LIKE WITH THEM WHEN YOU WERE GROWING UP?

We got into sibling rivalry, mostly with my middle sister. We fought a lot, but it was good. We're close now, and my younger sister, she was a baby when she came along.

GROWING UP DID YOU NOTICE ANY DIFFERENCES BETWEEN THE WAY YOUR ADOPTIVE FATHER TREATED YOU AND YOUR MIDDLE SISTER IN COMPARISON TO HIS BIOLOGICAL DAUGHTER?

No.

DID YOU TALK OPENLY WITH THEM GROWING UP ABOUT YOUR BIOLOGICAL FATHER OR ABOUT ANY OF THESE ISSUES?

My mom. If we asked a question, she answered us. We didn't ask much. She said when I was much younger, before she met my [adoptive] father, I would ask questions like, "Where is he?" But I think I blocked a lot of that out when my father started the process for adoption. He did have to talk to him on the phone because he had to get his consent, and he asked us if that's what we wanted. That was probably the second time in my life I had contact with him. He didn't want to let my dad adopt us, but he had no choice because the lawyer said, "If you don't want him to adopt them, then you've got many years of back child support to pay."

ABOUT YOUR MOTHER—WHAT IS HER HERITAGE?

Hispanic and Indian. I think she said my grandfather was Aztec Indian, and I'm assuming my grandmother was from Spain or Mexico.

AND YOUR BIOLOGICAL FATHER, DO YOU KNOW HIS BACKGROUND?

I think he is Hispanic.

AND HOW ABOUT YOUR ADOPTIVE FATHER?

He's Afro-American.

WHAT WAS IT LIKE GROWING UP IN A MULTICULTURAL HOUSEHOLD?

Not much different. I mean it was fine. Inside was fine, outside was different. I had to deal with prejudice. That was like a shocker to me as I got older. But inside the house was fine. We learned a lot being raised Hispanic, like different foods being introduced.

DO YOU HAVE ANY SIBLINGS BORN TO YOUR BIOLOGICAL FATHER THAT YOU KNOW OF?

I know he has one, but I don't know how many.

WHEN YOUR FATHER ADOPTED YOU, DID YOU NOTICE ANY CHANGES IN THE HOUSEHOLD, IN THE FAMILY DYNAMICS? OR DID ANYTHING CHANGE AT ALL?

Nothing changed.

DID YOUR PARENTS HAVE ANY FRIENDS WHO HAD ADOPTED CHILDREN?

I don't think so. Not that I can remember.

WHAT KINDS OF FRIENDS DID YOUR PARENTS HAVE? WERE THEY OTHER MILITARY FAMILIES?

Basically the military families.

DO YOU BELONG TO ANY RELIGIOUS ORGANIZATION TODAY? DO YOU STILL IDENTIFY WITH THE CATHOLIC CHURCH?

I identify with it a little bit. The church I go to is non-denominational. It's called Outreach Christian Center, but I still practice my Catholic religion a little bit.

IS IT MORE PART OF YOUR CULTURE?

Yeah, because I was raised with it. A lot of Hispanics are Catholic, so I try and hold on to it a little bit because now that I have my children, my mom wants to make sure that they know the Catholic religion.

WHEN WERE YOU MARRIED?

In 1994.

HOW DID YOU MEET?

I met him through a friend of mine who was dating his brother.

WHAT IS HIS FAMILY LIKE?

Oh, nice. Very nice. He has two brothers and his sister and his mom.

DO YOU FEEL THAT THEY'VE ACCEPTED YOU?

Oh, yeah, yeah.

DO YOU EVER TALK TO THEM ABOUT YOUR OWN BACKGROUND, ABOUT ADOPTION ISSUES, OR MULTICULTURAL ISSUES?

Well, I have told them some of my background when I was growing up, what I had to deal with. And he's asked me have I ever wanted to meet my real father or see him or anything. I have mixed feelings about it.

WHAT ARE SOME OF YOUR EXPERIENCES OR THOUGHTS ON INTERRACIAL DATING OR MARRIAGE?

It's hard sometimes. When I started dating interracially it was in Texas, so there was a lot of prejudice, but more so when they found out my father was black.

WHAT KIND OF MEN WOULD YOU DATE?

I dated whites. I dated Hispanics, blacks,

WHAT KIND OF PROBLEMS DID YOU ENCOUNTER THEN IN TERMS OF SOCIETY AND HOW THEY PERCEIVED YOU AS A COUPLE?

Like I said, a lot of prejudice and hostility. If you were military and you were traveling on base, it wasn't too bad because there were so many ethnic backgrounds—so everybody just accepted everyone. But when we got to a base that didn't have a school and you had to go off base—that's when you encountered a lot of hostility.

WAS THERE A CERTAIN GROUP THAT YOU FELT MORE COMFORTABLE DATING GROWING UP?

Probably the African American group because they just seemed to accept everybody.

WHAT WAS THE GENERAL REACTION WHEN THEY FOUND OUT THAT YOUR ADOPTIVE FATHER IS BLACK AND YOUR MOTHER IS INDIAN/HISPANIC?

You get the name calling. Got called the "n" word. I don't like to say that word. Got called "wet back" a couple of times. It's a Hispanic thing they say when you cross the border from Mexico.

DOES YOUR DAUGHTER KNOW THAT HER GRANDFATHER IS YOUR ADOPTIVE FATHER? DOES SHE UNDERSTAND THAT RELATIONSHIP YET?

Not really.

IS IT IMPORTANT TO YOU THAT SHE KNOWS ABOUT IT?

Not at this point, because it's weird. My mother has remarried, and my father has remarried, so they're not together anymore. And as for my husband's parents, his mom has been married but not his father, so she has four grandfathers.

TELL ME ABOUT YOUR MOTHER. WHEN DID SHE REMARRY?

Let's see. I've been married seven years. I think she married about nine years ago.

WHO DID SHE MARRY?

She married another military man. He is also Afro-American.

AND WHAT ABOUT YOUR FATHER?

He married an Afro-American woman, and they've been married for about ten years.

IS YOUR YOUNGER SISTER SUPPORTIVE OF YOUR CURIOSITY AND YOUR EMOTIONS REGARDING YOUR BIOLOGICAL FATHER?

Yes. Sometimes she'll say, "How do you feel about him?" And it's always hard to say because he's a total stranger. But probably a couple of years back, my cousin had told me that my real father had wanted to meet us and wanted to have more contact with us. So maybe I should do that. I don't know, it's hard to say. I keep thinking about it. It's been more on my mind lately.

IS THERE A REASON THAT IT EMERGED RIGHT NOW?

I guess because my mom's relationship with my grandfather just started mending not too long ago.

SO YOU'VE SEEN HOW RELATIONSHIPS CAN CHANGE.

She left and he was very upset. She lost him a couple years ago and thinks about all the time that was wasted over petty stuff. I think I started thinking about that.

YOU SAID THAT THE FIRST TIME YOU REMEMBER MEETING YOUR BIOLOGICAL FATHER YOU WERE ABOUT NINE?

Yes.

HAD YOU ASKED ANY QUESTIONS ABOUT HIM BEFORE THAT?

My mom said I used to ask where was he, why doesn't he write me.

DO YOU REMEMBER ANY OF THAT?

Not really. I try and think back. I think I remember writing some letters, but I remember the one time he showed up on our doorstep.

TELL ME ABOUT THAT.

It's all so clear. We were living in Colorado Springs, and there was a knock at the door. I opened the door, and I was just like looking at him. He knew our names and he said, "I'm your dad." I remember I was very excited and running. We went to Seven Falls, and we went to a rock-climbing place, and he took us to quite a few places that day.

WHAT WAS THAT LIKE FOR YOU?

I was excited, I was happy, but as excited and happy as I was, he was gone the next day without a good-bye or anything.

DO YOU KNOW WHY HE REEMERGED THAT ONE TIME?

I have no idea why. I never asked my mom why he showed up. I think it was a surprise to her too.

SO WHAT WERE YOUR FEELINGS OR THOUGHTS ABOUT HIM AFTERWARDS?

I guess I just thought, well, he's gone. He's here, he's gone. So maybe I never contacted him since because he left without saying good-bye or anything.

DID YOU EVER THINK ABOUT CONTACTING HIM AT ALL AFTER THAT?

No. No, not until just recently. I've been thinking about it.

GROWING UP, DID YOU CALL YOUR ADOPTIVE FATHER "DAD" THE WHOLE TIME?

Yes.

HE SAW YOU AS HIS DAUGHTER?

Yes.

IF YOU WERE ACTUALLY TO MEET YOUR BIOLOGICAL FATHER, WHAT KIND OF RELATIONSHIP WOULD YOU LIKE TO HAVE WITH HIM, OR WHAT KIND OF QUESTIONS WOULD YOU LIKE TO ASK HIM?

Boy. Probably why he showed up that day and why he left so quick. That would probably be one question. Why he never really contacted me before then, before I was nine, and why he showed up all of a sudden. I don't know what kind of a relationship I would want with him.

WOULD YOUR MOTHER AND YOUR FATHER BE SUPPORTIVE IF YOU WERE TO SEARCH FOR HIM?

I know my mom would. I don't know how my dad would be. I don't know if it would hurt him.

SINCE YOU'RE LIVING WITH YOUR BIOLOGICAL MOTHER, YOU HAVE SOME KNOWLEDGE OF YOUR GENEALOGY AND BACKGROUND. HOW DO YOU SEE YOUR SITUATION AS DIFFERENT FROM ADOPTEES WHO DON'T KNOW ANYTHING ABOUT EITHER OF THEIR BIRTH PARENTS?

I think I have an advantage, and it makes it a little easier.

AND IN YOUR SITUATION YOU HAD SOME ANSWERS. YOU COULD ASK YOUR MOTHER, AND SHE COULD TELL YOU WHAT SHE KNEW ABOUT YOUR BIRTH FATHER.

Yeah, whereas someone who doesn't know anything, it's just a loss. It's like you don't have an identity because you don't know where you come from, and you don't know who your parents are.

IN 1971, THE PRESIDENT OF THE NATIONAL ASSOCIATION OF BLACK SOCIAL WORKERS SAID, "BLACK CHILDREN BELONG PHYSICALLY, PSYCHOLOGICALLY, AND CULTURALLY IN BLACK FAMILIES IN ORDER THAT THEY RECEIVE THE TOTAL SENSE OF THEMSELVES AND DEVELOP A SOUND PROJECTION OF THEIR FUTURE." DO YOU HAVE ANY THOUGHTS OR REFLECTIONS ON THAT STATEMENT IN LIGHT OF YOUR OWN ADOPTION EXPERIENCE?

I know. I can't believe that. I don't agree with that. Anybody can be adopted as long as the adoptive family gives them some type of knowledge of their background.

WERE YOU TEASED GROWING UP BECAUSE OF YOUR FAMILY?

Oh, sure, I was called names.

AND THAT WAS STARTING EARLY?

My teens, my high school years.

HOW DID YOU REACT TO THAT?

Not very good. I didn't react too good. Fighting. I mean it was something that was totally new to me. Those words I was hearing, I had never heard before. It was in Texas. My sister didn't have any problem. It was me, all me. My little sister is more fair skinned than me, so she didn't have as much of a problem.

DO YOU THINK GROWING UP IN A MULTICULTURAL FAMILY HELPED PREPARE YOU FOR RACISM THAT'S STILL PREVALENT TODAY?

I think that helped a lot because it was like a wake-up call. I went to Texas—I never thought anything different until I got there. My father was Afro-American, and I started getting names called at me. It is like a slap in the face, like a shock.

DO YOU IDENTIFY WITH ANY ONE GROUP MORE THAN THE OTHER? DO YOU FEEL AS COMFORTABLE WITHIN THE AFRICAN AMERICAN COMMUNITY AS WITHIN THE HISPANIC COMMUNITY?

I haven't really been in the Hispanic community. I do feel uncomfortable because I don't know my own language. I've been approached by them speaking to me, and I feel so dumb. I'm like, "I don't know what you're saying."

WHAT DO THEY DO WHEN THEY FIND OUT THAT YOU DON'T SPEAK THE LANGUAGE?

They're like, "Ooh, I'm sorry." And I tell my mom, "Why didn't you raise us with it?" I'm going to make sure that my daughter learns the language, and my son, because I feel that's a part of me missing. I can't speak it. I can't read it. I can't communicate.

WHAT OTHER KINDS OF IDENTITY ISSUES HAVE YOU HAD?

It's hard sometimes, because people will look at me and they'll go, "What is she?" Then they see my husband, and then they look at me, and then they look at my mom and look at my dad, and then they look at my sisters, and we're all different complexions even though my middle sister and I have the same biological father. She's much more fair skinned than me, and then my younger sister is a little darker than me. I get to know people, and they go, "I've been meaning to ask you this—what are you?" I'm like, "Oh, if you must know, I'm part Hispanic and Indian, and I consider myself part Afro-American because that's the way I was raised, and that's the culture I was raised in."

HAVE YOU FOUND OUT ANYTHING ABOUT YOUR OTHER BIOLOGICAL SIBLINGS?

No.

DO YOU THINK YOU WOULD EVER CONSIDER SEARCHING FOR THEM?

No.

IS THERE A REASON THAT YOU'RE SO DEFINITE ABOUT THAT?

I think I would feel resentment because they had him and I didn't.

BESIDES YOUR PARENTS, ARE THERE OTHER THINGS THAT HAVE REALLY CONTRIBUTED TOWARDS SHAPING YOUR IDENTITY?

Being a military brat, I think that's helped a lot. I really think it's shaped me to be who I am because I've always had to learn to make friends real quick.

I IMAGINE IT'S HARD TO GROW UP HAVING LOSS AFTER LOSS.

Yeah, you need stability when you're a teen. You want to have friends, and then you move on and you've got to make new friends.

GROWING UP, HAS YOUR SELF-ESTEEM EVER SUFFERED BECAUSE OF YOUR FAMILY?

No. I've always had self-esteem, I think, because my adoptive dad always told me, "Don't ever let anybody put you down because of your race, because you are somebody. Always hold your head up high." My mom was the same way because she and my real father didn't have a good relationship; it was abusive. So she's instilled in me, "Don't let any man hurt you." So I think my self-esteem was really built up from both of them.

YOU SAID YOU FEEL VERY COMFORTABLE WITH THE AFRO-AMERICAN COMMUNITY AND NOT SO MUCH WITH THE HISPANIC COMMUNITY. WHAT ABOUT THE WHITE COMMUNITY?

I'm comfortable with that. Most of our community there is probably that, where we live now. I don't have any problem with it.

DO YOU THINK THAT THERE'S GREATER PRESSURE ON TRANSRACIAL ADOPTEES TO SOLIDIFY THEIR IDENTITY?

I would think so because you have two different cultures. And again, if you don't know your parents, that's another pressure put on you. I knew one of my parents, but just having my father to adopt me—that was a pressure in itself.

HAVE YOU EVER BEEN IN A SITUATION WHEN SOMEONE WAS REALLY DEGRADING OF THE AFRICAN AMERICAN CULTURE IN FRONT OF YOU, NOT KNOWING OF COURSE THAT YOU IDENTIFY WITH THAT GROUP?

Yes, I have had the problem. On my job, I've had it on my job. When I was younger, before I met my husband.

RACIAL SLURS OR COMMENTS?

Like jokes. I started putting pictures on my desk to alleviate the whole problem. I don't want to have to deal with it.

WHAT FACTORS SHOULD BE CONSIDERED WHEN SELECTING AN ADOPTIVE HOME FOR A TRANSRACIAL OR BIRACIAL CHILD?

Oh, man. I would say there definitely needs to be a lot of love because they're going to have problems when they get older. If they don't have that love and support to help them get through it, it's going to be hard.

WHAT DO YOU THINK WAS THE MOST DIFFICULT OR THE MOST ENJOYABLE PART ABOUT GROWING UP IN A MULTICULTURAL FAMILY?

I think the differences. Getting to meet my dad's side of the family. And I did meet some of my mom's sisters, so that was nice. With [my father] in the military, we got to see other cultures and see how they are.

DO YOU THINK IT'S GIVEN YOU AN APPRECIATION FOR OTHER CULTURES IN GENERAL?

Yeah.

DO YOU HAVE ANY SUGGESTIONS OR ADVICE THAT YOU WOULD GIVE TO PARENTS WHO ARE THINKING OF ADOPTING TRANSRACIALLY OR ADOPTING BIRACIAL CHILDREN?

Just to really think about it. I know when they adopt they think, "Look at the baby, oh, it's great." But you are going to have to really and honestly think about what you as parents are going to have to go through and what your children are going to have to go through when they get older. If you can give them the love and support it will be good.

IF THERE WAS AN AFRICAN AMERICAN CHILD BEING PLACED FOR ADOPTION, DO YOU THINK IT WOULD BE BETTER FOR HIM TO BE PLACED IN AN AFRICAN AMERICAN FAMILY INSTEAD OF A HISPANIC OR WHITE FAMILY, ALL THINGS BEING EQUAL?

That's hard to say because it depends on where they live, what kind of neighborhood it is, what kind of background they have. I don't know.

DO YOU THINK IT IS POSSIBLE FOR TRANSRACIAL ADOPTEES TO COME TO A SOUND CONCLUSION AS TO WHO THEY ARE, WHERE THEY'RE FROM, AND WHAT THEIR IDENTITIES ARE?

Yeah, I'm sure they can. It's just a matter of trying not to get caught up in society saying, "This is the way you should be because you're this, and this is the way you should be because you're this." If you can get past that and just finally say, "This is me and these are my parents," it doesn't matter, then I think they can.

WHAT DO YOU THINK IT'S LIKE FOR PEOPLE WHO DON'T KNOW THEIR BACKGROUND? I'VE MET SOME ADOPTEES WHO'VE KNOW THAT THEY'RE BIRACIAL, THAT THEY'RE PART X OR Y, BUT THEY DON'T KNOW DEFINITIVELY WHAT THE OTHER PART IS.

I think that's hard.

JUDITH CRAIG

GENDER:	Female
AGE AT TIME OF INTERVIEW:	23
RACE:	Haitian
MARITAL STATUS:	Single
OCCUPATION:	Student

Born on the island of Haiti, Judith was adopted in Canada by Caucasian parents when she was four months old. Her parents initially faced resistance by extended family members, who were against the idea of adopting a black child. However, they "did become more accepting of the idea." Her first few years were spent in Montreal and in Cincinnati, Ohio. Later, her family moved to Toronto and then settled down in the suburbs when she was nine. Judith has two non-adopted sisters, one non-adopted brother, and another brother adopted from Haiti, all of whom she was close to while growing up.

From her early childhood, her mother made it a point to talk about adoption, answer questions, and "insured that [they] felt comfortable" to the point where Judith would exclaim, "Ok, enough!" The multicultural nature of her family was celebrated by recognizing black history and culture, and her family enjoyed living in a diverse area of Toronto where she had friends of mixed cultures.

Judith's father was a Pentecostal minister, and her family was very involved with the church. Though her church congregation was very diverse, she was the minority among her group of friends. She was often asked ignorant and offensive questions by other church members, which she reacted to with embarrassment at some times, or with insight at other times. Though she loved being knowledgeable and teaching others, she was often offended by the way questions were asked, and when she would overhear racial slurs. Though her high school was very diverse and her friends were from all cultures, Judith never felt accepted by other black students. She was often teased about her appearance and remembered feeling as if she was being judged.

Regarding her thoughts on interracial dating or marriage, Judith expressed disappointment in seeing "one person's ethnicity or race or culture" displaced by the other's culture, or when the interracial aspect of the relationship is flaunted. Overall, she stressed the importance of educating children so that they gain knowledge of "both races." She expressed an interest in marrying someone with "more cultural similarities" to her, which was very different from her earlier years when she had "crushes mainly on white guys."

At the time of the interview, Judith was living in Toronto and pursuing her bachelor's degree in social work with a minor in sociology. When asked to describe her racial background, she identified herself as being black and stated that she has been able to "embrace the black culture a lot more." Noting the racism still prevalent within the white community, and her lack of knowledge regarding certain Caribbean traditions, she doesn't feel fully accepted by the white or the black community. Today, Judith is very active within an African and Caribbean Association at her university, where she has made friends from all cultures. She hopes one day to visit Haiti and search for her biological parents.

2005 update: Ms. Craig is completing her bachelor's degree in spring of 2005. Her immediate plans are to work in the U.K. for a few years, but her ultimate goal is to return to Haiti and work in the area of adoption. Ms. Craig has a strong passion to work within her community and to assist in progressive changes in the adoption process.

2006 update: Ms. Craig, now twenty-seven, resides in England working in the area of child welfare. She is in the process of working on a documentary about her life as a transracially adopted child and her journey back to Haiti, which is planned for 2007. She is very eager to work in the field of adoption with a focus on increasing the number of formal adoptions within the black community.

Her parents have displayed new attitudes towards the journey of self-discovery and searching for biological family.

PLEASE TELL ME YOUR FULL NAME.

Judith Craig.

HOW OLD ARE YOU?

I am twenty-three.

WHERE WERE YOU BORN?

I was born in Haiti, the island of Haiti, in the Caribbean.

HOW OLD WERE YOU WHEN YOU WERE ADOPTED?

I was almost four months old.

HOW WOULD YOU DESCRIBE YOUR RACIAL OR ETHNIC BACKGROUND?

Black.

SO YOU WERE LIVING IN AN ORPHANAGE RUN BY NUNS WHEN YOU WERE ADOPTED?

We were brought over by the nuns. I was actually in a documentary film that the Canadian government put out by the National Film Board on international adoption, and they showed us in Haiti. I was in the film—the orphanage and on our trip, on the airplane. They showed the nuns handing me over, and they showed other kids from Haiti. We were adopted mainly by white families.

WHERE ARE YOU PARENTS FROM?

They are both Canadian.

WERE YOU RAISED IN TORONTO?

For the first year and a half or so I was actually raised in Montreal. And then we moved to Cincinnati until I was four. And then we moved to Toronto. I grew up in Toronto until I was about nine. Then we moved out to the suburbs [of Toronto]. I was there from the time I was about nine years until I was nineteen. My family is still there, and I moved back to Toronto. That's where I am now.

Do you have any brothers or sisters?

I have one older sister, who is a biological child to my parents. She was three years old when I was adopted. When we moved to Cincinnati, my younger sister was born, so she is American and is my parent's biological child as well. Then we moved to Toronto and my parents adopted another child from Haiti, who was actually only six months younger than my little sister. They adopted him when he was four years old. He was a toddler when he came to us. Then just before we left Toronto in 1988, my parents had my youngest brother who was biological to them.

Growing up, what kind of relationship did you have with your siblings?

It was a pretty good relationship. From the time we were young, the girls all shared a room so we had to share stuff. We were little, so we grew up pretty close. We played a lot together and we shared bunk beds, so at night we would be talking and stuff. Then with my younger siblings, it was pretty good. We used to help my mom out with the younger kids and take care of them. I'd say overall when we were younger, we were definitely pretty close.

What about today? What kind of relationship do you have with them?

Today, it's interesting. My older sister and I are both out of the home. I'd like to be closer to my brother also because he is adopted. We have that in common in some ways, but he's never been as open about his adoption or the fact that he is a black young man. At this point in my life, I'm getting more in touch with who I am as a black woman, and I tried to instill that in him, and he is not really interested in that right now at this point in his life.

Have you ever been able to talk to them about any adoption issues that may come up?

Oh, yeah. I talk about it all the time. My mom is very much into the latest adoption things or whatever is going on. As I say, my brother who is adopted as well, he doesn't really care. And there have been times my mother has asked me to talk to my brother about different issues and I will. I have no qualms about it whatsoever. He is definitely more subdued about it.

WHEN YOU WERE GROWING UP, DID YOU EVER PERCEIVE ANY DIFFERENCES IN THE WAY YOU WERE TREATED BY YOUR PARENTS?

Not by my parents.

WHAT WAS IT LIKE GROWING UP IN A MULTICULTURAL HOUSEHOLD?

The first thing that comes to my mind is I don't know anything different, so for me it was kind of normal. We always knew we were a multicultural family, and we were different, and we celebrated it in our family more so than I think you would see in a lot of other families. I can think of times when my mother would be embarrassed. She would be put in situations, people were looking at her funny, like "What is she doing in the barbershop with a black kid?"

When I was younger, she used to force me to go to stuff on Black History Month and little classes, and I did not want to go. I thanked my mom a little while ago—I said thank you so much for making me go to those things because I realize the importance of learning about my culture and my history now. So growing up it was pretty normal family things.

CAN YOU TELL ME MORE ABOUT YOUR PARENTS?

My mom went to grade twelve, and she dropped out of high school. I guess she didn't really know what she wanted to do, and she was frustrated with high school, and so she lived with her parents. And my father pursued his education first at University of Toronto, then decided to change and felt called to go into the ministry.

DO YOU KNOW WHAT INFLUENCED YOUR PARENT'S DECISION TO ADOPT?

From my understanding, I think my mom was always interested in it. I don't think it was something that was really in her head since she was a kid, but as she got older, and she realized that there are kids who need homes. I think she was the one who pursued it and went to my dad and said, "I think we should adopt kids." They also knew they wanted to have biological children. My mom said, though, she didn't ever think she would have five children. So the five kids kind of fell upon them.

DO YOU KNOW HOW THEY CAME TO CHOOSE HAITI?

I remember my mother saying she didn't care where the child came from, she wasn't really concerned with where or what country or anything like that. Just somewhere where a child needed a home, basically. I think it was because the people they ended up coming in contact with had connections in Haiti.

WERE YOUR PARENTS' FRIENDS AND FAMILY MEMBERS SUPPORTIVE OF THEIR DECISION?

I think some people are very surprised by it.

WERE THEY SURPRISED BY THE ADOPTION, OR FROM WHERE THEY CHOSE TO ADOPT?

I think it was more the black child that came as a surprise. My mom's parents were very much against it. They were so much against it, they threatened to cut her off and not have anything to do with her. It didn't deter my mother, obviously. I am not sure how long it took them to come around, but eventually they did become more accepting of the idea, and they accept me now and my other brother.

HAVE YOUR PARENTS EVER GONE TO HAITI?

Never. It has been something my mom has wanted to do forever and ever. My younger sister actually went with a mission group. She went down last summer, and she's the first one in our family to go there. I was jealous out of my mind. "You're going to MY country." She ended up in the mountainous region.

DOES YOUR YOUNGER BROTHER HAVE ANY MEMORIES OF HAITI?

He does. His story was so different from mine. He actually lived with his biological family before he came here when he was four. He started life with his biological family. He was taken by his father to the orphanage, and his father lied and said, "My wife is dead." Men of course weren't really expected to care for their families by themselves, so they took my brother in. I don't know how or why, but they found out that his mother was indeed alive, and he had about twenty-three other siblings. We have pictures of his biological parents. We know what they look like, where they lived, and we have pictures of him with them.

COULD YOU IMAGINE YOURSELF ADOPTING FROM HAITI OR EVEN ADOPTING TRANSRACIALLY?

Yes, definitely. I always would say I'm going to have a rainbow family. I am in love with the Spanish culture. I don't know why. I love the music and dancing, the men. I can see myself adopting. I've never really thought of adopting a white child because I think white children are on such high demand. So many want that white perfect little baby, blue eyes, you know that whole stereotype. And I think for me, I can see myself adopting a five-year-old, a six-year-old. Because I have some of the skills of a social worker, I think I would be able to handle it.

YOU TALKED ABOUT BEING A SOCIAL WORKER. CAN YOU TELL ME MORE ABOUT YOUR EDUCATION?

I'm in my third year now at Ryerson University.

WHEN YOU ARE FINISHED, YOU'LL HAVE YOUR BACHELOR'S DEGREE?

I'll have my bachelor's degree in social work and my minor in sociology.

BEFORE YOU STARTED COLLEGE, WERE YOUR HIGH SCHOOLS DIVERSE?

Yes, my high school was. We went to school in Messessaga. My high school was very, very diverse. I hung out pretty much with a multicultural crowd, all different ethnicities. I didn't hang out with just black students, and that's probably for a few different reasons. I didn't feel like they accepted me. I wasn't highly accepted by my own kind of people, which did definitely play a big part of my becoming who I am and who I was at the time. It was difficult. It was very difficult, but I went on.

WERE YOU EVER TEASED IN SCHOOL FOR BEING DIFFERENT AND DID OTHER KIDS ASK YOU ABOUT YOUR FAMILY?

I got asked all the time. It is funny. A lot of my friends that I have now in school don't know that my family is white. And a girlfriend of mine a little while ago said, "You're adopted? You have a white family?" She was so surprised. She had no idea. It's funny now because I used to get told that I was whitewashed.

Back in junior high, I got teased for being different because my hair was always short. I used to braid my hair and do different things with it, but I would get teased for my appearance as well. I would go through the whole identity thing in different ways. And I did get teased. I remember in high school walking by areas and these black girls would look at me, and I just remember feeling that they were judging me. I wasn't good enough.

In high school, I would say the black, Jamaican culture was very prevalent, and that was kind of the norm. I guess because I didn't look like them, I felt very ostracized by a good number of them.

WAS THERE A SPECIFIC POINT IN YOUR LIFE WHEN YOU BEGAN TO IDENTIFY WITH YOURSELF AS A BLACK WOMAN, OR IDENTIFY MORE WITH YOUR HAITIAN BACKGROUND?

Definitely. As I aged up through school, I didn't think about it much of the time, but there would be different times when I would. I would say I was ignorant myself of different cultural things that unfortunately my mother wasn't able to teach me about, like cooking, language, music, dress, and attitude. She's a white woman; she couldn't have told me, or she could only tell me so much.

I'm aware of more issues that affect our community. I've taken up more causes. I've also gotten involved with a group from my school, the Asian/African/Caribbean Association and that's been great. In a lot of ways, I'm very happy about where I'm coming to. More and more I'm asserting myself as a black woman and becoming more proud of it.

DO YOU FEEL ACCEPTED EQUALLY BY THE WHITE AND BLACK COMMUNI-TIES?

I would have to say yes and no to some degree. In the white community in general, the racism is still there and will always be there. I would never say every white person is racist, nothing like that. But there's still a lot of racism within the white community towards blacks and other minorities, definitely. And I still feel that in everyday life, I guess because I don't live with my white family anymore. The black community is a little bit of a struggle because now that I've become more aware of who I am, the things that bother me most are things like I don't know how to cook any Caribbean dishes, and that seems so trivial. And I realize that more and more.

HOW WOULD YOU DESCRIBE THE WAY YOU'VE FORMED IDENTITY? WHAT KIND OF IDENTITY PROBLEMS HAVE YOU EXPERIENCED AND WHAT ARE THE WAYS YOU'VE DEALT WITH THEM?

I had problems identifying with my own culture and who I was just from a racial point of view because I didn't have the same experiences as other people. So that was a big problem for me. I went through a lot of hard times with other black people, with racial things, with racial slurs, with different aspects of race and being called "whitewash," and being told, "You act white," and different things like that. How are you supposed to know who you are when you are being told, "You act white" or "You act this way." How can I act a color? The black part is hard to identify with because what is being black? What is being white?

Also, I've always, always, been curious about who my biological family was. I think you definitely lose part of your identity just from not knowing, which is unfortunately my situation. It is like a closed book, pretty much. My parents have been looking since I was a baby. People they knew in Haiti are trying to find information. I'd like to identify more with my Haitian people, with my culture. I've been able to get into music a little bit more. It's easier because it is more readily available at your fingertips. Biologically, I've had to accept I don't really have a choice about what I know. So in that arena, I can't really identify more than I already have. I still have my little fantasies that I have a twin out there, and maybe we'll see each other and we'll be like, "Oh, my gosh!" Silly things like that. I don't really have a biological identity. I don't think I ever really will until I meet somebody who is in my family. I don't see how I could otherwise. So that is definitely a challenge for me, not knowing.

WOULD YOU LIKE TO MEET YOUR BIRTH PARENTS?

Definitely. I've always wanted to see them, physically, see what they look like and definitely talk to them. I've thought either she's really young, my birth mother, or she's really old. I wonder if she's pretty. I wonder what features and characteristics she had. And my mother always said, "They gave you away because they couldn't take care of you; you were sick. It was a love reason." So I've always carried that around.

AND YOUR PARENTS WOULD BE SUPPORTIVE?

Yes, totally. That's one thing that bothers me about people who adopt and who aren't into that. I think deep down it might cause a twinge of something for them, just because how could it not? Right? I'd be as sensitive as I could to them, but I think adoptive parents have to realize that when you don't know anything, it's very daunting. How can you not know anything about who gave birth to you? Who physically had you?

WHAT KINDS OF QUESTIONS WOULD YOU ASK YOUR BIRTH PARENTS? IS THERE ANY SPECIFIC INFORMATION?

As much as possible—everything, everything. I'd want to know of course, "How, why, when, how old were you?" I believe now I'm actually a carnival baby. In February, they have carnival down in Haiti, and all the islands have carnivals and a lot of sex goes on. You know sex and alcohol. I was born nine months after carnival; I was born in October.

I WANT TO READ YOU A QUOTE THAT THE PRESIDENT OF THE NATIONAL ASSOCIATION OF BLACK SOCIAL WORKERS SAID IN 1971: "BLACK CHILDREN BELONG PHYSICALLY, PSYCHOLOGICALLY, AND CULTURALLY IN BLACK FAMILIES IN ORDER THAT THEY RECEIVE THE TOTAL SENSE OF THEMSELVES AND DEVELOP A SOUND PROJECTION OF THEIR FUTURE." I'D LIKE TO GET A SENSE OF HOW YOU FEEL ABOUT THIS IN LIGHT OF YOUR OWN EXPERIENCE.

To some degree, I do agree with that. And you may think, "Oh, my gosh," but I do agree with that in some aspects. People who are fortunate enough to have families who instill as much as they can, but nobody can really give you that full experience. I think it is most important to have a home where you'll be loved and taken care of than getting culture instilled in you right from that age, but my counter-question to that would be: "Then why aren't more black families stepping up to the plate because there are tons of black children who need those loving homes?" and "Why aren't they adopting?" I don't oppose interracial adoptions at all, but at the same time I do see the importance of that statement because I think it is important. It would be a consideration, but if there's a family that's going to love this child, and they aren't the same race as the child, go for it.

DO YOU THINK THERE IS MORE PRESSURE PLACED ON TRANSRACIAL ADOPTEES TO DEVELOP THEIR IDENTITIES MUCH SOONER THAN OTHER PEOPLE?

Probably yes, I would say.

DO YOU THINK IT IS POSSIBLE FOR TRANSRACIAL ADOPTEES TO ACTUALLY COME TO A SOUND CONCLUSION AS TO WHO THEY ARE WITHOUT MEETING THEIR BIOLOGICAL PARENTS?

Without meeting their biological parents? I think yes. Again, I think a lot of it depends on their family, the type of family they have, the support they're given. I think it is possible, but the support system is very important. You need to access the right people; you need to access the right resources.

HOW MUCH OF THE ADOPTEE'S HERITAGE DO YOU THINK SHOULD BE INTRODUCED INTO HIS OR HER LIFE BY HIS OR HER PARENTS?

Everything.

AND EVEN IF THE CHILD RESISTS, DO YOU THINK IT IS IMPORTANT FOR THE PARENTS TO KEEP TRYING?

Definitely. I get very emotional when I hear of people who don't instill it in their children and try and pretend. If you are going to bring a black child into your home, (a) you should already have multicultural friends because otherwise what are you doing? and (b) if you have to move, move. You shouldn't live in a little tiny suburb where your child is the only black child. I don't think that is fair at all to the child. You need to be exposed. You can't deny who your child is.

IF YOU WERE TO BE ADOPTED ALL OVER AGAIN INTO A HOME THAT WAS JUST AS LOVING AND STABLE AS YOURS, WOULD YOU HAVE PREFERRED TO HAVE BEEN ADOPTED BY BLACK PARENTS? FROM A SOCIAL WORKER'S POINT OF VIEW, WHAT WOULD YOU THINK?

I would say yes. I've been curious enough to know what it would be like, and I think there are enough important things about it.

IF YOU WERE TO GIVE ADVICE TO ADOPTIVE PARENTS WHO ARE THINKING OF ADOPTING TRANSRACIALLY, IS THERE ANYTHING THAT YOU WOULD REALLY EMPHASIZE, ASIDE FROM CULTURAL EDUCATION?

I think they need to examine who they are as people and ask themselves why. They need to ask, "Why am I doing this?" They need to ask themselves, "How far am I willing to go to provide my child with as much of their culture and heritage as I can? How comfortable will I be in situations where all those types of questions come up?" They need to really examine themselves as individuals. You need someone who you can go to and ask these questions and find out answers. I think it is so important. You'll hurt your child if you don't do those things. Immerse yourself in the culture. If you can go to the country, go to the country. That won't do everything. It is like icing on the cake to get a little taste of what this culture is about.

18

TIM*

GENDER:	Male
AGE AT TIME OF INTERVIEW:	26
RACE:	Mexican
MARITAL STATUS:	Single
OCCUPATION:	Student

As a child, I always knew I was adopted even before I knew what the
word was . . . I ran around telling everyone "I'm adopted," and my parents definitely made me feel special because of that. . . .

Born in Mexico and adopted when he was only a few weeks old, Tim was
raised by Caucasian parents in an all-white suburb. His parents, who he described as "the most loving and supportive parents I can imagine," also
adopted his younger brother, who was born to Caucasian parents. From his
early childhood, his parents spoke openly and honestly to Tim about his
adoption, and they were nothing but loving and supportive.

Prior to college, Tim attended Catholic schools where he was usually the
only student of color. As a young child, he recalled not realizing that his skin
color was different until kindergarten, when he began to think about his

---

*Identifying information about this participant has been omitted or changed.

own ethnicity for the first time. This became a confusing time, especially when children at school would point to him and ask questions such as, "Are you black?" At home, Tim began asking his parents questions about his adoption, such as, "Why didn't my birth mother keep me? What did I do wrong?" Although his parents continually reinforced their love for him, Tim suggested that at some level, he feared his parents would get "rid" of him and he therefore became a diligent student, never getting in trouble.

During high school, Tim started coming to terms with his sexuality. He was surprised at how accepting and supportive his parents were when he told them he is gay. During the interview, Tim shared some of his experiences with interracial dating. He noted that dating within the Latino community has "been amazing" because he feels understood and has also been introduced to the Latino traditions and culture. His adoption has had a valuable role in his relationships, and he stressed how important it is that a partner understand that aspect of his life.

Tim has expressed an interest in working as a social worker to help adoptees "get to a place where they can embrace their history and who they are." When we spoke, he had also just completed a fellowship in Washington, D.C., where he worked on Capitol Hill and also with a leading Latino advocacy group. Currently, he is back in Illinois and pursuing his master's degree in social work.

———⚬❦⚬———

PLEASE TELL ME YOUR FULL NAME, YOUR BIRTHDAY, AND YOUR AGE.

My name is Tim. I was born in 1975. I'm twenty-six.

WHERE WERE YOU BORN?

In Mexico.

HOW OLD WERE YOU WHEN YOU WERE ADOPTED?

I was about six to eight weeks old when I was adopted.

DO YOU KNOW THE ETHNIC BACKGROUNDS OF YOUR BIOLOGICAL PARENTS? ARE THEY BOTH FROM MEXICO?

Oh, yes. They were both Mexican. I definitely am Mexican. No question about it.

WERE YOU ADOPTED THROUGH AN AGENCY?

I was adopted through an agency in ——— and I was actually one of the first adoptees that they had. The Bishop of Mexico, according to my mom, had been working really hard to get children adopted from Mexico to the United States and this adoption agency was their first go at international adoptions. I was actually the sixth child to be adopted from them and from Mexico. I don't know how many have come out afterwards. I have seen some statistics from the State Department, and they seem to be fairly low numbers ever since. I don't know why that is. I have been given various reasons why children are not adopted in larger numbers from Mexico, but honestly I don't know.

WERE YOU LIVING IN AN ORPHANAGE OR IN A FOSTER HOME WHEN YOU WERE ADOPTED?

It was an orphanage.

DID YOUR ADOPTIVE PARENTS TRAVEL TO MEXICO TO PICK YOU UP?

They did. They traveled to Mexico to get me. They stayed there for about three weeks while all the information was being processed.

WHAT ARE YOUR ADOPTIVE PARENTS' RACIAL BACKGROUNDS?

They are Caucasian. My mother is Polish, and my father is German.

DO YOU HAVE ANY BROTHERS OR SISTERS?

I have one younger brother who is twenty-four. He is Caucasian and he was born in and adopted from Chicago.

CAN YOU TELL ME A LITTLE BIT MORE ABOUT JUST YOUR RELATIONSHIP WITH YOUR PARENTS GROWING UP? DISCUSSING ADOPTION ISSUES, WHAT KINDS OF THINGS DID YOU TALK TO THEM ABOUT REGARDING YOUR ADOPTION AND YOUR BROTHER'S ADOPTION?

As a child, I always knew I was adopted, even before I knew what the word was. In fact, my mom says I used to run around the neighborhood and tell people I was adopted. I didn't even know what it meant, but I ran around telling everyone "I'm adopted" and my parents definitely made me feel special because of that, even though I didn't understand what it meant. My mom explained to me later that she wanted no one else to tell me. They wanted to be the first to tell me I was adopted. They made it very, very clear from the beginning, even when I didn't understand what the word meant, to tell me that I was adopted. And then later when I had questions about it, my parents would sit down and explain to me. The way my mom always tells the story about getting me—I just love it. Even as a kid she would tell the story about them coming to Mexico and getting me, and she had all these little stories about being in Mexico and adopting me. I knew that it was a very special thing for them and a very special experience for them, and so I thought, well, I must be special. So I automatically just assumed it was the greatest thing. And I had no problem with it. You know, I didn't even notice that I was any different from my parents. I really didn't. A lot of my parents' friends also adopted kids, and so it wasn't totally foreign to me to know someone who was adopted.

SO THEY WERE VERY OPEN ABOUT ADOPTION ISSUES AND ABOUT TALKING ABOUT IT AND EXPLAINING IT TO YOU?

Pretty much. Although, I didn't really ask a lot of questions. I really didn't know what to ask. So I just went with the flow and thought, "This is how it is."

WHAT ABOUT YOUR BROTHER? DO YOU THINK HE HAD A SIMILAR EXPERI-ENCE GROWING UP, TALKING ABOUT ADOPTION ISSUES?

I think he did. I think we both had very similar experiences. We're very different personality types. In fact, my brother and I have only talked about adoption once, literally. My brother, in many ways he acknowledges his adoption and what not. I am amazed at the way he has adjusted. From what I know, he seems to have adjusted really well. The only time my brother and I really talked about it was when I asked him if he wanted to search for his birth parents, and he said no, that he was just fine with everything.

IS HE A TRANSRACIAL ADOPTEE?

No, he is white. He doesn't look like my parents, but he is definitely Caucasian.

CAN YOU TELL ME ABOUT YOUR PARENTS, THEIR SCHOOLING AND THEIR WORK, THEIR BACKGROUNDS, HOW THEY WERE RAISED?

They were both raised pretty much in the same neighborhood, though they didn't know each other, on the West Side of Chicago. My mom grew up in a very Polish neighborhood and had a brother and a sister. My father has one brother and didn't graduate high school. Right now he is a foreman at a box company on the South Side. My mom graduated high school, didn't go to college, but she is currently a bookkeeper for an accounting company here in the suburbs.

DO YOU KNOW WHAT INFLUENCED YOUR PARENTS' DECISION TO ADOPT?

My mom can't have kids. They were trying to have kids for years, and my mom just couldn't. A couple of their friends had adopted through the agency that I was adopted through, and so they had heard about it. Then they just decided to go with that because their friends had gone through there. And they thought, well why not go through there too. And then they just happened to mention that they were starting these adoptions in Mexico. Actually, my mom said that before the prospect of me came up, they were thinking of adopting from Korea because they had known other people who had adopted children from Korea. They were looking into that About that time they heard of this agency that happened to be starting a program in Mexico.

IT SOUNDS LIKE YOUR PARENTS RECEIVED A LOT OF SUPPORT FROM THEIR FRIENDS, THEN?

Definitely.

WHAT ABOUT THEIR FAMILIES AND EXTENDED FAMILY? WERE THEY SUPPORTIVE AS WELL?

Oh, yeah. They all knew how badly my mom wanted children, and so they were all very supportive. In fact, my parents couldn't afford to adopt me. It was extremely expensive, and so my grandma actually helped to pay because it was very expensive to go down there. I probably wouldn't have been adopted if it weren't for my grandma.

DID YOUR PARENTS HAVE ANY FRIENDS WHO WERE MEXICAN OR MEXICAN AMERICAN OR LATINO?

No, they didn't.

HAVE YOU BEEN BACK TO MEXICO? HAVE YOUR PARENTS BEEN BACK TO MEXICO SINCE YOUR ADOPTION?

Interesting. My parents have gone to Mexico on vacation. In fact, my grandparents and a couple of my mother's siblings and their kids. I haven't really been ready to go back to Mexico, so I opted out of the two trips that they did go on. They want to go on the typical vacation—Puerto Vallarta, Acapulco. I think they are great areas, but I don't think that is the real Mexico. I want to go to the Chiapas. I really want to go with a knowledge of the language and with a better knowledge of the culture and the history so that I can really appreciate it on a different level then just going there on vacation. So I opted not to go. I'm getting to a place in my life where I'm getting ready to go. I will go back, but when I feel more comfortable with it. I'm not at that spot yet, but I'm getting there.

DID YOUR BROTHER GO WITH YOUR PARENTS?

He did. He went with my parents both times.

WHILE YOUR PARENTS WERE DECIDING TO ADOPT, DID THEY LEARN ABOUT MEXICAN CULTURE?

No. They didn't.

IF YOU GET MARRIED, WOULD IT BE IMPORTANT FOR YOU TO MARRY SOMEONE WITH A SIMILAR BACKGROUND?

It is for me, actually. That has been something more recently for me, definitely. I have dated Latinos, and there is definitely something that I feel that I get from that relationship that I don't get when I date other ethnic groups. I think part of it is that when I date Latinos, they specifically know the situation, and they want to introduce me to the culture, so that has been amazing.

DO YOU FEEL LIKE YOU CAN TALK ABOUT ADOPTION ISSUES AND HAVE YOU BEEN ABLE TO WITH PEOPLE THAT YOU'VE DATED?

Yes, although, of course, it depends on the length of the relationship, how in-depth it goes. Obviously, being adopted is a huge part of my life, and it's important to me, obviously, for a partner to understand this important part of my life. But people tend to believe that adoption is a taboo topic, that they can't talk to you about it, and they think they are going to make you cry.

DO YOUR PARENTS HAVE A PREFERENCE FOR A PARTNER FOR YOU? WOULD THEY PREFER YOU TO BE WITH SOMEONE WHO IS LATINO OR ARE THEY SUPPORTIVE OF WHOMEVER?

Well, it's interesting. They are supportive of whatever, but because of some of the things we have experienced as a transracial family, they want me not to be so race or ethnicity conscious. I think, in a way, they feel, although they don't blatantly say to me, that I'm sort of being discriminatory or racist about that. And they did say, "Well, you should love whoever you love." That's always their response, and I agree with that, but I think they are missing a part of why it would be important to me.

SO WHAT ARE SOME OF YOUR EXPERIENCES WITH INTERRACIAL OR TRANSRACIAL DATING?

For example, when I date Latinos, and when I go and see their family lives and traditions and the way they celebrate their culture, they do it in a way that I obviously haven't experienced, so for me to experience that is just incredibly awesome. I want to incorporate my Latino heritage into my everyday life, and I want someone who can appreciate and understand that, and also do it with me.

DO YOU THINK YOU'LL HAVE CHILDREN?

Sometimes. I don't feel that I am parental material, and maybe that's because of my age. I see what an awesome responsibility it is, so in many ways I think I couldn't provide what would be the best for a child. But at the same time, being adopted, I definitely feel almost a responsibility to adopt. There is an added complication because I am gay. I also feel that being adopted is enough to deal with. I look at what I experienced, and it was difficult enough for me just to be adopted and having people make comments and stare the way they did just because I was of a different ethnicity than my parents. I know people do it, but I think it would be really, really difficult, and in a way maybe be unfair for the adoptee. I've wanted to give back in another way. Maybe I can give back in another way to the adoptive community by being a social worker and helping people go through the bumps they go through just being adopted. Maybe that would be a better option because I think, honestly, the things that I've had to go through and the experience of being transracial and having to deal with that would be just over the top.

IF LAWS START CHANGING AND PEOPLE START SHIFTING THEIR PERCEPTIONS OF THE GAY COMMUNITY, DO YOU THINK THAT WILL HAVE ANY INFLUENCE ON YOUR DECISION TO HAVE KIDS?

Yeah. A long way to go. I think it would, but it is something that I feel would take generations to do. But I do know people who have done it, and the children are amazingly well-adjusted, so in a way I think maybe it could work. Right now, I'm just sort of skeptical.

WHAT DO YOU THINK IT IS ABOUT THOSE FAMILIES WHO MADE IT WORK?

I would say that from the families I know, I would say it mostly has to do with family environment and where they live. Everyone I know who has adopted—they live in very diverse communities in Chicago where it's not a big deal. Now, if you did that in the lily-white suburbs out here, you would have to deal with a lot of criticism. You know, it is amazing how people often treat people, even innocent kids. It has not been perfect for them, but I think that they have been able to have a better experience living in a city like Chicago than they would in a small suburb.

WHAT ABOUT YOUR EDUCATION? HOW MANY YEARS OF SCHOOLING HAVE YOU HAD?.

I have a BA, and I am finishing up a thesis for an MA.

WHAT IS YOUR MASTER'S PROGRAM?

It is sociology, and so is my bachelor's.

CAN YOU TELL ME A LITTLE BIT ABOUT THE SCHOOLS YOU WENT TO BEFORE COLLEGE?

I went to Catholic school my entire life, which is probably the reason I don't go to church anymore. A lot of it was my grandma's pushing, but my mom also believed in it. So, I went to a very, very small Catholic school about ten minutes from my house that had about thirty-five kids to a grade. It was very small. I grew up with the same kids my entire life. And then I went to a high school that only had about 515 students. That was in the next town over. In both schools, I was the only minority. It was when I entered school that I really started to have issues with my ethnicity. I started dealing with the difficulties that a lot of transracial families have.

COULD YOU APPROXIMATE AT WHAT AGE YOU REALLY STARTED TO EXAMINE THESE THINGS?

Consciously, I can remember kindergarten. I can remember people pointing out, because I was the only one, that I was different as far as my skin color. I had people asking me, "Are you black?" People would ask me all these questions, and I didn't understand it. And I ran home crying one day and asked, "Mom, am I black?"

THAT CAN BE SO CONFUSING.

It is very confusing. Especially when you are the only one. I was really thrown for a loop by it.

DID THAT SHIFT THROUGHOUT ELEMENTARY SCHOOL OR MIDDLE SCHOOL OR HIGH SCHOOL, OR AS YOU CAME TO KNOW YOUR CLASSMATES?

Yeah. I would say, I think people generally liked me. As a kid I was a really good student. I think because I was adopted, I always wanted to be really, really good. But at the same time, I did have this little streak in me where I would say funny things, and I did really good imitations of the teachers, so that made me popular.

WHO WERE SOME OF YOUR FRIENDS THEN?

All of my friends until really recently have been white. And throughout my entire life, I have had two friends in particular, two white friends, who live in my neighborhood.

So, going back to the children at school, did they ask you about your family and why you don't look like your parents? Or was it more just typical childhood teasing, you know, pointing fingers, laughing?

No, I wouldn't say they asked until we had functions where my family would come as a family unit. People would see us, and you'd get the stares and the gawks and the looks, and then people would ask us questions. Even as a kid, we used to be out as a family and you could hear people whisper, "That's not her kid" or "How can that be their kid?" My mom even had someone ask her, "How could you adopt a Mexican?"

Can you tell me a little bit about the neighborhoods where you grew up?

I live in a suburb that is all white, all Caucasian. I think I am the only Mexican. I have always grown up with just white people, and in fact, I just assumed that I was white. I didn't even realize I was different until other people pointed it out.

What age was that?

I would say in kindergarten because I remember being at a playground, and older kids in the neighborhood would say things to me like, "My mom says that you can't be your mom's kid," and I didn't understand it. I mean, I knew I was adopted, but I didn't really know what it meant. Then I'd go back and ask my mom, and she would say, "Well, you're adopted, that's why." And so that was when I really noticed—it was when I started getting into school, and I got more questions and more questions and more questions.

What questions did you ask your parents?

I would ask, of course, "Why didn't my birth mother keep me? What did I do wrong? Did I do anything wrong? I don't understand why you would give up your baby." My mom used to explain that my birth mother couldn't afford to keep me. "We wanted a baby, and we wanted to have you as our baby." And I always asked, "Will my mother come and get me?"

Did your family do anything special to celebrate Mexican culture and holidays or Latino culture?

They did not. And in retrospect, I can't blame them because they don't know. Obviously this doesn't come with a handbook, and they really didn't know. But I really wish that I had had it incorporated somehow into my childhood because I have this void in me, this cultural void, and for a while when I was growing up, I wanted to forget about it, forget about Mexico and live as an American. But obviously I would keep getting these questions from people, and even when I would encounter other Mexicans, I would be very inquisitive about them. For example, I would go to neighborhoods that are Mexican. When I'd go through them, I would be really perky and really interested in what was there, and so I always had an interest. I just didn't understand how to make it a part of my life, because it never was.

HAVE YOU FOUND A WAY TO INCORPORATE IT IN SOME MANNER RIGHT NOW?

I have. I am in the process of it. One interesting thing is that as a teenager in high school, I went through a brief period where I tried to reconnect with my Mexican heritage, and I would volunteer at some Latino organizations. The thing is, I never really felt totally a part of their culture because I felt like they didn't consider me Mexican. And so here I am trying to reconnect. Another thing is that Mexicans in particular don't consider me Mexican because I don't speak Spanish. That is a problem even for Americans who are of Mexican heritage here. If you don't speak Spanish, there tends to be some divide between those two groups. On top of that, I don't look Mexican. In fact, I look almost Asian. My mom says that it's because I have a lot of indigenous features. They believe that somewhere in my heritage, there is Aztec. Mexicans don't see me as being really Mexican. In fact, I oftentimes get more Filipinos who think I'm Filipino than I get Mexicans thinking I'm Mexican.

DID YOU HAVE ANY LATINO OR MEXICAN ROLE MODELS GROWING UP?

To be totally honest, I knew nothing about the culture. In fact, there came a point in my life where as a kid, my mom would say, "You're from Mexico," and then I would be interested in seeing things that represent Mexico. I would oftentimes turn on the TV as a kid, and I would watch Spanish TV. Unfortunately, the representations on Spanish TV aren't really all the best, and obviously I didn't understand what they were saying. I was conscious of seeing the darker skinned Mexicans always being maids. I was conscious of that even as a kid. And on top of that, when I would encounter Mexicans here, they were always cutting the lawn or being the maid, or on TV they were always being arrested for doing drugs. So in many ways, I started to equate being Mexican with being bad, so I tried to shy away from it for a long time. And then I would try to reconnect. I tried to reconnect in high school, and then I found myself not feeling accepted by Mexicans. So then I just completely wanted to not have anything to do with my Mexican heritage.

CAN YOU TELL ME A LITTLE ABOUT YOUR EXTENDED FAMILY? DO YOU FEEL LIKE YOU WERE ACCEPTED BY THEM?

For the most part. With my family, I do feel accepted. But there are some distant relatives, and this would make me mad when I was a kid, who would say derogatory things about Mexicans. I would comment that I thought it was inappropriate. This happened primarily in high school. And then they would say, "Well, we don't see you as being one of them." My aunts and uncles would say things like, "We don't consider you one of them."

YOU'RE THE EXCEPTION.

Yeah. I even get that sometimes in the neighborhood. There are some parents, and sometimes I will hear them saying—and sometimes I think they don't even realize I'm there—some derogatory things about Mexicans. I will call them on it because of my personality, and they'll say, "Well, we don't see you as one of them."

CAN YOU TALK A LITTLE BIT ABOUT YOUR ADOLESCENCE AND WHETHER YOU WENT THROUGH ANY PARTICULARLY DIFFICULT TIMES?

No. I was a very good kid. I think this actually stems back to the fact that I'm adopted. As a little kid, I used to kind of fear that they would get rid of me. Even though my parents never gave me any indication that that was the case, I still felt like it was a possibility if it happened to me once. I don't know why that was. My parents have been the most loving and supportive parents I can imagine, but at the same time it was always sort of there in the back of my head. So because of that, I wanted to be the best kid I could be. I got really good grades and never screwed around or did anything like that. And, in fact, if anything, when I started to come to terms with my sexuality and who I am, I felt a lot of guilt, that I somehow disappointed them in that of all the kids they could adopt, they get the gay one.

WERE THEY PRETTY ACCEPTING OF YOUR SEXUALITY?

They were very accepting, yes. In fact, I am so surprised at how accepting and incredibly supportive they are.

WAS THERE A POINT WHEN YOU TOLD THEM, OR DO YOU THINK THEY KNEW AS YOU WERE REALIZING IT YOURSELF?

Yeah, they knew, but my mom said she didn't want to. She said she suspected, but obviously wasn't going to make it an issue or bring it up unless I did. But I definitely felt a lot of guilt because I thought of all the kids they could adopt—you know. I felt very guilty about that. That was in high school. To overcompensate for that, I got really good grades, and I did really well.

WOULD YOU SAY THAT BEING ADOPTED IS HOW YOU DEFINE YOURSELF?

It is a big part of who I am because I've made more of an effort to find out and to examine my adopted self than anything else.

HAVE YOU EVER BEEN INTERESTED IN SEARCHING FOR YOUR BIRTH PARENTS OR LEARNING ABOUT THEM?

I was interested as a teenager in finding them, but I felt a lot of guilt about doing so and never did. Now I'm at a point where I'm content with not searching. I understand people who do, but for me, I love my adopted parents so much that it doesn't weigh on me. It is not something I feel that I have to do, but I do feel that I have to reconnect with my Mexican culture.

WOULD YOUR PARENTS BE SUPPORTIVE IF YOU DECIDED TO SEARCH?

They would be. They would never dare tell me not to, but I feel they would be hurt. There was a time in college where I wanted to. I was really struggling with understanding my heritage, and I wanted to change my last name. I could see on my mom's face. She told me, "I understand," but at the same time I could tell she was a little bit hurt, and I could tell she was trying not to show me she was hurt. I struggled with that, and in the end really realized this is who I am, Tim ———, not my birth last name. So I am happy with that now.

ARE THEY SUPPORTIVE OF YOUR LEARNING MORE ABOUT MEXICAN CULTURE AND RECONNECTING?

They told me they understand, but I don't think that they do because I just don't think they can understand what it is like to be a minority in this country. They've grown up American their whole lives. They don't have this ethnic heritage; they didn't grow up with it. They think I should probably be a happy old American, and I am for the most part, but in a way this is important for me. It is imprinted on my skin, and I look at the way Mexicans are—their position in our society. I think it is important for me to reconnect because it is so imprinted on my skin. It's in my blood and I have to have it. Part of the reason why I did that fellowship was because I really wanted the opportunity to connect with other Latinos who were in a similar position as me. When I went on my fellowship this last year, I really had an incredible time with the other fellows. They embraced me in a way I haven't had Latinos do. All of them were Mexican, fifteen of us were Mexican, and then five were other Latinos. The way they just embraced me and taught me about Mexican culture was amazing for me. Actually, my mom knows a lot of the things that I learned and is so happy for me because at the end, I wrote her a really nice card saying, "Thank you for being supportive of this and understanding. I learned more about myself than I ever have." In a way I know that they don't understand it, but they are supportive of it.

WHEN YOU WENT TO COLLEGE, WHAT WAS THAT LIKE?

I went to a small college that was primarily white and where I was actually one of the few Hispanics again.

HOW DO YOU DIFFERENTIATE HISPANIC FROM LATINO?

Oh, I sort of use them both the same, but there is a difference. Hispanic refers to anyone who speaks Spanish, and Latino is specifically someone from Latin America. I've always used the word Hispanic, and when I was on the fellowship everyone explained to me that it is the word white people use. No one who is actually Mexican calls himself Hispanic.

ANOTHER QUESTION I WANTED TO ASK YOU IS IN REGARDS TO THE NATIONAL ASSOCIATION OF BLACK SOCIAL WORKERS. BACK IN THE 1970S THE PRESIDENT SAID THAT—HE WAS TALKING, OF COURSE, ABOUT BLACK CHILDREN ADOPTEES—HE SAID THAT "BLACK CHILDREN BELONG PHYSICALLY, PSYCHOLOGICALLY, AND CULTURALLY IN BLACK FAMILIES IN ORDER THAT THEY RECEIVE THE TOTAL SENSE OF THEMSELVES AND DEVELOP A SOUND PROJECTION OF THEIR FUTURE." DO YOU HAVE A RESPONSE IN REGARD TO YOUR OWN ADOPTION EXPERIENCE?

I think if I was adopted by a Mexican family, I probably wouldn't have had to go through a lot of the cultural identity crisis that I've had. But saying that, I wouldn't trade my adoptive parents for the world. I absolutely adore them more than you can ever think. And I think in many ways, our experiences sort of transcend race and racial categories. So I agree with that statement to a point. There are things that my adoptive parents can't give me, but does that mean they can't be supportive and help me get that in another way? No. My parents have been very supportive in helping me. Mexican families who are native in America don't adopt children from orphanages in Mexico, so practically speaking, I would like to see children get adopted, period. If it happens to be by a white family, then so be it, as long as the family loves them. In a way, I agree with the statement, but I also don't.

DO YOU THINK THAT GROWING UP WITHIN A TRANSRACIAL FAMILY HAS PREPARED YOU FOR THE RACISM THAT IS STILL SOMEWHAT PREVALENT AGAINST LATINOS OR MEXICANS?

Yeah. I think I definitely had to learn from a young age how to deal with questions, how to deal with stares, and how to deal with people's perceptions.

In a way, I think it does make you a stronger person. It really made me think a lot about who I am and who I wanted to be and who I don't want to be. I don't want to be someone who's ignorant and racist in the way I've experienced it from certain people. So you know, it's definitely been an experience.

DO YOU GENERALLY FEEL ACCEPTED BY CAUCASIANS?

I feel accepted on certain levels, but I don't feel a part of the white majority. I definitely feel that the perceptions and the things people say make me feel I am not fully American. Even though I am American and white and I've grown up that way, I don't feel as though I've been fully accepted. I don't feel Latino, and in a way I don't think I ever can be fully Latino, fully Mexican. So I realize that I am sort of in my own unique spot. I've come to embrace my history in a way I never have before. I've come to realize the uniqueness that I have and the special place in history that I have. In a way, I feel that I understand the way white people perceive Mexicans the way they do, and in a way I feel like I almost understand why Mexicans perceive white people the way they do.

I THINK YOU'VE COME A TREMENDOUS WAY IN INTEGRATING EVERY ASPECT OF YOUR BACKGROUND.

Well, I'm trying.

DO YOU THINK IT'S POSSIBLE FOR TRANSRACIAL ADOPTEES TO COME TO A REAL FIRM CONCLUSION AS TO WHO THEY ARE AND WHAT THEIR IDENTITIES ARE?

I think you definitely can. I think it is still a work in progress. But I think it takes time and support and a lot of self-searching. One of the reasons I want to be a social worker is to help people go through this stuff, so that they can get to a place where they can embrace their history and who they are. I really feel as though I've come to a point in my life where I am content with my situation. I mean, there are still some issues I have.

I'M GLAD TO HEAR THAT. NOT A LOT OF PEOPLE SAY THAT THEY ARE PROUD OF THEMSELVES.

I have nothing to hide, and I'm proud of who I am. It's definitely been a process getting there, but now I feel such a strong need to give back and help other people.

WHAT IS IN THE BEST INTEREST OF A BIRACIAL OR TRANSRACIAL CHILD, IN YOUR OPINION? WHAT DO YOU THINK ARE THE BEST CRITERIA FOR AN ADOPTIVE HOME?

Well, number one, a loving family. People who are sincere and who want to adopt. I think for the most part, you get that with adoptive parents. My parents had to go through a lot to adopt me, so they really wanted a kid. I understand there are some cases that go through that aren't good. There are some adoptions that aren't good. But I think number one is a loving family. With that said, I think my parents had no idea that some of these issues were going to come up. My parents had no idea that they would get the stares and the comments from people. Adoption doesn't come with a handbook and neither does transracial adoption, so they were really dealing with something that was totally unexpected, that the adoption agency didn't prepare them for. Through it all, I think my parents have been very supportive and been great with helping me getting through it—more than I have with them.

HOW MUCH OF THE CHILD'S HERITAGE SHOULD BE INCORPORATED INTO THEIR LIFE BY THEIR ADOPTIVE PARENTS?

I think it should be incorporated quite a bit, but at the same time, my parents don't know how to raise me Mexican. And I don't know if it's fair to expect them to do so. At the same time, I think also there is the fear of tokenizing Mexican culture. That isn't productive, either. For example, my grandma would go to Mexico, and she'd come back, and she'd bring me like those little marionette puppets thinking that I would want it. I just didn't understand what Mexican culture was other than puppets and tacos and whatever, and that doesn't help either. So there is a danger, I think, in doing that. There has to be a better way to incorporate culture into a child's life. I think doing it by just giving them little tokens of their culture is bad as well.

ARE YOU GLAD THAT YOU WERE ADOPTED?

Very. Yeah. I mean people always make it a point to point that out to you. "Oh, you're so lucky." People just don't know that there's more to it than that. And they just think, "You should be so happy that you're adopted." Well, yes, in one way, but there's a heck of a lot more to it than that, thank you.

IF YOU WERE TO BE ADOPTED ALL OVER AGAIN INTO A HOME THAT WAS AS LOVING AND STABLE AND JUST AS WONDERFUL AS YOURS, DO YOU THINK YOU WOULD OBJECTIVELY PREFER TO HAVE BEEN ADOPTED BY LATINO PARENTS?

I think it would have been very important. Now the guilt comes in because you don't want to say anything bad about your parents, but yeah, in a way I feel it probably would have been. It probably would have been more of an ideal situation. But at the same time, obviously, I love my parents, and I am content with my situation.

19

TERESA DONIGER

GENDER:	Female
AGE AT TIME OF INTERVIEW:	30
RACE:	Born in U.S. and is Black-Hispanic-German
MARITAL STATUS:	Single
OCCUPATION:	Researcher, Northrop Grumman IT, Health Solutions and Services (June 2003)

Born in Washington, D.C., Teresa was adopted when she was one month old. The Jewish American woman who adopted her also adopted an older baby of Eurasian descent. Teresa explained "it was very rare at that time, for a woman to adopt children as a single mother, so it was really a sign of her determination." Her mother was the second single woman in D.C. ever to adopt children. When Teresa was two, her mother was killed in a car accident, and the two girls were then raised by their adoptive mother's sister and brother-in-law. Though they never legally adopted her, she considered them to be her parents. Born in 1917 and 1914, they were "more like grandparents in terms of age" and had four older biological children, all of whom were ten to twenty years older.

When Teresa was young, she had other friends who were adopted, and they formed an "adoptees' club." As a child, her parents and godparents tried to introduce Teresa and her sister to Asian, African American, and Hispanic culture and history. While her parents didn't necessarily go out of their way to make "cultural events…a regular kind of thing," these things were available. Growing up, Teresa's parents and others told her that she was "very special" and that she was adopted because her biological parents wanted the best for her. However, as she grew older, she began to wonder if she "may have actually been adopted because [her] parents didn't care . . . and didn't give a shit about [her]."

Teresa's childhood was spent mostly in a predominantly white neighborhood in upper northwest D.C. Most of her friends were white and/or Jewish, and for the most part she wasn't teased by or alienated from the other children in the neighborhood. She attended public schools up through junior high school, but her mother pulled her out so that she could attend a private school because she began to feel some tension and discomfort in the middle of junior high school around race and identity issues. At the primarily black public school she attended, she experienced difficulty fitting in as a biracial student. She felt more comfortable after transferring to what would end up being a predominantly Jewish private high school.

When Teresa turned twenty-one, she opened her adoption file and learned that she had birth siblings on her biological father's side. Although she "hadn't intended to meet anybody," her birth father mailed a letter to the adoption agency indicating his interest in meeting her. When Teresa opened the letter, it contained a "photo of himself and his second wife and their children." She immediately saw the resemblance between herself and her African American father and one of her biological sisters in particular.

Between 1995 and 2000, the same year of this interview, both of Teresa's parents passed away. In examining how the losses in her life have affected her as a person, she described herself as "somebody who as a part of [her] personality carries signs of loss and abandonment." She has found it difficult to determine which losses have changed her life "the most profoundly"—her sense of abandonment from being placed for adoption, her adoptive mother's death, her father's slow deterioration which lasted thirteen years after a stroke, or her mother's death.

Teresa has a BA from a college in California, where she designed her own degree to include "anthropology, sociology, Latin American studies and African American studies, and a little bit of literature and African religion." She also received her master's degree from NYU in Latin American and Caribbean Studies. Teresa is still unable to find "one particular race or culture that best meshes with [her]" or that she identifies with the most and has even felt like "a sort of spectacle" at times. She has begun to write about her life and the losses she has experienced and recently published an article entitled, "My Mother and Father."

—————— ⊗⊗⊗ ——————

CAN YOU TELL ME YOUR FULL NAME?

It's Teresa Elena Kate Doniger

HOW OLD ARE YOU?

Thirty.

AND WHERE WERE YOU BORN?

Here in Washington, D.C.

HOW OLD WERE YOU WHEN YOU WERE ADOPTED?

About a month.

WHERE WERE YOU LIVING BEFORE YOU WERE ADOPTED?

I think I was placed with a very short-term foster care family in Washington.

DO YOU HAVE ANY INFORMATION ABOUT THE FAMILY?

No.

AND WHAT IS YOUR RACIAL/ETHNIC BACKGROUND?

My background, as far as I know, on the mother's side is Hispanic and German, and on my father's side Afro-American. And I've been told I may also have some Mexican heritage. And at some point I was also told that my biological father was Puerto Rican, but then when I was twenty-one, I had my file unsealed, and it turned out that my biological father is not Puerto Rican. He is African American.

WHAT WAS IT LIKE FINDING THAT OUT AFTER HAVING ASSUMED OTHERWISE?

I think that for a lot of my life I kind of felt that my identity was pretty fluid, because I didn't really know what it meant to be Puerto Rican, because I didn't know anybody who was Puerto Rican. I mean, I always identified as having some kind of black heritage, some kind of Hispanic heritage, but I didn't really know what it would have meant to be Puerto Rican per se, so it didn't really make much difference.

AND WHAT ARE YOUR ADOPTIVE PARENTS RACIAL BACKGROUNDS?

My adoptive mother's cultural heritage is Jewish, and my adoptive father's cultural heritage is basically Anglo-Saxon.

DO YOU HAVE ANY ADOPTED SIBLINGS?

I was adopted with one other sister, but she is not my biological sister. She is Eurasian. She is half Chinese and half white.

GROWING UP, DID THE TWO OF YOU GET ALONG WELL?

Yeah, we were very close. I mean we had some sibling rivalry, you know, and we had our fights, but we were always pretty close, and we are still very close.

WOULD YOU CHARACTERIZE YOUR RELATIONSHIP WITH HER AS ANYTHING DIFFERENT THAN ANY OTHER SIBLING RELATIONSHIP?

For the most part, no. I think our bond is closer in some ways than many sisters because we have been through a lot together. We were actually adopted by a woman who died when we were young, and I think that loss made our bond a lot stronger than most people. What happened was that a woman named Joan Doniger adopted us, and Joan was a single mother. She was Jewish, but she died when I was two and my sister Kiyo was four. So the mother and father that I was just talking about—they are actually our aunt and uncle, and they raised us. When Joan died, her sister Naomi and her brother-in-law George—they were the ones who raised us from when I was two until the time we grew up.

DO YOU CONSIDER THEM YOUR PARENTS?

Yes. And they had four kids of their own, so we came to think of their kids as our sisters and brothers even though they were technically our cousins.

WERE YOU LEGALLY ADOPTED?

We were not legally adopted by them. They were our guardians.

CAN YOU TALK A LITTLE BIT ABOUT YOUR BROTHERS AND SISTERS?

We still consider them our brothers and sisters, but they are almost more like aunts and uncles agewise because when we moved in with them, they were already anywhere between ten to twenty years older than us. Now the youngest of them is forty-one. The oldest is fifty-three. So we're close with them, but their lives are very different than ours. All of them have kids. My eldest brother's kids are almost as old as I am.

ARE YOU CLOSE TO THEM?

Yes, we're pretty close to them. Yes and no. In some ways we're close, in other ways we're not that close because our lives are so different, and we live all over the place. Some are in Georgia, some are in Charlottesville, some are in Connecticut, and one of my brothers lives in Bethesda, so I see him and his wife pretty regularly. But I am not as close with them as I am with my sister Kiyo because we have a lot more in common, and we are just closer in general.

WERE YOU EVER ABLE TO TALK TO YOUR OLDER SIBLINGS ABOUT ADOPTION ISSUES?

Sometimes. It doesn't really end up happening because they just don't really relate. Recently, I was thinking that I might talk with them about some stuff because as I get older, I feel more and more disconnected from them, and I feel like I maybe should talk to them about that. At some point, I may do some kind of search for my birth parents because I feel I need to know where did I come from, and if I were to do that, I would probably need a lot of support from them so that I don't feel like I'm just kind of dangling out there, you know.

DO YOU KNOW IF YOU HAVE ANY BIRTH SIBLINGS?

I know I have birth siblings on my biological father's side. When I was twenty-one, my sister and I did open our files.

DID SHE OPEN HERS AT THE SAME TIME?

Yes, we had them opened at the same time. She did that because she had wanted to contact her biological parents. I wasn't ready to contact my biological parents, but I decided that I wanted to find medical information, medical history information, and what happened was ironic. In order to get medical history, since when my file was opened there wasn't any information that would have given the medical history, the adoption agency decided to contact the parents. They didn't find any leads to the biological mother, so they contacted the biological father, and ironically my biological father responded and was interested in contacting me. But my sister was the one who wanted to contact her parents. Her biological father was contacted, but said he didn't want to make contact, and please don't try to contact the biological mother because this would be a total nightmare for her. So my sister was really bummed out because she was the one who really wanted this to happen. Meanwhile, I didn't want any contact and my biological father was the one who was like, "Oh, yes, love to meet you."

YOUR SISTER WAS ADOPTED FROM WHERE?

She was also adopted in D.C.

DOES SHE KNOW HER CULTURAL BACKGROUND?

She's Chinese and white.

GO BACK TO YOU AND YOUR BIRTH FATHER.

Well, it was kind of crazy, because I wasn't trying to meet anybody. I just wanted to know my history, and then I get back this information that this guy wants to meet me. So what I did was—I said, "No, I'm not ready to meet anyone." And a little while later he responded by sending a letter to the adoption agency and the adoption agency said, "Are you interested in accepting this letter?" And I said, "Ok, fine, I'll look at his letter." And it turned out that with the letter he sent a photo of himself and his second wife and their children. So that's why I know I have siblings. And I think he has a couple of daughters from his first wife, and then he has one child from his second wife.

HAVE YOU EVER THOUGHT ABOUT CONTACTING THEM (HIS DAUGHTERS)?

I wouldn't contact them separate from him. I mean if I were going to contact anybody, I would contact him. They're young. One is in college, but the rest of them are younger than that.

CAN YOU TELL ME MORE ABOUT YOUR ADOPTIVE PARENTS?

Well, they're not alive anymore. They both died within the past five years. They were older. They were born in 1914 and 1917. So they were quite old. They were more like grandparents in terms of age. They were at Cornell in the '30s. They met there, fell in love, and then my father was an economist and my mother was interested in agriculture, and she went to the agricultural school at Cornell. They had pretty interesting careers. They were both very serious and pretty political, and they were also both kind of artists, and they were very progressive, very liberal, very strong democrats.

DO YOU REMEMBER A LOT ABOUT JOAN DONIGER?

No. I was too young. I was two years old when she died.

My dad said that when I was little, I used to say to him, "Why did mommy leave me and not say goodbye?" But I don't really know how my sense of loss manifested itself in any other ways. Or trauma—like I don't know what signs of trauma I displayed. I don't really know.

You don't look back and feel a pervasive sense of loss?

Well, I think it has probably affected me pretty profoundly. Because I know that I'm somebody who has in my personality signs of loss and abandonment, but I think a lot of adopted people have that, so I don't know to what extent Joan's loss complicated that, I mean I am sure it did, but I don't know to what extent.

First I was adopted, then I lost Joan, and then when I was twelve my dad had a massive stroke, and I saw him have the stroke. I thought he was going to die, so that's another loss. And I saw him basically deteriorating from when I was twelve until I was twenty-five, which is when he died. I was always worried that he was going to die. So that's an ongoing sense of loss or worrying about losing somebody. And then my mom became sick, and again I was worrying that I was going to lose somebody. So I've almost always worried that I was going to lose somebody. It's hard to say which part of the losses that I've experienced in my life have affected me the most profoundly.

Do you know what influenced your parents' decision to adopt?

Well, Joan, I think, basically just wanted to have kids and she wasn't married, and I guess she pretty much knew she wasn't going to get married. So I think she just wanted to have kids. Everybody says that Joan was determined to have kids, and she decided she was going to do whatever it took to get kids. And one thing that's interesting about Joan is that in 1968, when she adopted Kiyo, it was very rare for a woman to adopt children as a single mother, so it was really a sign of her determination. She was supposedly the second (single) woman in all of D.C. to ever have adopted children. Apparently, the woman who was the first single woman to adopt here in D.C. is someone that I know. A family friend of my mother's knows this other woman; she's a black woman. She was the first one, and Joan was the second one.

What did she die of?

She was hit by a car. It was an accident.

Did your parents belong to any religious organizations?

No. We were not raised religious. We were baptized by a Unitarian minister, but we didn't even go to the Unitarian church. But Joan and the mother who raised us, Naomi, their cultural background was Jewish; but Joan, I think, identified more as Jewish than Naomi, who raised us. Naomi had basically abandoned her Jewish heritage.

Do you identify with any religious group right now?

Not really.

Are you married?

No.

When you think about a future partner, does race or culture or ethnicity play a part in that?

Yes, definitely. These days I kind of wonder about who or what kind of a partner is really going to work out with me because I date a lot of different kinds of guys. These days it seems like I've been dating Latino men and black men. I haven't dated a white guy in a while. It used to be that I dated mostly white guys. But for most of my life, I've been surrounded by white people. And I am attracted to all kinds of guys.

Regarding the people you have dated, have you been able to talk to them about adoption or have they been curious about your background?

Yeah, I mean pretty much anyone, whether it's someone that I'm dating or whether it's just a friend. Most people get curious. Most of them question when they find out what my background is, and I don't tend to have a problem talking about my background. Sometimes I do feed into the curiosity a little bit too much, and then I realize, "Oh, this is getting a little bit silly" because it is almost like I become this spectacle or something. But if I feel like it's an interesting, engaged kind of conversation, then I'm fine with it.

Has anyone that you've been dating ever really pressured you to acculturate more into their group?

Not too much. Sometimes people will make comments that make me feel that I should acculturate too much, but sometimes people will say things to make me feel like I'm too this or too that, like I'm too "bougie." Basically a lot has to do with class. They'll talk about how I'm too Ann Taylor or I'm too whatever. Or they'll tease me because I have good hair or about how I dress or the color of my skin, the fact that it is light. Or something about my eyes, or the way that I talk, the fact that I speak kind of white. They weren't necessarily pressuring me to acculturate, but they'll kind of criticize me for not being more something.

Do you think you might have children?

I think so. I don't know when.

How would you like for them to share your background and your culture?

I think that I would want them to share my background and culture, but it will be interesting because I will have to really think hard about what aspect of my culture and background are the most important, that I'd want them to share. Because like I said, I don't have a religious grounding, and I don't know exactly what my culture is. I mean my heritage is Hispanic and black and white, but I wasn't raised that way. So I can only expose them to a little bit of what I've learned. The cultural background that I've had has been basically some kind of white. But I don't even know what.

Do you think you might ever adopt?

That's a good question. My gut instinct is no because I think that from my experience it complicates one's life too much. And I don't think that I want to do that to somebody else. But at the same time, especially because there are so many children of color who are not being placed in families as readily as other children, I think that maybe I would feel like I was doing a good thing to adopt them.

Can you talk about your education and about how many years of schooling you've had? And what you've done afterwards?

I went all the way through high school, and I have a BA. My BA was a degree that I self-designed in something called intercultural studies where I basically put everything that I liked in my life together and made a degree. It was anthropology, sociology, Latin American Studies, African American studies, and a little bit of religion.

Where did you go to college?

I went to one of the Claremont colleges in California—they're a group of schools outside of L.A.

What graduate school did you go to?

NYU.

Can you talk a little bit about the student composition?

Scripps was pretty much white. Scripps was very small, only about 700 students. It's predominantly white, and the minorities are probably mostly Hispanic and Asian because that's what California is. Although it's funny because it was the first time that I had met a number of biracial people. That's where I made several friends who were biracial, and that's where I really kind of began to identify myself as black. I began to realize that I was comfortable with seeing myself as partly black. I still thought of myself also as Hispanic and white, but I was comfortable with seeing myself also as black.

WERE YOU UNCOMFORTABLE WITH THAT GROWING UP IN HIGH SCHOOL?

Not that much. I was kind of like, "Yeah, I know I'm part black." It wasn't really something that I dealt with easily, whereas in California it was like a positive thing. For some reason, in southern California it was much easier to be who I was. I felt more attractive; I just felt much more comfortable. Even now when I go to California, I feel much more comfortable with who I am. It's like people are much different there. I think California is more laid back.

WHEN YOU WERE APPLYING TO SCHOOLS AND HAD TO INDICATE YOUR RACE, WHAT DID YOU DO?

I think I always put Hispanic and black. On the 2000 census, I put everything. I put white, Hispanic and black.

CAN YOU TALK ABOUT THE NEIGHBORHOODS IN WHICH YOU GREW UP AND ABOUT SOME OF THE FRIENDS YOU HAD WHILE GROWING UP?

I grew up in a D.C. neighborhood. It's a neighborhood called Cleveland Park, and Cleveland Park is predominantly white. It used to be a lot more interesting in my opinion. It used to be you'd find more intellectual and kind of progressive types, more writers, artists, kind of like public interest lawyers. It's not like that now. . . . So I grew up around a lot of white families and my friends were pretty much white. It seemed like there were a lot of Jewish families. My best friend was Jewish, half Jewish, and we all went to the little elementary school just down the street. I went to the public school for junior high school, and then I went to private school for high school. But it was a pretty friendly, comfortable environment. My sister and I never felt uncomfortable.

SO YOU WERE NEVER TEASED OR ALIENATED?

No, not really. We had a couple of friends who were also biracial. Not adopted necessarily, but also biracial.

WHO WERE SOME OF YOUR CLOSEST FRIENDS IN HIGH SCHOOL?

The private school I went to was predominantly Jewish, and even though my mom doesn't identify with being Jewish, I think she had a feeling that maybe I would be more comfortable with that. She was right.

IN YOUR ADOLESCENCE, DID YOU GO THROUGH ANY SORT OF DRUG/ALCOHOL TIMES?

No. For some reason I wasn't really into that. I didn't rebel, and I didn't do anything reckless. The harmful things were much more internalized. I was depressed basically.

DID YOU EVER SEEK ANY SORT OF MENTAL HEALTH TREATMENT FOR THAT?

Well, unfortunately my mom tried to get me to see a psychologist at one point, and I just refused. I went to the person and I didn't like her and I just said, "I'm not seeing you." But I wish that either my mom or my family friend had kind of pushed me more because I really needed that. When I was about sixteen, I really should have been seeing somebody on a regular basis because I was totally depressed.

Basically, my parents were just at a loss as to what to do because they were so caught up in their own failing. They didn't know what to do, and they were often kind of in and out about the fact that they were failing physically and emotionally. And then also my dad . . . he was really upset about not being able to function basically. He was sometimes verbally abusive. So it just would have been good for me to have somebody for me to talk to about that kind of stuff instead of going to my room and crying all the time, or ending up suffering, or not talking it out, but having it manifest itself in ways that were really negative, like not doing well in my school work and not getting sleep.

WAS YOUR SISTER GOING THROUGH A SIMILAR FEELING?

Not really, because she was in college, so she had that distance.

GOING BACK TO YOUR CHILDHOOD, WHEN DID YOU FIRST START TALKING ABOUT YOUR ADOPTION, AND WHAT KINDS OF QUESTIONS DID YOU ASK YOUR PARENTS?

You know, it's funny. I don't really remember. All I know is that for as long as I could articulate my thoughts and ideas, I've also known that I'm adopted. And I remember being told I come from one of those families where we were always told we were adopted because our parents wanted the best for us. I think for a long time I was like, "Oh, yeah, because we were very special." I sort of believed that whole myth that because we're very special, and because they loved us so much, that we're adopted. And now that I'm older, I feel like that's a nice idea, but you have no idea why you were adopted. You may have been adopted because your parents may not have cared and may not have given a shit about you. I mean, they needed to get you out of their life because they made a mistake and they had you. You have no idea, and it doesn't really matter. You know the bottom line is that probably you're lucky that you're alive and that the parents who adopted you, adopted you and gave you what you have. But why it happened, you just shouldn't even think about it. You just have the life that you have, and there you go. But I did definitely come from one of those families that sort of talk about that whole story because what else are you going to say? You have to give your child that story.

YOU HAVE TO CUSHION THE BLOW SOMEHOW.

You have to. And I think that I probably would too. But as far back as I can remember, what I remember is hearing, "You were adopted because your birth parents loved you very much, just like we love you very much, and we've wanted you, and everybody wanted you to have a wonderful life." But that's all that I remember.

WHEN YOU WERE LITTLE, DID YOUR PARENTS TRY TO INTEGRATE ANY CULTURAL EVENTS OR ARTIFACTS INTO YOUR LIFE?

Yes and no. I mean we always had a sense of the importance of, respectively, for my sister, Asian American people in history, and for me, African people and African American history and Hispanic people and history. I don't know that our parents did necessarily everything that they could have. She became very close with a number of black people who became her closest friends. So I felt like that was always good for me, kind of having these role models, these people who I looked up to, and when I was older, kind of became mentors of mine. And Kiyo's godmother is actually Asian American, so that was always kind of nice and important. None of the family goes to tons and tons of different cultural events; it wasn't like we incorporated it into our lives as much as it could have been. We did some cultural kinds of things with my mom and dad, but not as much, probably more with Kiyo's godmother and father. So Edee, the godmother, really wanted to be involved with us as much as possible, so she kind of went out of her way to do things with us. She actually formed something that we called the Adoptees Club when we were little girls. It was myself and my sister and a friend of ours who was also an adoptee. She was adopted from Korea. There was another girl, Vanessa, and then that was it. So we would do stuff from when we were seven to twelve, because Vanessa, unfortunately, was killed in a car accident. So we did cool stuff when we all came together as part of the Adoptees' Club.

DID YOU EVER WANT MORE? DO YOU REMEMBER?

I don't know. I'm only saying as a thirty-year-old that there could have been more. As a kid, I don't think I thought to myself, "God, you know, we really should go to more performances."

COULD YOU TALK A LITTLE ABOUT YOUR EXTENDED FAMILY? DO YOU FEEL LIKE YOU WERE ACCEPTED WITHIN THE FAMILY?

Well, I didn't know my grandparents very well. We really only knew my grandmother. The rest of them died before we were born. My grandmother I hardly even knew because she died when I was six or something. But as far as extended family, mostly it's cousins that I know, and for the most part I feel that my relationships with them are pretty good. But like last weekend I went to see my cousins in New York, and I kind of feel like—and it's sort of the same with my brothers and sisters—this is my family, but yet there's definitely a way I feel a sense of disconnection. I feel like these are people who I care for very much, but I feel like they don't really know who I am. They don't really know about me. They don't really know what kind of struggles I have and why I have those struggles and what kind of issues I'm dealing with.

DO YOU THINK THAT IS MORE OF AN AGE FACTOR, OR SOMETHING TO DO WITH BEING ADOPTED?

I think more about the adopted stuff. But part of that is because I don't see them that often, and so I don't talk to them that often.

NOW YOU TALKED A LITTLE BIT ABOUT YOUR OPENING YOUR FILES. DO YOU THINK YOU WILL DO THAT IN THE FUTURE?

I think so. I just don't know when because people are always telling me it's hard to know when the right time is.

WAS THERE EVER A TIME WHEN THE ADOPTION BECAME A FOCAL POINT IN YOUR LIFE?

Maybe in college. It kind of comes and goes. I'm not just this person who was adopted, and then sometimes I feel that having been adopted really does make me who I am. I have been for a while conflicted because I tend to feel that, in a way, I don't thoroughly agree with the social workers flat out that white people should not be able to adopt black children. I do think that if there is a shortage of parents to adopt children—if there are parents who can adopt them and who are in a good position to adopt them and raise them and give them a good life, no matter what the color of the parents' skin is, they should be able to adopt them. But I do think that if you have a white family and a black family, and both families basically come out the same in terms of being financially prepared and emotionally well-equipped and psychologically well-equipped, and they're going to provide a good cultural environment, I would give that child to the black family because I think the child will be better off.

SO LOOKING BACK ON YOUR ADOPTION, DO YOU THINK YOU WOULD HAVE PREFERRED, ALL OTHER THINGS BEING EQUAL, TO HAVE BEEN ADOPTED INTO A LATINO OR AN AFRICAN AMERICAN FAMILY?

I think that basically what I would have wanted is the kind of life I've had. If I were going to be raised by a black or Latino family, I guess I would have wanted them to have been able to be very comfortable, because I've grown so accustomed to having a very comfortable life.

ARE YOU GLAD THAT YOU WERE ADOPTED?

Yes, I think so. I mean all things considered, I have a very nice life.

SO THROUGH YOUR AFRICAN AMERICAN, LATINO, ANGLO HERITAGE, IS THERE A PART YOU IDENTIFY WITH MORE?

I think at this point in my life, I'm trying to meld the three together. I think by default, I probably seem pretty Anglo, but I don't necessarily identify the most with the Anglo. Am I Jewish? My mother didn't raise me Jewish; we're something else. It's sort of that ill-defined white.

ARE THERE ANY OTHER ASPECTS OF ADOPTION OR YOUR STORY THAT YOU WOULD LIKE TO TELL?

With a number of losses that were beyond my control, and usually they are out of control, but then also with the whole sort of nature of adoption, I think that I feel as if being adopted has sort of resulted in the sort of perpetual search for identity. I think it would be interesting to talk to other adoptees about how they come to some sense of closure, or how they come to developing a sense of identity that satisfies them. Because just now, when you asked which of the three—the Anglo, Spanish, or black—which I identified most with, I don't know that I can give you an answer.

WHAT TYPES OF STEREOTYPES OR DISCRIMINATION HAVE YOU ENCOUNTERED?

Some stereotypes that are not necessarily negative, but they are stereotypes—I get stereotyped about having light skin, bright eyes, good hair. In the Latino community, it's a little bit weirder. People think that I'm either

Dominican or Puerto Rican, and they don't know exactly what to do with me. And white people often don't know whether I'm black or Latino or what, and so they don't know how to respond sometimes. But I don't usually face major discrimination—just a little bit. The thing about being a person of color but not necessarily looking the way most people might look in that group—like I don't look like your average black person, so I don't get as much discrimination as most people do, but I still always wonder if I might. It's a little complicated. I might go into a store, and sometimes I get almost a little bit paranoid because sometimes I think, "Oh, it feels like someone's watching me." But I don't know how much of that is me being paranoid or if it could happen. But that's really annoying. It could be me. It is just kind of hard to tell.

WHAT ADVICE WOULD YOU GIVE PARENTS WHO ARE CONSIDERING ADOPTING BIRACIALLY, OR TRANSRACIALLY?

I think that probably one of the key things is exposure. Exposing your child to that child's culture and also exposing them to other children who are like them, so they see some of the same pieces. My aunt said that when I was a kid, mom used to try to get me to play with the other biracial kids, and I didn't want to play with them. I wanted to play with my other friends, and the other friends would be white kids. Because I just wanted to play with the kids I thought were cool. I didn't want to play with them just because they looked like me. But if you expose kids at the age where they are too young to be able to think for themselves, maybe you can decide things for them. But I think exposure is probably the most important thing initially, and just always having that exposure and just always educating and always teaching the child about themselves and their culture and never stopping that education. And always being available to talk about issues that come up.

WAS THERE EVER A TIME WHEN YOU FELT BAD OR RESENTFUL ABOUT YOUR PARENTS ADOPTING YOU?

Yeah. I think that I started more so when I was in college. Even within the past five years, I've had periods of time when I was very upset and very emotionally unstable because I really couldn't deal with a lot of the confusion I was feeling, and I felt like, "Why did this have to happen to me?" There are just too many issues that are just too confusing for me to handle as far as my father being an embarrassment when I was younger, and especially with my mom who was so old. It was a combination of her being this white woman who looked nothing like me, and she was old. People would say, "That's your *MOTHER*?" I think the fact that she was old was more embarrassing than the fact that she was white. That would come up off and on when I was in middle school and high school.

Was your family very loving?

Yes. That's why I think when I say that I had a lot of confusion and struggles and feelings and all that, I don't feel that I wouldn't ever say I was never happy. Maybe at some point I said that to myself, but I don't feel that I wish I could do my life over again, because in the end I have had a very nice life. I've had a very interesting life. I mean it's been a difficult life, but not that difficult. I would have had a difficult life if I had not been adopted, and it may have been an even more difficult life. And if I'd been raised by either a black family or a Latino family, and they had been comfortable—that might not have been so good either. There might have been traumatic events that could have taken place in that life.

20

ADAM SACKETT

GENDER:	Male
AGE AT TIME OF INTERVIEW:	21
RACE:	Caucasian
MARITAL STATUS:	Single
OCCUPATION:	Student

Born in Detroit, Michigan, Adam was placed into foster care when he was eight years old. His biological mother had "a problem with alcohol and drug abuse," and he was removed from her care. Soon after, Adam was adopted by a single black woman who was raising two other adopted children and one stepchild. Because Adam and his biological mother were the only white family in their all-black neighborhood, he was not bothered by being brought up in a transracial family.

Adam was raised in a predominately black area of Detroit where his best friends were all black. At times other children would make fun of him, or he would be associated with "all those niggers." His elementary and high schools were also all black. Only in high school, did he have friends who were white. When asked if this was a problem, Adam replied, "No, not at all." On occasion, his mother would talk to him about his unusual situation, and sometimes his friends were puzzled by his family situation. In describing his extended family, Adam felt that he was accepted by his black relatives.

Overall, Adam's experience of being adopted into a black family has provided him with "insight into certain areas." He feels more comfortable with black people and feels fully accepted by the black community. Adam has stayed in contact with his biological mother and describes their relationship as more of a friendship. Adam's mother had encouraged him to contact his biological mother when he was in high school, as she had "always kept in some kind of touch."

After high school, Adam moved to Washington, D.C., where he worked before returning to Detroit for college. Currently in D.C. again, he lives with three black roommates. He is working at American University where he would like to pursue a degree in justice, law and society.

FIRST OF ALL, LET'S START WITH SOME DEMOGRAPHIC INFORMATION. HOW OLD ARE YOU, ADAM?

I'm twenty-one.

WHERE WERE YOU BORN?

In Detroit, Michigan.

DO YOU KNOW ANYTHING ABOUT YOUR BIOLOGICAL PARENTS?

Yes.

COULD YOU TELL ME WHO THEY WERE, AND SO ON?

My mother was married to a man in the army, and I have a brother and a sister by my mother and a sister by my father.

HOW OLD WAS SHE WHEN YOU WERE BORN?

Probably around eighteen or nineteen. They were divorced, and I was with her until I was around seven or eight, and then due to circumstances, I was put into foster care.

DO YOU WANT TO TALK ABOUT WHAT THOSE CIRCUMSTANCES WERE?

She had a problem with alcohol and drug abuse.

WERE YOU TAKEN AWAY FROM HER?

Yes.

AND YOU WERE PUT INTO FOSTER CARE, WHEN YOU WERE AROUND SEVEN OR EIGHT?

Yes. Eight.

WHAT HAPPENED? TELL ME ABOUT THE FOSTER PARENTS.

The first foster family was a black pastor and his wife, Church of God of Christ. They were a black family, and I stayed with them for about a year, year and a half. And then a lady in their congregation—I went with her and her mother, and they ended up adopting me.

THIS WOMAN ENDED UP ADOPTING YOU?

Yes, and I lived with her and her mother.

SHE WAS A SINGLE WOMAN?

Yes.

I MEAN, I HOPE YOU KNOW HOW UNUSUAL IT IS BECAUSE I HAVEN'T BEEN ABLE TO FIND ANYBODY—

Oh, yes.

HOW WAS IT THAT BOTH SETS OF FOSTER HOMES WERE BLACK FAMILIES?

I think it was just the area I was in. Detroit is predominantly black.

HOW OLD WAS THE FOSTER MOTHER WHO FINALLY ADOPTED YOU?

She was in her thirties.

IS SHE STILL ALIVE?

Yes.

IS SHE MARRIED NOW?

Yes.

DO YOU HAVE BROTHERS AND SISTERS?

Yes.

BIRTH OR ADOPTED?

They are adopted. Two of them are adopted and one of them is a stepchild.

DOES YOUR MOTHER WORK OUTSIDE THE HOME?

Yes, she does.

WHAT DOES SHE DO?

She is a medical biller at a doctor's office.

AND WHAT DOES HER HUSBAND DO?

He is a construction worker.

HOW OLD WERE YOU WHEN SHE MARRIED HIM?

Oh, that was just last year!

SO, IN FACT, YOU WERE REARED BY A SINGLE MOTHER AND HER MOTHER.

Yes.

THIS WOMAN CAME TO ADOPT YOU BECAUSE SOMEONE IN HER CHURCH RECOMMENDED THAT SHE DO SO?

Yes. And I went into foster care with them, with her, and then she adopted me.

DID YOU SPEND THE REST OF YOUR CHILDHOOD IN DETROIT?

Yes.

TELL ME ABOUT THE NEIGHBORHOOD. WAS IT MOSTLY A BLACK NEIGHBOR-HOOD?

Predominantly black.

WORKING CLASS BLACK?

Yes.

AND THE ELEMENTARY SCHOOL AND THE HIGH SCHOOL THAT YOU WENT TO?

All black.

AS YOU WERE GROWING UP, WHO WERE YOUR CLOSEST FRIENDS? WERE THEY BLACK KIDS, WHITE?

Black.

DID YOU HAVE ANY WHITE FRIENDS?

A couple, but not in school. I would meet some outside of school, and I would get to know them, but not until after high school did I ever have any white friends.

WAS THIS A PROBLEM FOR YOU?

No, not at all.

NOW, YOUR MOTHER BELONGED TO A CHURCH?

Yes.

WERE MOST OF THE PEOPLE IN THAT CHURCH BLACK?

Yes.

IN MY OTHER STUDIES, MANY OF THE WHITE FAMILIES WHO ADOPT ACROSS RACIAL LINES SEEK OUT FAMILIES WHO HAVE ALSO DONE THAT. DID YOUR ADOPTIVE MOTHER TRY TO FIND ANY FAMILIES WHO HAD ADOPTED ACROSS RACIAL LINES?

No.

SO, YOU WERE TREATED AS HER CHILD. DO YOU VIEW HER AS YOUR MOTHER?

Oh, yes.

DID SHE TRY AND TALK TO YOU ABOUT HOW UNUSUAL YOUR SITUATION WAS?

She did occasionally.

WITH BLACK FRIENDS, WEREN'T THEY PUZZLED AS TO WHAT YOU WERE DO- ING IN THIS BLACK FAMILY?

Sometimes. I know there were some times when we would go out places, and my sisters are a lot younger than me, and my mom would say, "Adam, grab your sisters," and I would grab them up and people would kind of look at us crazy. Once I moved actually out of Detroit and moved here, I ran into more of that.

WHEN DID YOU MOVE FROM DETROIT TO WASHINGTON?

Just within the last year.

WHAT DID YOU DO AFTER YOU GRADUATED FROM HIGH SCHOOL?

I worked, and then I went to college.

WHICH COLLEGE DID YOU GO TO?

University of Detroit.

WHY DID YOU COME TO WASHINGTON?

I have friends here, so I decided to come here, and one of my uncles lives here.

NOW, YOUR UNCLE IS BLACK OR WHITE?

Black.

YOUR MOTHER'S BROTHER?

Her "play" brother. . . . He is an old close friend, not a blood relative.

ARE YOU CLOSE TO HIM?

Yes.

IN WASHINGTON, WHOM DO YOU LIVE WITH HERE? DO YOU LIVE ALONE?

No, I have roommates, three roommates, all black.

AND THEY KNOW ABOUT YOUR CIRCUMSTANCES?

Yes.

DID YOU KNOW THEM FROM DETROIT?

One of them I did.

DO THEY ASK YOU A LOT OF QUESTIONS ABOUT YOUR ADOPTION?

They do! Yes.

FOR EXAMPLE, WHAT KIND OF QUESTIONS?

They just ask wasn't it strange, or how do you cope now with people of your own race, and how does it feel being here? Because Detroit is large, but it is still relatively small enough so that everyone in my neighborhood knew who I was, and people from the church knew who I was. So whenever I went into a new environment, I was with people who knew who I was, and they were like, "This is Adam; he's cool." Now coming here, I find myself in a situation where I've always been around black people, and when I enter certain situations, people are like, "What are you doing here?" And it is different.

DO YOU HAVE GRANDPARENTS, AND YOU DO HAVE AN UNCLE?

Yes.

WERE YOU ACCEPTED BY YOUR BLACK RELATIVES?

By the whole family, oh, yes.

BUT YOU ARE STILL THE ONLY ONE?

Yes.

CAN YOU REMEMBER AT WHAT AGE YOU RECOGNIZED THAT YOU WERE DIFFERENT THAN YOUR MOTHER? DID YOU RECOGNIZE IT AS SOON AS YOU MOVED IN?

Yes. As soon as I moved in.

WERE YOU BOTHERED BY IT?

No, because I think the area I was raised in even before I was with her and my family, we were around all black people. We lived in an all-black neighborhood; we were the only white family in the neighborhood.

WITH YOUR BIRTH MOTHER?

With my birth mother. So I always have been in that environment. So it wasn't too abnormal to me.

HOW COME YOU WERE IN A BLACK NEIGHBORHOOD WITH YOUR BIRTH MOTHER?

She preferred the company of black men.

WAS YOUR BIRTH FATHER BLACK?

No.

WERE THERE SOME TIMES IN YOUR LIFE THAT YOU FOUND THAT THE RACIAL DIFFERENCES WERE HARDER THAN OTHERS? FOR EXAMPLE, WHEN YOU FIRST MOVED TO WASHINGTON?

Yes. There were different times. I remember when I was younger, when kids would make fun of me.

BLACK KIDS?

Yes. That would hurt. I would go into areas where it was white. I remember one time there was a birthday party for a friend of my mother's out in the suburbs, and I walked in and I said, "I'm here for the Ward party," and the lady went to walk me towards a white birthday party that was going on, which was totally understandable. And I said, "No, I'm with this party over here," and she said, "Are you with all those niggers?" And I was like "uh . . ." because that was my mama.

AND HOW OLD WERE YOU?

I was a teenager. And so I mean there were different times when I felt it was tense.

WHAT ABOUT YOUR TEACHERS? DID YOU HAVE ANY PROBLEMS WITH THEM IN ELEMENTARY SCHOOL? HIGH SCHOOL?

No, no problems with teachers. In elementary school kids made fun of me, but my mama was like, if they make fun of you, you tell them to stop. And if they pick on me and push me and stuff, she told me to fight them back. And once I did that, there was no problem anymore, and we were cool. And we played forts together, once they saw I was going to stand up for myself .

WHAT ABOUT THINGS THAT YOUR FAMILY DID TOGETHER? YOU WENT TO CHURCH TOGETHER. DID YOU DO ANY TRAVELING TOGETHER?

Yes.

WAS THAT COMPLICATED IF YOU'D GO INTO STRANGE CITIES OR SOMETHING?

Yes.

MY KIDS IN MY STUDIES TELL ME ABOUT GOING INTO A RESTAURANT IN NORTH DAKOTA, AND EVERYBODY IN THE RESTAURANT WOULD STARE AT THEM BECAUSE THEY HADN'T SEEN BLACK PEOPLE, AND SO ON.

I don't think it was so much strange when I went with my family because my mom is an older woman, you know what I'm saying, so people would look a little bit, but they wouldn't say anything. Now, I know that there were times when I was hanging out with my cousins, and we would go into the suburbs, and I would drive out to Farmington Hills all the time and never have a problem. My cousins would get in the car, and we would go to Farmington Hills and get pulled over like every five minutes. Literally, one night we got pulled over three times right in a row. That's when I really started to notice a lot of things that I think a lot of people, even my age that are white, don't understand. They don't see it personally. They think black people are exaggerating, but I've seen it up front. It's not an exaggeration. You get pulled over three times in a row when you cross the line into a white neighborhood. It happens. And there were times when I was younger, I felt guilty about that because I knew that I could always just exit out of that situation, but my family couldn't. I could be white, and they never could.

DID YOU TALK TO YOUR MOM ABOUT THINGS LIKE THAT?

Yes. And you know she was always "everything happens for a reason." God has a reason for everything.

DID SHE GO TO CHURCH REGULARLY?

Yes. And she would tell me, you know, that she believed there was a reason that I was put in this situation, and she said even different things like that maybe white people would be more willing to hear it from me, being white, than from someone who is black.

THE MINISTER IN YOUR CHURCH WAS BLACK?

Yes, Pentecostal.

DO YOU STILL BELONG TO THE SAME CHURCH, OR THE SAME KIND OF CHURCH?

No. I don't go to church anymore.

WHAT ABOUT DATING? DO YOU DATE?

Yes.

AND DO YOU DATE MOSTLY WHITE, MOSTLY BLACK?

Mostly black.

DO YOU THINK YOU WILL END UP MARRYING A BLACK WOMAN?

Maybe.

HERE IN WASHINGTON NOW, YOU'RE DATING MOSTLY BLACK?

Yes.

AND HOW DO THEY RESPOND TO YOU, BLACK WOMEN?

It depends. They seem cautious, some of them. You know, is it just an experiment that he's going through. Then they find out about my background.

DO YOU TELL THEM THAT PRETTY SOON IN THE RELATIONSHIP?

Sometimes. It depends how I'm feeling them out. Sometimes I don't want to tell them right away because I don't want them to think only about that. Sometimes people can see, in the black community especially, well, I was adopted by a black family. Then it seems kind of like, well, what are you trying to do? I don't try to run around. . . .

WERE YOU DATING WHEN YOU WERE STILL LIVING IN DETROIT?

Yes.

WHEN YOU SHOWED UP, WERE BLACK PARENTS SURPRISED, OR DID THEY KNOW AHEAD OF TIME THAT THEIR DAUGHTER WAS GOING TO BE GOING OUT WITH A WHITE MAN?

I think most of them knew ahead of time. Not all of them were comfortable with it, but they knew ahead of time.

ON THE OTHER SIDE OF THE STORY, I HAD EXPERIENCES WITH YOUNG MEN WHO SAY, WELL, THEY DIDN'T MENTION . . . AND A COUPLE OF TIMES THEY WERE THROWN OUT.

I never had that experience.

SO THE FAMILIES PRETTY MUCH WELCOMED YOU? THE OLDER BROTHERS AND SO ON?

Yes. There were some parents I could tell were uncomfortable with it, but they were never rude.

AND HERE IN WASHINGTON, MOST OF YOUR DATES AND FRIENDS ARE BLACK?

Yes.

DO PEOPLE AROUND HERE, BRIDGET AND ANYONE ELSE, KNOW OF YOUR BACKGROUND, BECAUSE I'VE NOT SAID ANYTHING.

Yes. Bridget does, and Professor Johnson does.

DO YOU KNOW OF ANYONE LIKE YOU, A WHITE PERSON ADOPTED BY A BLACK FAMILY?

I know a friend of my mother's from church had two little foster boys, and they were white.

DID SHE ADOPT THEM?

I am not sure. She was talking about it.

COULD YOU ASK YOUR MOTHER?

Yes.

TELL ME A LITTLE BIT ABOUT HOW YOU DECIDED TO LIVE WITH WHOM YOU ARE LIVING NOW. ARE THESE FRIENDS FROM DETROIT?

My uncle owns the house and asked me if I wanted to move down here. And my mama agreed with it because I think she thought I needed a heftier male influence at this point in my life, so I decided to move down here. He owned the house; he said I could move in there. One of his friends and one of his cousins were already living there. So I just moved in with them, and then a friend of mine from Detroit came with me. It's a big house.

SO THIS IS SOMEONE YOU KNEW FROM HIGH SCHOOL?

Yes.

ADAM, WHAT DO YOU SEE AS YOUR LONGER TERM INTERESTS? ARE YOU STAYING HERE AND WORKING FOR A WHILE?

I am going to work and go to school here.

WHERE ARE YOU GOING TO SCHOOL?

Here, at American University.

OH, I DIDN'T KNOW THAT. YOU'RE STARTING HERE?

In the fall. I want to study justice, law and society. I would like to eventually teach on the college level.

IT MEANS YOU HAVE TO GET A PHD. A LONG TIME.

Yeah, I know. But I'd like to work in this area as well as race relations kind of stuff. It interests me.

SO YOU HAVE BEEN ACCEPTED HERE?

Professor Johnson and I sat down and talked about it. Because I'm working here now, he said it is not difficult to take classes. They will let you take classes.

AND YOU HAVE FINANCIAL ASSISTANCE?

If you work here full time, you get to go to school for free.

SO YOU ARE GOING TO WORK FULL TIME AND GO TO SCHOOL?

Yes, in the evenings.

WE'VE HAD STUDENTS WHO HAVE DONE THAT, BUT IT'S HARD.

But I am determined.

HOW MANY CLASSES WILL YOU TAKE?

I think only three, three a term.

THEN I GUESS YOU COULD ALSO GO DURING THE SUMMER.

Yes, I could.

FROM THE FEW REFERENCES YOU MADE TO YOUR MOTHER, I TAKE IT YOU ARE VERY CLOSE.

Yes.

TELL ME A LITTLE BIT ABOUT YOUR SIBLINGS. HOW MANY ARE THERE?

My sisters are eight and seven, and my stepbrother is fifteen. We are all pretty close. Brittany and I are real close.

NOW, THIS WAS YOUR MOTHER'S HUSBAND'S SON?

Yes.

AND ARE YOU CLOSE TO HIM?

Yes, we are pretty close. He just graduated. Now he's in college.

WHERE IS HE GOING?

UM in Dearborn.

WHAT DOES YOUR MOTHER'S "PLAY BROTHER" DO FOR A LIVING?

He works for the government. He works for GSA.

DOES HE HAVE A BACHELOR'S DEGREE?

Yes.

WE TALKED A LITTLE BIT ABOUT YOUR LONG-TERM ASPIRATIONS. SO YOU REALLY THINK YOU WOULD LIKE TO SPECIALIZE IN JUSTICE, LAW AND SOCIETY AND TEACH?

Yes. I always wanted to teach, and I always wanted to do something in that area, but I wasn't really sure of what area of study to do that type of work in.

AND YOU PLAN TO GO BACK TO SCHOOL IN THE FALL?

Yes.

DID YOU EVER TRY AND FIND YOUR BIRTH PARENTS?

Yes. I know my mother.

CAN YOU TALK TO ME ABOUT THAT?

We get along now. We're friends.

WHEN DID YOU MEET HER?

We started getting back in touch when I was in high school. Actually, my mama tried to encourage that.

HOW DID SHE DO THAT?

She just encouraged me to . . . I always knew where she was.

YOU ALWAYS KNEW WHERE YOUR BIRTH MOTHER WAS? THAT ISN'T ALWAYS THE CASE.

Yes. She always kept in some kind of touch.

THAT WAS GENEROUS. ARE THEY FRIENDS, THE TWO OF THEM?

No. They don't really talk.

WHAT DOES YOUR BIRTH MOTHER DO NOW?

She's a bookkeeper.

DID SHE REMARRY?

No.

HOW OFTEN DO YOU SEE HER, OR HOW DO YOU STAY IN TOUCH WITH HER?

Mostly through email. I haven't seen her in a couple of years. I did see her a couple of years ago. I spent a weekend there.

BUT YOU ARE NOT CONFUSED ABOUT WHO YOUR MOTHER IS?

Not at all.

HOW DO YOU FEEL ABOUT HAVING BEEN ADOPTED BY A BLACK FAMILY?

I think that it was a good thing, that it gave me insight into certain areas. A lot of times I think that racism in this country isn't so much. . . . I think it is more the only time average white people see black people is in court. Maybe at school, because they don't really socialize, they don't see what happens in each other's communities. The white people don't know black culture. They don't understand. A lot of the stereotypes and prejudices are based on what you see in the media and hear in the music and different things like that. They don't apply to the majority of black people.

DID YOUR MOTHER DO ANYTHING TO TEACH YOU DIFFERENTLY THAN SHE WOULD HAVE FOR AN ADOPTED BLACK CHILD?

She didn't treat me differently at all. She was an ambulance driver for years, and her partner was white. She was around white people, and they were around us, so it wasn't necessary.

DID YOU TALK ABOUT RACE RELATIONS AT DINNER OR WITH THE FAMILY?

Yes. Mostly my grandmother and I.

TELL ME A LITTLE BIT ABOUT THAT.

My grandmother and my mother especially came up with the race riots in Detroit in 1968. And my grandmother was telling me stories about 18th street. It was an area in Detroit where all the businesses were owned primarily by blacks, and there were some famous hotels and jazz clubs and things like that; and the property was seized by the government, and the black people had businesses taken from them. And she told about that, and then after the businesses were taken, they couldn't get loans because the grandfather clause—because the grandfather was a slave and up to your great grandfather, so you couldn't get a loan to open a business in this country, so I really was raised knowing. My mother taught me a lot about different things.

HOW MUCH EDUCATION DID YOUR MOTHER HAVE?

She had high school, and then she went to a paramedic school and graduated from that.

HOW OLD WAS SHE WHEN SHE ADOPTED YOU?

About thirty-five.

AND HAD SHE HAD BIRTH CHILDREN?

No.

SO YOU WERE HER FIRST CHILD?

Yes. I was also raised really close to a couple of my cousins because my uncle was shot and killed.

WAS THIS HER BROTHER?

Yes.

DID YOUR GRANDMOTHER LIVE WITH YOU AND YOUR MOTHER?

Yes. Still does.

WAS SHE BORN IN DETROIT, YOUR GRANDMOTHER?

She was born in the South.

HOW MUCH EDUCATION DID SHE HAVE?

High school.

THAT'S UNUSUAL.

Yes.

DID SHE HAVE A HUSBAND? DID HE DIE?

She was a single parent. He left. They were married, but he left.

SO YOUR MOTHER, THEN SHE HAS A SON WHO WAS KILLED, AND THOSE WERE HER TWO CHILDREN?

Yes.

ARE YOU CLOSE TO YOUR GRANDMOTHER NOW?

Yes.

HOW OLD IS SHE?

She is going to be ninety this year.

HOW DO THEY FEEL ABOUT YOUR LEAVING TO GO TO WASHINGTON?

They both miss me, and I talk to them a lot. My mama thought it was a good idea and thought that I needed to get out and see more of the world. She sees a lot more ethnic mix than before, plus she thought that I needed someone to really kick me in the ass to get back to school.

WAS SHE WORRIED ABOUT THAT?

Yes, very much.

WHAT SORT OF WORK DID YOU DO AFTER YOU GRADUATED FROM HIGH SCHOOL?

I did administrative assistant sort of work. The kind of work in security and personnel. You know, office staff, who issued IDs.

THAT'S INTERESTING.

Yes, it was fun.

DO YOU HAVE ANY SUGGESTIONS THAT YOU WOULD MAKE TO BLACK PARENTS WHO MIGHT HAVE AN OPPORTUNITY TO ADOPT A WHITE CHILD ABOUT WHAT THEY SHOULD OR SHOULDN'T DO? DID YOU LEARN ANYTHING FROM YOUR EXPERIENCE THAT YOU WANT TO EMPHASIZE OR THAT YOU WANT TO WARN AGAINST OR ANYTHING LIKE THAT?

Really, I don't know if there are any specifics to something like that. It depends on the child and the parents.

DID YOU FEEL EARLY ON, PRETTY SOON AFTER YOU WERE IN THE FAMILY, THAT THIS WAS YOUR HOME, THAT YOUR MOTHER WAS YOUR MOTHER?

Yes. And there were times when I acted up when I first got there, and my grandmother and her both let me know it doesn't matter if you are white or black or brown. Whatever your race is you have to live under the same rules, and you are going to get the same benefits and the same everything that everyone else does who lives here. And I think that was important, that I knew I was in the family.

WHAT HAPPENS VERY OFTEN WITH ADOPTED CHILDREN, EITHER THE SAME-RACE ADOPTION OR TRANSRACIAL, IS THAT ADOPTIVE CHILDREN TEST AND MIS-BEHAVE. AND YOU DID YOUR SHARE OF TESTING?

Oh, yes.

DID YOU GO THROUGH A PERIOD OF EXPERIMENTING WITH DRUGS OR ANY KIND OF ILLEGAL ACTIVITY?

Yes, yes I did.

DO YOU WANT TO TALK ABOUT THAT? WAS IT SERIOUS? DID YOUR MOTHER GET INVOLVED IN IT?

She got involved. Put her foot down. In black communities and black families, they are a little stricter than a lot of times in white families from the things I hear. And I mean there were times when I got whipped. It was not uncommon, even though it is more uncommon in white households, but it really helped me to know limits. It was not like every time I was bad it happened, but I knew when I did get one, it was a very serious thing.

WHEN DID THE FIRST INCIDENT OCCUR?

I was about fifteen, and I stayed out all night.

WAS IT JUST MARIJUANA, OR WAS IT MORE SERIOUS?

It was marijuana and drinking. And I stayed all night with some friends, and my mother was at work when I got home, which I knew she would be. So I came home and my grandmamma was sitting at the door, she had pushed this chair up right in front of the door, and I walked in the door, and she got up out of that chair real fast; and she started slapping me and yelling at me, and telling me I wasn't that grown, and I wasn't going to stay out. And I went downstairs. I was upset. But then when my mama came home and she said, "You know your grandmamma was up all night worrying about you," and I was sitting there, and she was like, "You know, when my brother died, he was messed up in all this stuff." So then I started to see her point and how I had actually worried her, and I understood her anger. Then I felt bad, you know, real bad. Because I knew what she had been through.

WAS THAT THE ONLY INCIDENT?

Yes.

YOU LEARN FAST. IS THERE ANYTHING YOU WISH YOUR GRANDMOTHER AND MOTHER HAD DONE DIFFERENTLY? AS YOU THINK BACK, AT ANY TIME?

Not really. I'm not saying they were perfect, but I didn't have a bad childhood at all. And I look at the way they are raising up my little sisters now and I look at the things she goes through. Like my stepbrother, he was getting in trouble there for a minute, and she didn't treat him any different than she treated me. I think that's very much who she is. She loves, and it doesn't matter; she doesn't love you because of who you are or what you are, she loves you because she loves you.

DO YOU HAVE A GOOD RELATIONSHIP WITH HER HUSBAND?

Yes. We get along pretty good.

HOW LONG HAS HE BEEN INVOLVED IN THE FAMILY?

About two or three years.

WAS HE SURPRISED TO MEET YOU?

Probably a little bit at first. But he was very accepting and very good about it.

WHAT DOES HE DO FOR A LIVING?

He's a construction worker.

IS IT A GOOD MARRIAGE, DO YOU THINK?

Oh, yes. They seem to enjoy each other.

THAT'S GOOD. DO YOU FEEL AS COMFORTABLE WITH WHITE PEOPLE AS YOU DO WITH BLACK? DO YOU FEEL MORE COMFORTABLE WITH ONE GROUP THAN ANOTHER? DO YOU THINK IN TERMS OF THOSE CATEGORIES?

I tend to feel more comfortable with black people.

DO YOU FEEL FULLY ACCEPTED BY THEM, AT LEAST ONCE THEY KNOW WHO YOU ARE?

Yes, I do.

YOU ARE VERY UNUSUAL.

And white people have consistently treated me different once they find out, that's probably why.

HOW HAVE THEY TREATED YOU DIFFERENTLY? GIVE ME AN EXAMPLE.

Some people take interest in it, and ask a lot of questions, and some people are just turned off or disgusted by it. It is not even so much what they say, it's what they don't say after that. Or they have general misconceptions: he's a wigger.

WHAT'S A WIGGER? THAT'S A TERM I HAVEN'T HEARD.

It is a term used nowadays that describes white kids who want to be black. A lot of people say he's a wigger. And then I'm very comfortable with the fact that I'm white.

ONE OF THE THINGS THAT I HAVE DONE SOME RESEARCH ON, AND MAY DO SOME MORE RESEARCH ON, IS THE WHOLE NOTION OF MIXED-RACE PEOPLE. IT USED TO BE THIRTY YEARS AGO, TWENTY YEARS AGO, IF YOU WERE MIXED RACE, YOU WERE BLACK. BUT NOW I THINK THERE IS REALLY A SEPARATE IDENTITY FOR MIXED-RACE CHILDREN. HERE IN WASHINGTON, YOU LIVE WITH BLACK FRIENDS, AND THIS IS YOUR UNCLE'S APARTMENT AND SO ON. WHERE DO YOU MEET WHITE PEOPLE, OTHER THAN HERE AT THE UNIVERSITY?

At the university! That's about it, because most of the social places I go are black. You know, I am starting to meet more white people. That is one thing that I really said that I probably should do too, but it is strange. I was thinking about different things about it, with the fact that a lot of people know about white culture. But being raised around black people, of course I know about white culture. But like popular music right now, I've heard of the different artists that the white kids my age listen to, but I've never really heard any of the music, so when they start talking about music, all I know about is rap, and R&B, jazz, blues, Motown because that's what I was raised on. So I'm like, I've never heard what they're talking about. Even stylewise, when I'm not dressed for work, I dress a little more urban. I wear the jeans and the shoes and the sweatshirt. It's different.

WILL THE DATING THING TURN OUT TO BE COMPLICATED, DO YOU THINK?

I've dated white girls and black girls. It is not really an issue for me. I remember the first time I brought a white girl home, my mama was a little disappointed, because she was looking forward to having pretty little mixed grandbabies she said.

AND SHE STILL MIGHT.

And she still might. But it is interesting.

AND YOU ARE CLOSE TO YOUR SISTERS? DO YOU VIEW THEM AS SOMEONE THAT YOU HAVE SOME RESPONSIBILITY FOR AND WANT TO TAKE CARE OF?

Yes. I love my sisters.

DO THEY ASK QUESTIONS?

When they were little they did. I remember the older one . . . because they are not biologically sisters either. When Brittany first came, because she came first, she's a little bit older—I was holding her, and I was wearing my hair to right about here, and she was running her fingers through it, and she said, Who does your hair?"

HAIR IS ONE OF THE BIGGEST THINGS.

Oh, I know. And she said, "Who does your hair?" And I said, "Mama cut it," and she kept running her fingers through it. "How did it get like that?" I said, "Brittany, it grew like that." And she looked at me all seriously and leaned back a little and said, "When do you turn black?"

HOW OLD WAS SHE?

About five or six. And my mama was like, "No Brittany. . . ." She was all concerned I was going to be upset. I was like . . . no that is really what starts a lot of problems. We keep things so secret, and we make things sound so taboo that people get afraid to ask.

THAT'S EXACTLY RIGHT.

So I told her, "I don't turn black. I'm white. But I'm still your brother."

AND SHE ACCEPTED THAT?

Yes. When I walk in the door, they say "Big brother, big brother," like Orson Welles. A friend of my mother's models in Detroit, and she has a really pretty little girl, hair almost down to her waist, long black straight hair. And she took the little girl over to a little girl's house who was white for the two little girls to play, and after they were done playing they had gotten so dirty, that the lady decided to let them take a bath so they would be clean, throw the clothes in the wash. By the time my mom's friend got there, everything would be clean. When she got there, the lady was in tears because as soon as the water hit her [the girl's] hair it just shrunk back up on her head and she [the lady] didn't know what to do and she was crying; and she didn't know, she didn't know it would do that.

IT'S A BIG DEAL.

And it is difficult to do. I know how to do it though.

WHEN YOU DID HAVE ANY TROUBLE, DID YOU TELL YOUR MOTHER ABOUT IT?

I told her. And there was a friend of hers I had been raised around for years, at a barbecue she asked me about who did my hair, and how I got my hair so straight. And I was like, "Woman, don't you know I'm white? I've been white ever since I was adopted." It's interesting, but I did go through a kind of identity crisis when I was a teenager, where I was kind of uncomfortable. It was around the time when I started driving and stuff, and I would go places with my friends, and I would see them get pulled over by the police, and I saw a few people that I knew shot and die. Then you go into school, and in Detroit you had metal detectors to go through, and shooting and different things. At that time in an average young black man's life, he goes through—it is very common to go through a lot of anger towards white people in general. So all my friends and I would sit around and talk about white people, and they'd always say, "I don't think of you as white" and stuff like that, which was to make me feel more comfortable, but it still made me feel guilty and almost wish that I wasn't white at times, because I felt real guilty. Because I could see it too, just as clearly as they could; living in the community, I could see the things. I could see how the little stores in the area were buying used meats from the white suburbs, and our meat quality wasn't as good. You had to go to the suburbs to get good groceries. All these things that they've done studies about, I was living through.

So I did go through a time where I felt like I was dangling . . . you know, I'm never going to be quite white all the way. The white community is always going to see me as different, but I am never going to be black, because I'm white. So I felt like I was just a pendulum swinging between the two.

THAT'S A GOOD WAY OF PUTTING IT. DO YOU STILL HAVE SOME OF THOSE FEELINGS?

Sometimes. You know, I am very pleased to be where I'm at right now, at the university and things, because it's a lot more open atmosphere. The job I was working right before I got to the university was a lot less of a friendly atmosphere.

HERE IN WASHINGTON? WHAT WERE YOU DOING?

Yes. I was an administrative assistant and receptionist at a business in D.C. They weren't politicians and stuff. These were real nice people from Reston and areas like that, and I remember the first time my roommate came up there to get me. They treated him very shabbily because they didn't know who he was and he was black; and he was coming into the building and nobody who worked there was black, and they treated him differently. And then my uncle came up there sometimes, and they just started treating me a lot differently after they found that out. Like I wasn't quite right . . . like what's wrong with him? There are times I still see it or feel it. When I go to a place like this, and I am with all black people, and I'm the only white I know, people look at me like. "What's he trying to do? What's he doing?" And I know people look at me and think the same thing. There are times it is still uncomfortable. It is sad that there are still those types of issues in society in the '90s, the year 2000.

IT'S A LOT BETTER, BUT THEY ARE STILL HERE.

And I was listening to Whoopi Goldberg talk about that one day, and she talked about we can all manage to get so frustrated about things and think why is this like this and why is this like that, but if you just look back thirty years, there was segregation. Racism is only generations away. There are still implications for men. Women complain because they don't have equality to men, but look how far they've come since the '30s. So everyone has issues, but really, we've gone so far that you have to expect there to be some backlash still.

DO YOU HAVE ANY TIES WITH YOUR BIRTH FATHER?

Not at all.

BY CHOICE OR YOU JUST DON'T KNOW WHERE HE IS?

I know where he is. But I never knew him, and I think that it's just that now I know where he is and he knows where I am, but it's been so long, and he has another family now, so I don't think that . . . there's not bitterness there; it's just that there's no reason. Whereas with my mother, it was important to her to have a relationship with me, so I wanted to do that. My mama always raised me, you should love and respect your mother.

YOUR MOTHER SOUNDS LIKE SHE IS QUITE AN EXCEPTIONAL WOMAN, IN TERMS OF HER GENEROSITY OF SPIRIT.

Yes. But I think it is very common in the black community. It is like even now, when I hear the white kids at school and they'll be dogging out their mothers, and it seems in the white community kids go through a phase where they just hate their mothers for some reason. In the black community, the mom is everything. And you don't see that as much in the white community. My mama was that way with me. Think of what she was going through; she was going through her own thing too.

NOW, IF YOU SHOULD MARRY A WHITE WOMAN, DO YOU THINK SHE WOULD ACCEPT HER?

Yes. She liked Audrey. She did tell me she didn't know how a white girl would be able to handle me. I don't think Audrey understood, never having been around black people, because she hadn't been. I could see she wasn't a racist person, but she was going through a lot of stereotypes, and she would hold on to a lot of things that I didn't see the same way, and we were getting into arguments about different things.

THIS IS A WOMAN YOU DATED IN DETROIT?

Yes. But her and mama got along real well.

ALL THINGS CONSIDERED, WOULD YOU HAVE PREFERRED TO HAVE BEEN ADOPTED BY A WHITE FAMILY?

No. I feel very close to my family.

SAY A LITTLE BIT MORE ABOUT WHY YOU FEEL CLOSE.

I think that it—it's hard to explain. She's my mother, I love our relationship and can't imagine having any other mother.

IF YOU WERE ADVISING BLACK PARENTS WHO MIGHT HAVE THE OPPORTU-
NITY TO ADOPT A WHITE CHILD, WOULD YOU HAVE SOME SPECIFIC SUGGES-
TIONS ABOUT WHAT THEY SHOULD AND SHOULD NOT DO WHILE THEY ARE PAR-
ENTING A WHITE CHILD?

Not really. I just would say love them and treat them as you would your
birth children.

IS THERE ANYTHING THAT YOU WISH YOUR MOTHER OR YOUR GRAND-
MOTHER HAD DONE DIFFERENTLY WITH YOU?

No.

YOU SOUND AS IF YOU FEEL PERFECTLY COMFORTABLE IN THE COMPANY OF
BLACK PEOPLE.

Yes, I do.

IT IS UNUSUAL.

Yeah, I guess it is.

IS THERE ANYTHING, ADAM, THAT I SHOULD HAVE ASKED YOU THAT I
DIDN'T? IS THERE ANYTHING YOU WANT THE OPPORTUNITY TO SAY?

I can say a little bit about how I see blacks and whites in our society. I
think in this society, that when you are a minority, you understand in general where white society comes from. Whereas if you are white, you don't
understand how minority people function. You don't really know the intri-
cacies of black people's families. A lot of the people I work with do not understand how black people think about things, even for example, the television shows they like to watch. I never start talking about television shows
like *Friends.* I never watch many of the shows I hear white people talking
about all the time.

SO YOU AS A WHITE PERSON FEEL A LITTLE BIT OUT OF THE REACH OF
WHITE SOCIETY?

Yes. Whereas I can talk with blacks, and I don't run out of things to talk
about because I was raised very similarly.

WHEN YOU AND YOUR MAMA TALK ABOUT YOUR FUTURE, FOR EXAMPLE, WHOM WOULD SHE LIKE YOU TO MARRY?

She would like me to marry a black woman and raise my kids as a black family would.

AND DO YOU THINK YOU WILL MARRY A BLACK WOMAN?

Probably.

THANK YOU.

21

FLUTIE*

GENDER:	Male
AGE AT TIME OF INTERVIEW:	35
RACE:	Caucasian
MARITAL STATUS:	Married
OCCUPATION:	Doorman

Flutie, thirty-five years old at the time of the interview, is a Caucasian man who was adopted by a black family when he was nine years old. Along with seven siblings, five of whom were adopted, Flutie was raised by a single mother in Michigan. His biological family was a "totally dysfunctional family," but his adoptive mother always encouraged him to stay in contact with his birth mother. His adoptive extended family was open-minded and supportive.

Prior to his adoption, Flutie was struggling at school, getting into fights, taking drugs, and physically abused in his home. His adoption "saved [his] life" and helped him get through high school. Today, Flutie is married with three young children. He has completed three years of college.

———— ⬤⬤⬤ ————

*Identifying information about this participant has been omitted or changed.

WHAT IS YOUR NAME?

Flutie.

WHAT IS YOUR AGE?

Thirty-five.

WHAT AGE WERE YOU WHEN YOU WERE ADOPTED?

About nine.

WERE YOU BORN IN THE U.S.?

Yes.

WHAT DO YOU CONSIDER YOUR ETHNICITY OR RACE TO BE?

White.

WHAT WAS THE ETHNICITY OR RACE OF YOUR ADOPTIVE PARENTS?

All black, actually a single mother, but the whole entire family was black.

HOW MANY SIBLINGS DO YOU HAVE?

Six brothers and one sister.

WHAT ABOUT YOUR BIRTH PARENTS? DO YOU KNOW ANYTHING ABOUT THEIR
ETHNICITY OR RACE?

They were a totally dysfunctional family. My mother was German/Irish.
She is white. And then my father, American/Irish.

SO YOU KNEW YOUR BIRTH PARENTS?

My mother, I know very well. My dad, I don't really know. And I have a
stepdad.

YOU HAVE STAYED IN CONTACT WITH HER?

Yes. My adoptive mother always stressed that they were still my parents.
Those are my parents.

YOUR ADOPTIVE MOTHER STRESSED THAT YOU SHOULD STAY IN TOUCH WITH
THEM?

Yes. They gave me life, and so I should respect them for that.

WHERE WERE YOU RAISED?

Ann Arbor. That's where all the families lived, except for my real father.
Basically, all my family lived in Ann Arbor.

Did you live with your birth parents up until you were nine years old?

My mom and dad were divorced when I was two, so we were all together until I was two. He was away in the Marine Corps—he really wasn't there at all. She was single from two to four. From four until now, she's married to my stepdad.

If you feel comfortable talking about it, can you tell us about the transfer from your mother's house to your adoptive mom's house?

In hindsight, it was a pretty irresponsible family. I was getting in trouble at school, staying away from school, fighting, grades were poor. I was getting high.

Did all that change when you went to the family?

Yes, it did. I'd get beaten to death at my old house. I'd get beaten to death at my new house, too. They were a lot more strict. No eye rolling or not, coming in when you're supposed to come in.

At your birth mom's house, she beat you?

Yes. You know they were so dysfunctional. He was an alcoholic; she was on prescription pills. They were so dysfunctional, and they made everybody else in the house dysfunctional.

What year of school did you finish? What was your last year of school?

I graduated from high school. I graduated twelfth and have spent three years in college . . . I don't have a degree though.

What type of work do you do?

I'm a doorman at a hotel.

How long have you had that job?

Thirteen years.

Are you married?

Yes.

What race is your wife?

White.

AND YOUR CHILDREN?

I have three.

HOW OLD ARE THEY?

Nine, eight, and seven.

AND ARE THESE YOUR BIOLOGICAL CHILDREN?

Yes.

HOW LONG HAVE YOU LIVED IN INDIANAPOLIS?

About fourteen years.

WHAT MADE YOU MOVE TO INDIANAPOLIS?

I came here about four years after high school to go to JC, to walk on to play football.

HOW WOULD YOU DESCRIBE YOUR EXPERIENCES IN SCHOOL?

School is great. I love the academics, the sports. I learned social skills and sports.

HOW WAS IT WITH YOUR BROTHERS AND SISTERS? DID THEY GO TO THE SAME SCHOOL?

The oldest boy and the oldest girl went to another school, Huron. Mostly they went to Pioneer, a few went to the other high school.

DID PEOPLE KNOW THEY WERE YOUR BROTHERS AND SISTERS?

Yes, no problem.

WHAT ABOUT YOUR FRIENDS IN YOUR SCHOOL? WHAT RACE WERE THEY?

Everything. It had to be fifty-fifty.

WHAT ABOUT YOUR CLOSEST FRIENDS?

I would say one of each. The godfathers—one is white and one is black.

WERE THERE ANY OTHER MINORITIES, LIKE ASIANS?

Yes. And Indian and Chinese or Japanese—probably Chinese—Vietnamese.

WERE YOU FRIENDS WITH ANY OF THEM?

Yes, I got along with most everybody. In Pioneer, it was not so racially divided, and they didn't have us separated by race.

WHAT ABOUT YOUR EXTENDED FAMILY? LET'S START WITH YOUR ADOPTIVE
FAMILY. HOW DID THEY RECEIVE YOU?

Fine. They were all educated, open-minded, supportive. Just family.

WHAT ABOUT YOUR BIOLOGICAL FAMILY? SINCE YOU HAVE CONTACT WITH
THEM, WERE THEY OK WITH THAT?

My mother, she has some issues. My grandparents on my stepdad's side
have trouble with it because they're racist.

SO HAVE THEY EVER MADE A COMMENT TO YOU AT ALL?

Not really directed toward me or at me, but it is always tense.

WHAT ABOUT YOUR ADOPTIVE MOTHER, ROSE, WHAT IS HER LEVEL OF ED-
UCATION?

I don't know to be honest, but I think it is high.

SO SHE HAS HAD SOME COLLEGE?

Yes.

WHAT'S HAPPENED TO THE BROTHERS AND SISTERS? ARE THEY ALL FROM
THE SAME FATHER?

Actually, none are from the same father. She has one boy and one girl
from different fathers, and all the rest are adopted. They are all black.

HOW DID YOU COME IN CONTACT WITH HER?

My dad had sent me over there to sleep. He said, "You take him," and
Rose said yes.

AS FAR AS GROWING UP WITH ROSE AND THE PEOPLE SHE HUNG OUT WITH,
WHAT KIND OF PEOPLE WERE THEY?

I would have to say the majority were black because we lived in the projects which was all black. There were dinners and parties and functions
where there were white kids and black kids. Most of the people were neighborhood people, and they were black.

WERE YOU MEMBERS OF A CHURCH?

Yes. My little white brother, my stepdad's real son, we used to walk to
church and it was a United Methodist.

SO DID ROSE BELONG TO CHURCH AT ALL?

She was a Ba'hai. I would go to some of those programs. There's not a
church; there's a temple in Chicago. They have prayers there.

WERE THE MEMBERS OF THE UNITED METHODIST CHURCH WHITE?

All white.

ARE YOU GLAD THAT YOU WERE TRANSRACIALLY ADOPTED?

For the most part, it saved my life. I was losing fast. I would probably not have finished school, even high school, and I definitely would have been on some kind of substance.

DO YOU HAVE ANY SUGGESTIONS FOR PARENTS WHO ARE THINKING OF ADOPTING A CHILD OF ANOTHER RACE?

I would suggest a lot of love.

SOMEONE LIKE ROSE?

Yeah. The old school.

IF YOU LOOK BACK NOW, WOULD YOU RATHER HAVE BEEN ADOPTED BY WHITE PARENTS?

No. I am a better person for that.

SO WOULD YOU RECOMMEND TRANSRACIAL ADOPTION?

I would say very much so. It would be your responsibility to try to find out something about the culture and such to help that child along. The biggest thing I can think of with me was the food. Black kids will eat whatever is put in grease. White people wouldn't know that, for the most part.

HOW WAS IT LIVING IN A BLACK FAMILY? WERE THERE ANY EXPERIENCES OR SITUATIONS WHERE YOUR CULTURE WAS DIFFERENT THAN THEIRS? LIKE THE FOOD?

Nothing really. I don't mind answering; I just don't think different of it. The food, because that is always the big joke still. I really hate stereotypes, and it makes the hair on my neck stand up, but if I had a stereotype, I would say that black folks seem to be stronger in the sense that they take ridicule and punishment better. White people always worry about hurting somebody's feelings, trying to be polite all the time where it is not necessary. I would say that is different.

IS THERE ANYTHING ELSE THAT YOU THINK YOU COULD TELL ME THAT WOULD GIVE ME INSIGHT INTO YOUR EXPERIENCE?

I don't really think about it.

IV

SUMMARY AND CONCLUDING REMARKS

SUMMARY AND
CONCLUDING REMARKS

Seven men and fourteen women participated in the study. The seven men range in age from eighteen to thirty-five. Two of them were adopted before they were six months old. The female respondents range in age from eighteen to forty-three. Two of them were adopted at birth, four before they were six months old, and eight when they were between one and nine years of age.

Nine of the respondents were adopted from Korea, four were adopted from Vietnam, five from Mexico, Colombia, Haiti, and the Philippines, and three from the United States. One of the three is African American and Hispanic. She was adopted by white parents. Two are Caucasians who were adopted into African American families.

Nine of the women are single, as are five of the men. Four women are married, and one is divorced. One man is married and one is divorced. Four of the women hold postgraduate degrees and three hold a bachelor's degree. Three are currently students studying for a bachelor's degree, three have high school diplomas, and one woman dropped out of high school in the eleventh grade. One of the male respondents holds a postgraduate degree, three completed a bachelor's degree, and three are currently university students working towards a bachelor's degree.

Unlike all of the respondents in *In Their Own Voices,* and three quarters of the participants in this study, we do have two respondents who describe their experiences with their adoptive families as having been very sad and bitter. The two women, Maria and Terry Boesch, describe having been emotionally, physically, and sexually abused by their mothers. Tony did not report being abused, but he talks about his family experiences in a negative tone and describes the current relationship with his parents as "definitely distant." Fifteen of the remaining nineteen describe their family relationships in positive and very positive terms; three express some ambivalence. Ryan Killacky describes having run away from home many times between the ages of fifteen and sixteen, having been arrested twice for criminal trespassing and possession of marijuana, and drinking in high school. He is currently a member of Alcoholics Anonymous. Ryan states he would have preferred to have been adopted by Vietnamese or Asian parents so that he could have been raised in that culture and have Vietnamese language facility. Although he feels somewhat alienated from his family, he is thankful he was adopted. For two of the respondents, Jennifer and Polly Bettencourt, their less than fully positive experiences are primarily the result of the death of one of their adoptive parents—Polly's father when she was eleven, and Jennifer's mother when she was in high school.

Of the fifteen positive experiences, Adam Sackett, Flutie, Casey Stell and Carrie are the most effusive. Flutie, for example, stated, "Being transracially adopted saved my life. I would not have finished high school, and I would have used drugs." Adam Sackett told us, "I can't imagine having any other mother." He also commented that his adoptive mother "would like [him] to marry a black woman and raise [his] kids as a black family would. [He] probably will." Casey Stell feels she had "a perfect childhood." Carrie reports that in high school her mother was her best friend and that then and now, she is "extremely close to both [her] parents."

The major theme in almost all of the interviews is the respondents' ethnic or racial identity. Those who are comfortable with their identity, be it as Korean or Asian, or Asian or Korean American or African American or Hispanic, are also happier and more satisfied with their lives.

BIBLIOGRAPHY

Benson, Peter L., Anu R. Sharma, and Eugene C. Roehlkepartain. "Growing Up Adopted: A Portrait of Adolescents and Their Families." Search Institute, Minneapolis, Minn. (June 1994).

Clauss, D. and S. Baxter. "Rainbow House International Survey of Russian and Eastern European Children." *Bulletin of the Joint Council on International Children's Services* (Summer 1998): 6.

Cole, Jill C. "Perceptions of Ethnic Identity among Korean Born Adoptees and Their Caucasian-American Parents." Dissertation Abstracts International-A, vol. 54, no. 1 (July 1993): 317. University Microfilms, #9504358. Also cited in FACE FACTS (July/August 1995): 24–26.

Essley, Mary, and Linda Perilstein. "Eastern European Adoptions." *Bulletin of the Joint Council on International Children's Services* (Spring 1998): 8; and www.cradle hope.org/survey/html.

"Intercountry Adoption: Procedures Are Reasonable, but Sometimes Inefficiently Administered." GAO/NSIAD-93-83.

Kim, D. S. "Intercountry Adoptions: A Study of Self-Concept of Adolescent Korean Children Who Were Adopted by American Families." Unpublished PhD thesis, University of Chicago, 1976.

Lewin, Tamar. "South Korea Slows Export of Babies for Adoption." *New York Times*, February 12, 1990, p. B10.

Maass, Peter. "Orphans: Korea's Disquieting Problem." *Washington Post*, December 12, 1988.

Mainemer, Henry, Lorraine C. Gilman, and Elinor W. Ames. "Parenting Stress in Families Adopting Children from Romanian Orphanages." *Journal of Family Issues*, 19, no. 2 (March 1998): 64–80.

National Broadcasting Corporation. 10:45 p.m., September 19, 1988.

Politte, John. "Self Esteem Among Korean Adopted Pre-Adolescents." University Microfilms, #9504358, 1993.

Porter, Bruce. "I Met My Daughter at the Wuhan Foundling Hospital." *New York Times Magazine*, April 11, 1993, p. 24.

Simon, Rita J., and Howard Altstein. *Adoption Across Borders*. Lanham, Md.: Rowman & Littlefield, 2000.

"South Korea to Restrict Adoptions by Foreigners." No author. *Baltimore Sun*, December 26, 1993, p. 16.

Suh, Edward. "Life Adjustment Problems among Adopted Korean Children." *Open Door Society News* (October 1987): 3.

U.S. Department of State, The Bureau of Consular Affairs, Overseas Citizens Services, Office of Children's Issues. "Numbers of Immigrant Visas Issued to Orphans Coming to the U.S." Retrieved January 20, 2004. www.travel.state.gov/family/adoption/stats/stats_451.html

U.S. Department of State and Immigration and Naturalization Service. Reported in *The Bulletin of the Joint Council on International Children's Services*, (Spring 1999); and "Immigrant Visas Issued to Orphans Coming to U.S." www.travel.state.gov/family/adoption/stats/stats_451.html

Westhues, Anne, and Joyce S. Cohen. "The Adjustment of Intercountry Adoptees in Canada." *Children and Youth Services Review* 20, nos. 1–2 (1998): 115–34.

Wickes, Kevin Lee. "Transracial Adoption: Cultural Identity and Self-Concept of Korean Adoptees." Dissertation Abstracts International-B, vol. 54, no. 8 (February 1994): 43–74. University Microfilms, #9504358. Also cited in FACE FACTS (July/August 1995): 24–26.

INDEX

ABOUT THE AUTHORS

Heather Ahn-Redding is assistant professor of Criminal Justice at High Point University. She received her doctorate in Justice, Law and Society from American University's School of Public Affairs. She is coauthor of *Illicit Drug Policies, Trafficking, and Use the World Over* (with Caterina Gouvis Roman and Rita J. Simon, Lexington Books, 2005) and *The Crimes Women Commit: The Punishments They Receive* (with Rita J. Simon, Lexington Books, 2005).

Rita J. Simon is University Professor in the School of Public Affairs and the Washington College of Law at American University. She is author or editor of numerous books, including *Women's Roles and Statuses the World Over* (with Stephanie Hepburn, Lexington Books, 2006), and *Adoption Across Borders* (with Howard Altstein, Rowman & Littlefield, 2000).